Silencing Shanghai

Silencing Shanghai

Language and Identity in Urban China

Fang Xu

LEXINGTON BOOKS
Lanham • Boulder • New York • London

Published by Lexington Books
An imprint of The Rowman & Littlefield Publishing Group, Inc.
4501 Forbes Boulevard, Suite 200, Lanham, Maryland 20706
www.rowman.com

6 Tinworth Street, London SE11 5AL, United Kingdom

British Library Cataloguing in Publication Information Available

Library of Congress Cataloging-in-Publication Data

Names: Xu, Fang, (Professor of sociology) author.
Title: Silencing Shanghai : language and identity in urban China / Fang Xu.
Description: Lanham : Lexington Books, 2021. I Includes bibliographical references and index. I Summary: "Silencing Shanghai examines the paradoxical and counterintuitive contrast between Shanghai's emergence as a global city and marginalization of the Shanghai dialect. The endangerment of the vernacular exposes how state-sponsored social exclusion silences a significant voice of the people and shakes the linguistic foundation of the local identity"—Provided by publisher.
Identifiers: LCCN 2021018544 (print) I LCCN 2021018545 (ebook) I ISBN 9781793635310 (cloth) I ISBN 9781793635327 (ebook) I ISBN 9781793635334 (pbk)
Subjects: LCSH: Language attrition—China—Shanghai. I Language policy—China—Shanghai. I Chinese language—Dialects——China—Shanghai. I Chinese language—Social aspects—Shanghai. I Group identity—China—Shanhai. I Migration, Internal—China—Shanghai.
Classification: LCC P40.5.L282 C4595 2021 (print) I LCC P40.5.L282 (ebook) I DDC 306.44/0951132—dc23
LC record available at https://lccn.loc.gov/2021018544
LC ebook record available at https://lccn.loc.gov/2021018545

For grandma Sun Yucheng and grandma Xia Zhiqing

Contents

List of Figures and Tables

FIGURES

TABLES

Preface

Born into a Manchurian-Han Chinese family with close ties to the Western theatrical world in Shanghai, I always say I grew up backstage. My early memories of summer months and after-school time are images of workshops making stage backdrops and props, scenes of students' rehearsals, and the smell of dry ice at the Shanghai Theatre Academy. In Shanghai in the 1980s and 1990s, the theatrical world was in Mandarin Chinese, the standard national language of the country. It was the language associated with high educational level, and in my mind, beautiful and elegant people on stage and intellectual conversations in our living room. In contrast, the Shanghai dialect was the tongue associated with quotidian life that was banal and practical. Nevertheless, I spoke and still speak Mandarin Chinese with a Shanghai dialect accent, which means it is nearly impossible for me to distinguish words ending in "n" as in *chen* (morning) from "ng" as in *cheng* (city) when speaking. It also creates difficulties when I romanize Chinese words in *pinyin* in my writing. It is this element of being a person from Shanghai and having the Shanghai dialect as my mother tongue that will never leave me regardless how long I live in an English-speaking society.

Besides the linguistic element, the demolition of my Northern European style family house next door to the Theatre Academy in 2006 by eminent domain led me to reflect and examine my attachment to my home city. Rose and mock orange bushes, oleander and cypress trees in the front garden, pomegranate and fig trees in the middle, and grape vines over bamboo canopy frames covering the path leading to the backyard with clothing lines. Pebbledash outside walls, turquoise colored tiles around fireplaces, and velvet curtains that smell slightly musky in Shanghai's humid climate. Years before the demolition, the house and garden started to sink when commercial and residential towers more than twenty stories tall were built in the immediate vicinity. The garden would flood during the annual summer typhoon season and we could no longer see a piece of open sky. My world before college encompassed an area one mile in any direction radiated from home, the center of my life. After the demolition, Shanghai is still my city, but I no longer have a home. I do not mean physical dwelling, but a place one ties their identity to. On future visits to Shanghai in 2009, 2010, and 2013, I avoided the area because even after years I did not have the courage to look at the new wing the adjacent hospital built on the land where our house and garden once were. That experience led me to study gentrification and urban transformation in the doctoral program in the sociology department at the Graduate Center of City University of New York.

Eminent domain and state-led gentrification in the last three decades displaced millions in Shanghai. However, the Shanghai alleyway housing that most of the displaced once inhabited was unfamiliar for me. After reading multiple books about the floor plan and layout of alleyway housing units, I still had difficulty picturing its intricate structure and imagining life within. I felt inadequate and unable to write about urban transformations in Shanghai from an urban sociology perspective. What else is quintessentially Shanghai, something that transcends time and space to signify to ourselves and others that we are Shanghairen (Shanghai people)? The Shanghai dialect.

I never took any linguistics or sociolinguistics courses, so the task of writing a dissertation about the decline of the dialect was daunting. It took roughly three years for my research and dissertation to take shape. Through all of their forms and drafts, Sharon Zukin, my dissertation supervisor, has provided sage guidance, thoughtful feedback, and sharp critiques. She has pushed me to produce important, practical, and insightful research. She has continuously provided invaluable support and mentorship throughout my academic career during and beyond the PhD program. I also greatly benefited from the encouragement of Philip Kasinitz, who read through all my early dissertation drafts and has provided me with unique perspective to structure the work when I was lost in the details. I am also grateful to Jillian Cavanaugh, whose expertise in linguistic anthropology has opened up an entirely new field for me, and she has helped me tremendously to navigate the said field in positioning my research. Thanks as well to Xiangming Chen for his support throughout the research and writing of the dissertation.

I am grateful for the help and support from informants, acquaintances, and friends in Shanghai at different stages of the dissertation and later this book project. Without them spreading the word about my research, the snowball sampling used for my survey would not have been able to reach multiple generations of Shanghairen. Without them frankly revealing their lived experiences in our shared home city, I would not have been able to tell a story of Shanghai from the ground up. I have nothing to show reciprocity but this book recording their smiles, sighs, and resolutions.

The dissertation was completed in 2016 when I landed a lecturer position in the Interdisciplinary Studies program at the University of California Berkeley. The move from New York to San Francisco brought me geographically closer to Shanghai while challenging me to build another home, in various senses. Overtime, I find intellectual homes in all three cities, New York, Berkeley, and eventually back in Shanghai too. First, I would like to thank a number of Graduate Center peers who helped shape my research and dissertation. Those under the mentorship of Sharon Zukin met monthly to share and discuss our research and dissertation. I greatly value the feedback and edits from Jacob Lederman, Aneta Kostrzewa, and Jinwon Kim. Thanks for being the sounding board and providing consistent support for me, helping me complete the dissertation in a timely manner. Among other peers at the Graduate Center that I am grateful for, my good friend Sara Martucci, who graduated from the same PhD program and Chun-Yi Peng from the linguistics PhD program have continuously provided support and help that nurture and enrich my academic and personal life.

At Berkeley, I am grateful to the former director of my program, Peter Sahlins, who supported my creation of the course Language and Identity and introduced me to the campus community. My appreciation also goes to Andrew Jones, who provided valuable feedback on my book proposal and inspired the title of the book. Multiple other faculty provided me with opportunities to share work with their students, among them I am especially grateful to Lanchih Po. I am also greatly appreciative of the Found in Translation group at the Berkeley Language Center where I was twice invited to give talks about my research. One of the talks was based on chapter 3 about language policies and the other on chapter 5 about language attitudes among Shanghairen and internal migrants. I am thankful for the audience's questions and comments. Lastly, the academic connections in Shanghai provided me deeply appreciated opportunities to share my work with the audience living and breathing the decline of the Shanghai dialect. Among them, I thank Yu Hai in Fudan University and Zhu Weijue and Shen Qi in Tongji University for their interests in my research. The sense of home and solace the Shanghai dialect has provided me over the years have sustained the efforts to turn the dissertation into this book project.

I am also grateful to other faculty and friends around the world for their support by connecting me to resources, guiding me in the publishing process, and commenting on my book proposal and versions of various components of the book. They are Jerome Krase, John Mollenkopf, Elina Vesselinov, the late Neil Smith, and the late William Helmreich at City University of New York, Jan Rath at University of Amsterdam, Amy Hanser and Sanjeev

Routray at University of British Columbia, and Gina Anne Tam at Trinity University.

I would also like to extend my special appreciation to James Rowe for his incredible editing work that helped to polish my dissertation and fine tune this book to its final form. I am grateful for the editors at Lexington Books, Courtney Morales and Shelby Russell for their support and patience during the COVID pandemic that helped me to carry this project to fruition.

I am grateful for the financial support from various grants and the dissertation fellowship at the Graduate Center of City University of New York, the Write-up Grant from the Foundation of Urban and Regional Studies at Oxford University, and the Professional Development Fund from University of California Berkeley. I am also thankful to John Wiley and Sons for allowing me to reuse portions of my 2020 article published in *City & Community*. Volume 19, Issue 2:330-351, "Pudong is not My Shanghai: Displacement, place-identity, and right to the city in urban China" in chapter 3 of this book. A small part of my 2020 chapter, "Chapter 11: Only Shanghainese Can Understand: Popularity of Vernacular Performance and Shanghainese Identity" in *Revealing/Reveiling Shanghai: Cultural Representations from the 20th and 21st Centuries*, edited by Lisa Bernstein and Chu-chueh Cheng, 215-238 (Albany: State University of New York Press) was incorporated in chapter 1 of this book.

Finally, I want to express my deepest gratitude to my mother, Wei Long, for being my most ardent supporter and honest critic. In terms of "tiger mom," the Shanghainese kind might be the worst, or the best.

Introduction

To celebrate International Mother Language Day on February 21, 2014, Shanghai online news outlet Kankanews interviewed Haoliang Xu, an assistant secretary general of the United Nations and director of the United Nations Development Programme in Asia and the Pacific.[1] A Shanghai native, Xu commented on the importance of linguistic diversity, in general, and the importance of preserving regional dialects, in particular. In the brief video, Xu says, in the Shanghai dialect:

> If everyone in China speaks Putonghua, it would mean the disappearance of diversities, of regional cultures in the country. If in twenty years or so, I go back to Shanghai to live, it would be odd to hear Putonghua everywhere, which is not the environment I was familiar with, or grew up in. That is to say, regional dialects and cultures everywhere should be protected and preserved.

Xu chuckled when describing the "unimaginable" scenario of hearing Putonghua (which literarily means "common speech") or Standard Mandarin Chinese, spoken everywhere on the streets of Shanghai during that 2014 interview. Unfortunately, this unthinkable scenario has already happened. Today, on the streets of Shanghai, one hears Putonghua everywhere, and only rarely the Shanghai dialect. This change renders Shanghai unfamiliar and alien to a native Shanghairen (Shanghai people) like Xu, who regards the Shanghai dialect as his mother language. Xu believes that cultural and linguistic diversity should not be sacrificed for the sake of economic development. However, this sentiment is not necessarily shared by policymakers in China, or even by ordinary Shanghairen living through the country's economic reforms.

This book investigates the paradoxical and counterintuitive contrast between Shanghai's emergence as a global city and the marginalization of its native population, captured in part through the decline of its distinctive language, the Shanghai dialect. The dialect is a hybrid of several branches of Wu Chinese, with loanwords from Western languages. It belongs to a different language family from China's national language, Mandarin Chinese. As Sihua Liang writes about Cantonese in Guangzhou, the ideological issue of categorizing a linguistic variety as a language or a dialect is resolved by the central state officially defining all major Chinese languages, such as Cantonese, Wu, Hakka, or Min as dialects of the Chinese language, a.k.a. Mandarin Chinese, despite the fact of their mutual unintelligibility.[2] Linguistically, we can only say the Shanghai dialect is a dialect of Wu rather than of Mandarin Chinese. However, linguists in the West, such as Mair, who advocates for the recognition of those officially labeled dialects as languages eventually concedes that non-linguistic factors, such as politics, ethnicity, and culture, are impossible to separate from linguistic ones in the classification of the languages in China.[3] Following the lead of Liang, I decide to use the Shanghai dialect instead of Shanghainese in this book. As Bourdieu writes about language and symbolic power, the power to classify is the power to make others see the world in a particular way.[4] It is the dominant ideology sponsored by the central state and the resulting widely accepted dialect status of Shanghai speech that makes this whole investigation meaningful.

Unintelligible for Mandarin Chinese speakers, the Shanghai dialect has served as a significant marker of Shanghairen identity over the last century. However, the dialect has experienced a rapid decline over the last two decades and is on the brink of endangerment. How can this have happened while Shanghai has risen to global prominence as the showcase for China's economic development?

This is not a story about the Shanghai dialect itself, but rather a story told from the vantage point of the dialect's decline as an aspect of broader transformations in urban China. After all, changes in language use do not take place in a social vacuum. Instead, changing social circumstances prompt and explain linguistic change. And changes in language use in Shanghai reveal how the city's globalization process has transformed the daily life of Shanghairen in myriad ways. In this book, I argue that three sets of state policies in areas of language use, urban redevelopment, and internal migration have contributed to the endangerment of the Shanghai dialect. Each of these policies has favored the rich, the resourceful, and the highly educated. The result of these policies has been confusion and conflict around local identity: who counts as Shanghairen?

In the last two decades, the state has vigorously promoted Putonghua through legal and administrative means, as well as the public school system. This has severely limited linguistic space for regional dialects across the country, including the Shanghai dialect. The symbolic power of dialect proficiency lies in its indication of the speaker's Shanghairen identity and claim to this globalizing city. However, claims based on legal residency and language use have been challenged by waves of urban redevelopments and a continual influx of internal migrants. When the urban built environment was overhauled and upgraded to accommodate global capital, millions of native Shanghairen were marginalized geographically. They were displaced from vernacular alleyway housing in the urban center to the periphery, in previously rural counties away from the Shanghai proper in their mental mapping. At the same time, millions of internal migrants converged to provide the labor force necessary for Shanghai to become a global city. All of these migrants, from laborers to executives, were given some form of legal status, and thus access to public services, though in a tiered fashion and not entirely on par with those provided to native Shanghairen. Since migrants' entry and claim to the city is granted by the state, there is little incentive for them to acquire the Shanghai dialect against the state's language policies.

The overall linguistic space for the Shanghai dialect has rapidly shrunk as a result of conscious choices by both native Shanghairen and migrants. To emphasize the latter's standing in Shanghai or to highlight their attachment to Shanghai, I will refer to them as non-natives or non-native Shanghairen in the rest of the book. Since there has been a significant decrease in everyday use, the Shanghai dialect functions mostly to maintain the boundary between native and non-native Shanghairen. Because of this ultimate linguistic barrier, the educationally and socioeconomically privileged migrants developed what I call flexible resident identity. Their personal wealth and skillsets afford them a global citizen lifestyle, with permanent resident permits in both foreign countries and Shanghai, while they live in Shanghai most of the year. Instead of identifying with their hometown, or Shanghai, or any other country they may have legal status in, these migrants instead enjoy their flexibility as a sense of security. The recent shift in the urban linguistic scene from almost solely the Shanghai dialect to predominantly Mandarin Chinese sprinkled with English has been overlooked as a consequence of global city-building. Ultimately, the disappearance of both vernacular architecture and vernacular dialect in Shanghai renders it a global city with homogeneous, state-sanctioned *Chinese* characteristics.

This book tells the story of language as an aspect of power relations in a cosmopolitan metropolis closely monitored and shaped by an authoritarian state. The shift in language use reflects not only the changing demography of globalizing Shanghai but also exposes how state-sponsored linguistic exclusion silences a significant local voice. Furthermore, it is apparent that anger about socioeconomic inequality is expressed in the form of cultural and linguistic discrimination and xenophobia instead of being communicated as discontent with the central state. Such prejudice goes both ways. Native

Shanghairen feels marginalized when the dialect is shunned in public by non-natives and is labeled as backward and vulgar by the state. Meanwhile non-natives feel discriminated against when the unintelligible dialect is spoken to, or even around them, and when they are criticized for the refusal to learn the dialect. Language shift has been largely overlooked in studying urban trans-formation in China. In giving voices to the people, we need to pay attention to which language(s) they speak. Most importantly, changes in patterns of language use reveal a performative acting-out of social class and new social identity in formation.

LINGUISTIC BACKGROUND

The Shanghai dialect's current endangerment is set against the backdrop of two aspects of the complex linguistic landscape of China. One is what Charles Ferguson characterizes as a diglossia system, which means the literary and the vernacular forms of the Chinese language coexist and have distinctive functions that rarely overlap.[5] Literary Chinese is the so-called High Language used in court or other formal situations, and vernacular Chinese is the so-called Low Language used in everyday conversation. Chinese language scholars point out that the two forms diverged in ancient times and have coexisted for millennia. The literary Chinese learned through the school system by the privileged across feudal China was not spoken by anyone as a native language.[6] Rooted in canonical writings of the Warring States (403–255 BC), literary Chinese has been the preemi-nent written language in China for the past 2,000 years.[7] Throughout this period, literary Chinese was preserved and maintained by literati, taking on an archaic form while vernacular Chinese, by and large, went through an independent grassroots development.[8] Yet, even though every literate person was trained to write in the rigid style of the ancient writers until the early twentieth century, they resorted to their varied native tongues in speaking.[9]

The second aspect of the linguistic background is that regional vernacu-lars of the modern Chinese language are roughly divided into two groups. The northern varieties, conventionally known in English as Mandarin dia-lects, were variations, with regional accents, based on the educated speech in Beijing of the fifteenth century, when the Ming Dynasty established the national capital there. Mandarin dialects cover more than three-quarters of the Chinese language region, while southern regional vernaculars, so-called non-Mandarin dialects such as Cantonese, Hakka, or Wu, to which the Shanghai dialect belongs, occupy only the southeast coastal regions. More importantly, the Mandarin dialects are more or less mutually intelligible;

the non-Mandarin dialects, on the other hand, differ greatly from each other, and from any variation of Mandarin. For example, there are five phonetically distinguishable tones in the Shanghai dialect and nine in Cantonese. The Shanghai dialect also has a series of voiced consonants b, d, g that Mandarin does not have.[10]

These vast differences between literary and vernacular Chinese, and between Mandarin and non-Mandarin dialects, prevailed during feudal China but sat awkwardly against the political ideology for building a modern nation-state with a uniform national language. The diglossia system started to erode when both Guoyu (national language) and Guoyin (national pronunciation) were created and promoted under the rule of Kuomintang during the Republic of China in the early twentieth century. The victory of the Chinese Communist Party over Kuomintang and the founding of the People's Republic of China in 1949 introduced more thorough measures to replace the diglossia system with a standardized language and pronunciation to serve the functions of both High and Low Languages. The official language of the People's Republic of China, Putonghua, inherited the Beijing-pronunciation-based Guoyin, which is not a native tongue for anyone in China. Using Putonghua as both the written and the spoken language eliminates a functional separation in non-Mandarin dialect regions. Unlike Mandarin dialect speakers, non-Mandarin dialect speakers, such as Shanghairen, were forced to adopt a new spoken language in their daily lives. However, top-down policies promoting Putonghua were less effective than anticipated during the Maoist era, as evidenced by the linguistic environment in Shanghai, which was still dominated by the Shanghai dialect in the 1990s.

The endangerment of the Shanghai dialect documented in this study is one recent example of the battles lost by a Low Language to a state-backed High Language.[11] As Alan Hudson points out, the end result of the erosion of the diglossia system is usually that the Low Language loses ground, driven out by younger generations educated in the more prestigious and more economically viable High Language.[12] Joshua Fishman points out that the High Language is more likely to win out, given the better rewards and stronger sanctions associated with it.[13] The rewards are more attainable and tangible in China's economic reform era, when upward social mobility can be achieved through education and on the job market rather than being predetermined by one's birthplace or family's political background, as I will detail in chapter 2.

GLOBALIZING SHANGHAI

Shanghai is one of the most studied Chinese cities, and scholars tirelessly remind readers of the city's past glory in the early twentieth century as the

"Paris of the East."[14] Shanghai is also the epitome of contemporary Chinese urban conditions; as Xiangming Chen puts it, "Shanghai is a timely urban laboratory for understanding how local transformations occur in global or globalizing cities as a combined function of global impact and state power."[15] Over the last two decades, studies on Shanghai have examined multiple dimensions of the globalization process, from economic achievements, urban redevelopments, the proliferation of Western consumer goods, to the influx of foreign and domestic talents. Here I will briefly address the four dimensions of Shanghai's globalizing process, which provides crucial context for my story of the dialect's endangerment.

It was not until the 1990s that economic reforms reached Shanghai. Contrary to its previously designated role as an industrial producer at the heart of China's centrally planned socialist economy, by the turn of the millennium Shanghai was ready to embrace the status of a global city, with tertiary sectors, Fortune 500 companies' regional headquarters, and the professionals necessary to staff them. The quick pace of Shanghai's economic globalization explains the urgent need for upgrading and expanding its urban infrastructure. The city needed to be made physically capable of sustaining its economic vitality.

The transformation of the urban built environment is the second dimension of globalization in Shanghai. The unprecedented scale of Shanghai's urban transformation resulted in scholars like Hanchao Lu proclaiming that "[b]y the late 1990s, much of the city had been literally destroyed."[16] Large-scale redevelopment projects demolished most of the city's central residential neighborhoods, which contained many varied examples of vernacular architecture. In place of old central-city alleyway housing neighborhoods rose glass-façade skyscrapers, elevated inner-city expressways, shopping centers carrying transnational fashion brands, and a brand-new subway system with gleaming marble platforms and spotless stations. These building forms are transplanted from elsewhere to project an "imagined" global image, as Anthony King and Abidin Kusno argue.[17] Leslie Sklair points out that viewed as representations of capitalist globalization, these typical urban architectural forms can be found almost anywhere in the world and are venues that transcend differences between geographical, ethnic, and cultural communities in the practices of consumption.[18] Once the backbone of China's industrial production, Shanghai has been turned into a city devoted to consumption.

Emerging from the ration system and sea of blue and grey Mao suits, consumerism, and the abundance of consumer goods are the third dimension of globalization in Shanghai. Global retail chains replaced mom-and-pop stores and wet markets in residential neighborhoods, luxury and fast fashion brands such as Louis Vuitton, Hermès, Cartier, Forever 21, and H&M line the Huaihai Road and Nanjing Road, two major thoroughfares. Increased access to Western consumer goods extends, in some degree, to Western cultural products. Side by side with selected Western popular culture—fashion magazines, TV shows, and Hollywood movies that successfully pass state censors, Western high culture has also been strategically promoted in Shanghai. Considering the rigid censorship of Western culture in general during the Cultural Revolution (1966–1976), the municipal government's financial support for the construction of cultural venues such as the Shanghai Grand Theatre, and for the organization of performances of Western classical music, ballet, and opera indicates a social engineering effort to promote consumption of global culture[19] and to elevate Shanghai to its global city status.

While international capitals globalize urban commercial spaces, members of the transnational capitalist class act like agents.[20] Among these agents that Sklair identifies, major transnational corporate owners and executives and their local affiliates, globalizing professionals and merchants play significant roles in brokering and facilitating the prevalence of consumerism in Shanghai. Compared to the so-called floating population who recently migrated to cities from rural or small-town China and work manual labor jobs at the bottom of socioeconomic hierarchy, the transnational capitalist class is a much smaller non-native population in Shanghai. However, they are capable of wielding great power in the local economic, social, and cultural realms. Studies on this latter group explain the fourth and last aspect of globalization in Shanghai.

Members of this group of non-natives are the returning Chinese expatriates who have been educated abroad. Many of them are hired by foreign corporations for managerial positions or higher, in recognition of their English language skills and familiarity with Western corporate culture. According to Aihwa Ong, among these there are also cultural entrepreneurs in the businesses of fashion, art, and culinary industries, who selectively deploy business management in combination with cultural forms in an individualistic, instrumental manner to encourage consumerism.[21] Both groups, together with their highly educated domestic counterparts, serve as the base for urban China's new upper-middle-class, who are globally oriented and expect their living and working environments to resemble other global cities. For them, a rooted, fixed identity, such as Shanghairen, or the acquisition of the Shanghai dialect as part of the assimilation seems irrelevant, as I will illustrate in chapter 5.

Shanghai, after more than a decade of concentrated foreign direct investments, large-scale urban redevelopments, embrace of capitalist consumerism, and the arrivals of a transnational capitalist class and domestic labor force, has regained its pre-1949 cosmopolitan reputation. The city's pre-1949 glories were rediscovered and memorialized in the official rhetoric to encourage great changes in Shanghai in the early 1990s. This nostalgia for the past served to justify the city's —or rather China's—ambition to participate in globalization and to play a bigger role in the global economy. As Tim Bunnell puts it, building a global city is a nation's "means of 'plugging in' to global political, economic and social networks."[22]

Saskia Sassen, who coined the term "global city," acknowledges that the state remains a powerful actor in any global or globalizing city, mediating forces and local responses, even though transnational financial and social forces permeating national borders and setting up global networks.[23] Indeed, the fast-paced global city–building process in Shanghai is attributed to the Chinese Communist Party's sweeping state power. It is the state's will and national wealth that have arranged and orchestrated the globalization of Shanghai. As a result, the city first and foremost represents the country on the global stage. Equally important, Shanghai's achievement and significance point inward, to the rest of the country, and that's why the state needs to make sure, though channeling global economic and cultural influence, the voice of this global city is essentially national rather than local.

ANALYTICAL FRAMEWORK

To interpret the social dynamics both produced by state power and in response to it in a globalizing city, I employ theoretical concepts of language ideology, right to the city, and nationalism in my analysis. The dominant language ideology valuing Putonghua over the Shanghai dialect works its way into both native and non-native Shanghairen's everyday language attitudes and choices, consequentially threatening the vitality and survival of the dialect. I bridge the environmental psychological concept of place identity with the applied sociolinguistic concept of linguistic justice to highlight a thus far overlooked but essential component of metropolitan living. That is, language attitudes and choices in the context of both globalization and a strong national language. Lastly, the development, implementation, and enforcement of a national language and its wide use is closely associated with nationalism and the ruling elites' political agenda. Converging in this study, these three sets of concepts help to decipher the changing face of Shanghai and the silencing of its native tongue in the state-led globalization process.

Language Ideology and Linguistic Capital

My analysis of social conflicts surrounding language choices, specifically the rising preference for Putonghua over the Shanghai dialect, is anchored by the linguistic anthropological concept of language ideology. It is in this analytical framework that I examine the Chinese Communist Party's state policies that institutionalize the dominance of Putonghua and the marginalization of the Shanghai dialect, engendering a rapid language shift in Shanghai in the last two decades.

Linguists and linguistic anthropologists have long treated language ideology as a field of inquiry for studying social dynamics and processes. These ideologies are not only about linguistic forms or uses but also about individuals and social groups using the languages and social institutions affected by their language use.[24] Judith Irvine emphasizes the social dimension of language ideology that it is "the cultural system of ideas about social and linguistic relationships, together with their loading of moral and political interests."[25] That is to say, language ideologies are by definition always multiple, omnipresent, and held by diverse speakers to a varied degree to aid the understanding of their social world. Extending the significance of the concept of language ideology beyond users of a particular language in examining social dynamics, Judith Irvine and Susan Gal highlight that language ideologies "are ideas with which participants and observers frame their understanding of linguistic varieties and map those understandings onto people, events, and activities that are significant to them."[26] This interpretation of language ideology means both speakers and non-speakers of a particular language have their own ideas not only about the language itself, for example, whether it sounds beautiful or is difficult to learn but also about the speakers of that language, for example, imagining them to be either vulgar or sophisticated. Language ideologies vary based on their believers and the social standings of the believers in a particular social milieu.

In cases similar to my study, which involves a national language projecting dominance and a vernacular associated with local identity, the concept of language ideology is employed to explain a dichotomy, differentiating uses of languages among diverse social groups. Nancy Dorian generalizes from various studies on endangered languages how language ideology usually assigns varied meanings and status to different languages, that the standard language is typically rich, rational, and suitable for wide usage, while dialects and ethnic minority languages are crude and inadequate.[27] From her study on Catalan speakers in Barcelona in the 1980s, against the backdrop of Castilian Spanish being the country's official language, Kathryn Woolard identifies "two competing social dimensions of language use: on the one hand is power, prestige, dominance, status, and on the other hand, covert prestige, solidarity."[28] Other linguistic anthropologists' studies in Western Europe, such as Alexandra Jaffe's study on the Corsican language under the French state's language ideology and linguistic policies,[29] or Jillian Cavanaugh's study on the struggles of Bergamasco, a northern Italian dialect, exemplify the power dynamics inherent within language practices and the varied degrees of acceptance of the dominant language ideology.[30] In those cases, the dominant language ideology associates the country's national language with power, prestige, and higher status while regional dialects are associated with lower aesthetic values and status. Meanwhile, among speakers of those endangered languages or regional dialects, an alternative language ideology endows vernaculars with covert prestige to ensure that they remain relevant and alive.

Language ideology typically manifests in two ways, as Kathryn Woolard points out: first, in behavioral proficiency, which involves the recognition, knowledge, and control of a linguistic standard; and second, in attitudes about language use and opinions of the character of its speakers.[31] In these ways, dominant language ideologies assert indisputable power, often backed by the state. As for language proficiency, Pierre Bourdieu argues that modern national educational systems play an important role in maintaining and reproducing the dominant language ideology, hence the dominance of the official language, through codification in dictionaries and grammar books.[32] Thus, a linguistic standard would be disseminated across the country. In terms of language attitudes, in a case involving Mandarin Chinese outside of Mainland China, Shuanfan Huang illustrates the ramifications of the dominant language ideology in Taiwan. Participants in his study associated the official language, Mandarin Chinese, with young, elegant, white-collar urbanites, and dialects with old, vulgar, blue-collar, rural folks.[33]

The presence and reach of dominant language ideologies tell only half of the story. The alternative is vernacular usage, which connotes local solidarity and covert prestige, acknowledged and honored by its speakers. This alternative language ideology serves as an important symbol of group cohesion and exclusive identity, as James and Lesley Milroy reveal in their study on Singaporeans and Singaporean English.[34] They identify a paradox in their study; namely, Singaporeans view standard British English as the "ideal" form of English, while at the same time practicing Singaporean English to signify their Singaporean identity.[35] Local resistance to the dominant language ideology in Singapore has a postcolonial, political tone. In other cases, the economic strength of dialect speakers supports the alternative language ideology regionally, such as the case of Catalan. By examining the economic structure in Catalonia, Kathryn Woolard points out that although Castilian Spanish is imposed by the state, local Catalans in Barcelona in general fare better socioeconomically than Castilian-speaking migrants.[36] This lays the economic foundation for the higher status of Catalan locally. Besides the political and economic circumstances prompting the status of dialects, William Labov, in his influential work *Language in the Inner City: Studies in the Black English Vernacular*, points out that African-American Vernacular English is a group-identity-oriented speech associated with a sense of black pride.[37]

In all three studies above, though the roots of local acceptance and resistance to the dominant language ideology vary, the covert prestige and values associated with illegitimate languages coexist with the recognition of the authority and status of the official language. Against this background, a social group with a minority language as their mother tongue, such as Shanghairen in my study, strategizes their linguistic practices for varied gains. To understand such calculated practice, I employ Pierre Bourdieu's argument about the conversion of different types of capitals.

Bourdieu differentiates four types of capital in an individual's possession: economic capital rests on ownership, control, or proximity to wealth or property; cultural capital refers to knowledge or experience usually associated with upbringing and educational achievement; social capital is based more or less on social connections and network; and lastly symbolic capital refers to status, recognition, or prestige that results from certain knowledge or practices.[38] These four types of capitals matter for an individual's life chances in two dimensions: the total volume of diverse capitals and the particular composition of them. To give an overly simplified example, a struggling artist possesses a relatively high volume of cultural capital but a low volume of economic capital. In the event that the artist is introduced, by a friend or acquaintance, to a wealthy patron who buys his art, the artist's social and cultural capital are successfully converted into economic capital and potentially symbolic capital if his work gains attention or wins awards. In the case that the patron later sells the artwork, his social capital—knowing the artist—and cultural capital, in the form of the artwork, are converted back into economic capital. These conversions go on. The identification of various capitals is not only important to pinpoint the social position an individual occupies in a given society but also demonstrates an individual's ability to successfully convert them.

In the case of language practices, Bourdieu distinguishes linguistic capital from other knowledge grouped together under cultural capital. He argues that the family initially endows children with linguistic capital, but it is the school system that recognizes the composition and convertible values of this capital and makes future conversions possible. The school system actively reproduces the authority and legitimacy of particular linguistic forms by issuing educational credentials.[39] In other words, proficiency in the official language and the recognition of its dominance—the two dimensions of linguistic capital—are assets produced and rewarded through the school system. Later, this linguistic capital, associated with the official language, will be available for conversion to symbolic, social, and economic capitals on the job market and beyond. In chapter 2, I explore how the proficiency and beliefs in Putonghua's convertibility facilitates the upward mobility of native Shanghairen.

Extending linguistic capital conversion to the alternative market of illegitimate languages—regional dialects such as the Shanghai dialect, the proficiency and belief in a marginalized vernacular are convertible among their speakers into symbolic, social, and to a certain extent, economic capitals. It is especially true when proficiency in a minority language is associated with a regional or ethnic identity. Bourdieu's reflection on regional identity is useful here. The practice and preservation of a regional language are meaningful for the speakers' mental image of who they are as a distinct people and potentially useful for aiding the speakers' symbolic and material request and satisfying their interests.[40] However, compared to the state-sponsored conversion market used to promote the dominant language ideology and the official language, this alternative market has limited resources and often dwindling participants. Furthermore, the coexistence of dominant and alternative linguistic markets strengthens the sense of distinction and the awareness of othering, instead of mitigating the pressure for linguistic conformity. Alexandra Jaffe argues from her study on French versus Corsican speaking in Corsica that the resistance communicates a sense of disenfranchisement.[41]

To interpret that feeling of loss, I use the concept of place identity and right to the city to disentangle the association of the Shanghai dialect proficiency with a Shanghairen identity and a sense of belonging to a changed place. During the last three decades of economic reforms and global city-building, native Shanghairen have experienced geographical displacement and have been trying to use dialect proficiency to reclaim their right to the city. At the same time, millions of internal migrants with legal status overlook the linguistic element in articulating their own right to global Shanghai.

Right to the Global City

To examine the role the Shanghai dialect plays in individuals' claims on and identification with the globalizing Shanghai, three theoretical concepts are useful. First is right to the city, coined by Henri Lefebvre to highlight the disenfranchisement in liberal-democratic capitalist societies in the late 1960s. The second is place identity, developed by Harold Proshansky in 1978 to describe the intricate relations between an individual's identity and the physical space they inhabit. And lastly, Saskia Sassen's concept of global city, which refers to a network of cities that are financially significant globally and host clusters of specialized services such as banking, insurance, and law, like New York, London, and Tokyo.[42] I situate my study of Shanghairen identity and the right to geographic and linguistic space in Shanghai at the intersection of these three concepts. Through language attitudes and practices, and access to housing, native and non-native Shanghairen articulate, challenge, and claim their right to Shanghai.

The right to the city concept has recently been widely used in social sciences, in literature about urbanization and gentrification, as well as by advocates for accesses to public services and other resources in cities. But what exactly does it mean? Lefebvre's conceptualization can be theoretically complex, even though it makes intuitive sense, that urban inhabitants cry out and demand participation in the decision-making process in cities, especially when it concerns the production of urban space.[43] Peter Marcuse deciphers the concept this way: "The demand is of those who are excluded, the aspiration is of those who are alienated; the cry is for the material necessities of life, the aspiration is for a broader right to what is necessary beyond the material to lead a satisfying life."[44] There is still ample abstraction here, in terms of the ideas of exclusion, alienation, material necessities, or a satisfying life. They certainly mean different things for different people. In my research, the sense of exclusion is exemplified by native Shanghairen displaced from their urban central housing to the periphery or by non-natives who do not understand the Shanghai dialect but work and live in a predominantly dialect-speaking environment. And for both groups, overall quality of life has increased significantly since the 1990s, raising the bar for what are viewed as material necessities or as a satisfying life.

The world historical context of the changes described above and the conditions that inhabitants of Shanghai find themselves in is what David Harvey terms "neoliberalism with Chinese characteristics."[45] Economic reforms in China since the late 1970s have seen the central state retreat in various areas where local initiatives and the private sector have flourished. Local governments have emerged to take a bigger role in the production of urban space and in the implementation of regulations regarding economic activities and internal migration. Harvey goes on to argue that the declining power of nation-states to control multinational monetary flows also allows local governments to attract and to negotiate with international finance capital for specific investments.[46] With freedom comes responsibility, as a result municipal governments have shifted from a managerial role to an entrepreneurial one.[47] Under the planned economy, before reforms, the municipal or district governments in Shanghai were not autonomous enough to conduct such negotiations directly with foreign investors. That historical shift fueled the municipal and district governments' aspiration to become more profitable and prominent in the region, which coincided with the central state's ambition to build Shanghai into a global city.

The economic reforms that allow the municipal and district governments in Shanghai direct contact with international capital inevitably entail a subjection of them to "external coercive power" under interurban competition, which "brings individual cities closer into line with the discipline and logic of capitalist development" as Harvey writes.[48] To realize the ambition to become the next global city, Shanghai had to provide a "good business climate" to attract international investment, on par with those in long-established global cities, in terms of infrastructure, labor force, and supportive services.

According to Saskia Sassen, a global city is a significant production point for the specialized financial services that command the globalized economy.[49] For Shanghai to grow into such a role, to become a new node in this network of global cities, particular and expensive infrastructure, such as airports and office towers, highly trained and specialized labor forces, such as professionals in law and finance, and lifestyle developments, such as waterfront recreation areas, upscale condominiums, and shopping malls were required. With the construction of international and domestic airports, the maglev train and subway system, the establishment of special economic and industrial parks for foreign direct investors, and reforms in migration policies that attract foreign and domestic talents, Shanghai is swiftly reaching its goal.

The large-scale urban redevelopments in Shanghai made the sparkling new global-city-look possible. You-tien Hsing points out that land-centered urban politics is not necessarily predetermined by the grand scheme of decentralization policies under "neoliberalism with Chinese characteristics." Rather, the municipal government needed to negotiate with both socialist land masters and local agencies to achieve control of urban land, which it later leased to real estate developers, thus realizing capital accumulation.[50] Taking as a case study the development of the Lujiazui Central Business District in Pudong in the 1990s, Zhengji Fu argues that Shanghai's urban restructuring is neither entirely internally induced, as it was in the pre-reform era nor solely externally produced by global capital; rather, it is the outcome of the interaction of global capital and the central and local governments.[51] Scholars have identified this as state-sponsored gentrification, in the sense that land ownership remained in the hands of the state, while huge incentives were given by the local government to real estate developers.[52] In return, the municipal and district governments saw land value, revenue, and the fame of their jurisdictions rapidly increase.

This newly vacated and highly desirable inner-city land soon became crowded by modern office towers, shopping malls, and luxurious condos as a direct result of the private-public partnership in Shanghai. Famed as the first lifestyle center in urban China since the reforms, Xintiandi and its immediate surroundings are composed of all three types of space standard to global cities. Its redevelopment exemplifies the private-public partnership, one that involved the Shui On Group based in Hong Kong, Luwan District Government, and the Shanghai Municipal Government.[53] Furthermore, an urban built environment devoted to lifestyle-based consumption patterns helps the city achieve its new status by appearing "as an innovative, exciting, creative, and safe place to live, or to visit, to play and consume in," as Harvey point out.[54] In the last three decades, a plethora of such consumption spaces have been built, such as the Shanghai Grand Theatre, Shanghai Museum, Shanghai Stadium, Shanghai Ocean Aquarium, and most recently

Shanghai Disneyland Park; the flourishing of luxury shopping malls, upscale restaurants, and waterfront recreation areas by both Huangpu River and along Suzhou Creek; as well as the organization of the Shanghai Biennale, the annual Shanghai International Arts Festival, the 2010 Shanghai Expo, and the newly built Shanghai International Circuit that hosts the Chinese Grand Prix, part of the Formula One World Championship. These amenities and events not only caught the world's attention but also provided the necessary proof of global city status.

Naturally only those who can afford it have the right to occupy those newly built residential and commercial spaces. Swept out of sight before Shanghai's glamourous new look was presented to the world, more than one million households of native Shanghairen were displaced and dispossessed starting in the 1990s. However, the story is not simply about bitterness and a sense of rejection or exclusion. Even though Shanghai's urban center has been transformed beyond recognition, and in many cases, now denies access to native Shanghairen, the displaced still try to claim a Shanghairen identity associated with the physical space.

This pride tied to being native to a famed city translates into what Marco Lalli identifies as positive self-esteem associated with a prestigious place.[55] Furthermore, such self-esteem is maintained through the symbolic qualities of the place, as Twigger-Ross and Uzzell conclude in their study in London.[56] This means that even though the majority of native Shanghairen cannot afford to frequent such upscale consumption spaces, they are proud inhabitants of the city that hosts such lifestyles and provides those amenities. Their very geographical closeness still gives them hope for future access. D. Asher Ghertner shows a similar mentality in his study of urban redevelopment in Delhi that even slum-dwellers take up the vision of "world-city aesthetics" and aspire to live in such an exciting global city of the future.[57] To a certain extent, this aspirational self-esteem extends the right to the global city even to those who cannot afford to physically enjoy it. In this light, it is easy to understand why displaced Shanghairen feel ambiguous about urban redevelopments in Shanghai. The bitterness and sense of marginalization do not dampen the pride of being a native to this global city.

Beneath the possession of spacious new residences with modern amenities in the city's periphery, displaced native Shanghairen grieve for their demolished neighborhoods. Those neighborhoods are regarded by Shanghairen as a sort of homeland, which according to Yi-fu Tuan, is a place viewed as "an archive of fond memories and splendid achievements that inspire the present."[58] Tuan points out that people are attached to their homeland in two important ways; first, the homeland has landmarks of high visibility and social significance and second, daily routines in the homeland create a safe and familiar environment.[59] Though many historic landmarks survived the redevelopments, such as the neo-classical buildings of the Bund on the west bank of Huangpu River, their significance has been replaced by iconic new skyscrapers on the opposite side of the river, including first the Oriental Pearl TV Tower, and later the Shanghai Tower and the Shanghai World Financial Center, which are the second and the eleventh tallest buildings in the world, respectively.

The diminished significance of former architectural icons and the demolition of alleyway residential neighborhoods robbed native Shanghairen of the specific place they can attach their Shanghairen identity to. Harold Proshansky coined the term "place identity" to differentiate the aspect of an individual's identity that is developed and maintained in relation to the physical environment they inhabit or frequent. This involves conscious and unconscious beliefs, feelings, preferences, values, and behavioral tendencies.[60] Yi-fu Tuan's argument about sense of place echoes Proshansky's concept that an individual's connections with a specific place is essential for the reconstruction of the past and for the understanding of one's identity.[61] The demolition of the places where native Shanghairen once anchored such personal connections and experiences means those connections are severed, and place identity itself is threatened. These are not the type of objects that can be packed up and moved to a new home; rather, it is a loss of way of life, the imprint of urban history, community life, and personal past.

Emotional attachments and sense of belonging to particular places are only part of Proshansky's conceptualization of place identity. A fuller understanding of the term makes the concept even more useful for capturing recent migrants' meaning-making in relation to Shanghai's urban space. Proshansky and others argue that place identity also includes an individual's attitudes about, evaluation of, and preferences for places.[62] The highly educated and well-off non-natives in my research successfully navigated the bureaucratic system and acquired legal status in Shanghai, but their decision to settle down in the city does not necessarily lead to the development of a place identity associated with the city. Their preference for modern urban amenities, opportunities for career advancement, and the meaningful relationships they have built over years living in Shanghai cannot overcome the ultimate obstacle, dialect proficiency. Instead of a Shanghairen identity, they develop what I call "flexible resident identity," which suggests a voluntary in-betweenness, embodied by the group of privileged Chinese urbanites in relation to their hometowns, legal statuses, and long-term residency in Shanghai; in some cases, it includes their aspirations as well, including acquiring permanent resident status abroad. Their attachment to a place is conditional, but concrete at the same time. The personal wealth, knowledge, and skillset they possess afford them such mobility. Instead of a flexible citizenship, they feel more comfortable and secure with flexible resident status combined with a Chinese citizenship. Their non-commitment to a single place makes them true cosmo-politans living in a city that is forgetting its native tongue.

Together with this relatively small number of highly educated profession-als and entrepreneurs, less-educated manual laborers, who account for the majority of the more than nine million internal migrants in Shanghai, have also established long-term legal residency. They share not only the physical space with sixteen million native Shanghairen[63] but also the linguistic space. To foster a good and welcoming business environment befitting a global city, the entrepreneurial municipal government actively promotes Putonghua to eradicate language barriers, coinciding with the central state's nationalist agenda. The nationwide public school system guarantees the acquisition of Putonghua for everyone across the country. And state-owned mass media reinforce the practices of Putonghua. Together, these forces drive the replace-ment of the Shanghai dialect with Putonghua. The dispossession of linguistic space experienced by native Shanghairen is a latent, though no less intended consequence of the urban entrepreneurialism that seeks to attract and accom-modate investment capital and a Putonghua-speaking labor force.

Extending the concept of right to the city to linguistic space—what Peter Marcuse elaborates above as a wide range of rights beyond material neces-sities to enjoy urban living,[64] it generates contentions about language use between native and non-native Shanghairen. For the former, exemplified by the UN official quoted at the beginning, the dominance of Putonghua on Shanghai streets alienates native Shanghairen in their own city. Many of them perceive it as a deprivation of their linguistic right to speak their mother tongue. For non-natives with little knowledge of the dialect, discrimination resulting from their lack of dialect proficiency challenges their hard-earned right to the city. This is a complex situation; both parties can claim a disad-vantageous minority position and feel victimized. As I will untangle in this book, since everyone in Shanghai lives under the power of an authoritarian state, each group viewing the other as the force of oppression is misguided.

The application of the concept of right to the city in Shanghai is situated at the intersection of urban entrepreneurialism with Chinese characteristics, place identity, and the disappearance of the linguistic space for the Shanghai dialect. An insight of Tuan's is instructive here; whenever a person feels the world is changing too rapidly to comprehend and is beyond their control, they evoke an idealized and stable past, which supports their sense of identity.[65] Facing urban transformation, one generated and controlled by national elites and their delegates in Shanghai and fueled by international capital, native Shanghairen feel dispossessed and bewildered. They yearn for stability and continuity and locate it in the linguistic sphere. Most of them are nostalgic for a linguistic space dominated by the Shanghai dialect, though they are resolved to accept reality. This sentiment is anchored in uneasiness with the political agenda that promotes a uniform national identity through a national language.

Nationalism and National Language

Nationalism underlies both the state's promotion of Putonghua and its construction of Shanghai as a global city. This is another crucial dimension to understand the language conflict currently ongoing in Shanghai, a city famed for its cosmopolitan past. It is a clash between state power working to globalize the city and the forces intent on maintaining Shanghai's local character, all within the broader context of economic globalization and authoritarian regime. This is the unique dilemma Shanghai faces in the ongoing globalization process. The city and its people must negotiate between a nationalist agenda and the city's historical connection with the world being selectively revived.

Theories of nationalism and national language focus on the political and economic need for a standardized language and a culturally homogeneous population. One important figure in the field is Ernest Gellner, who defines nationalism as a political principle that reflects the objective need for a modern industrial state.[66] Such a state "can only function with a mobile, literate, culturally standardized, and interchangeable population."[67] The implication of Gellner's argument for this study is that to maintain political and ideological control throughout Mainland China,[68] particularly under economic reforms, the Chinese Communist Party requires an educated, culturally homogenous, and politically loyal labor force. Linguistic standardization and cultural conformity are tightly associated with the rise of nationalism, even though, as Florian Coulmas points out in the Western European context, that many languages were well-established as national languages before the surge of nationalism in the nineteenth century.[69]

Shanghai in early twentieth century was a counterexample to the argument that a national language is necessary in countries undergoing industrialization, since the rest of the country lagged so far behind Shanghai's development at that point. A standard national language appears essential in an industrial society, which according to Gellner, "requires sustained, frequent and precise communication between strangers, involving a sharing of explicit meaning, transmitted in a standard idiom and in writing when required."[70] In this formulation, the roots of nationalism lie in the distinctive structural requirements of an industrial society, when a large proportion of the population are centrally educated to be adequately employable, geographically mobile, and participate in a modern, standardized mode of production. However, this line of thinking does not suggest the replacement or annihilation of vernaculars. Differing from this utilitarian view, Coulmas writes that under conditions of foreign domination and political fragmentation, an ardent nationalist would regard the language as the only culture marker that could serve as a common bond and symbol of the nation.[71] That was precisely the mindset when Guoyu and Guoyin, the national language and the national pronunciation, respectively, were developed in the post-feudal, anti-colonial context of early twentieth-century China. However, as mentioned earlier, that historical period witnessed the rise of cosmopolitanism in polyglot Shanghai, when the Shanghai dialect served as a *lingua franca*. As detailed in the next chapter, this was also a time period of urbanization, labor migration, and an influx of domestic and international capital, which are characteristics Gellner identifies as early industrialism.[72]

Similar processes have been happening again in the recent economic reform era, but the linguistic landscape is very different this time around. Industrialism and the practical need for communication across a diverse population are not sufficient explanations for the replacement of the Shanghai dialect with Putonghua. Forces for modernization and economic development were present in Shanghai a century ago, when the dialect came into shape and thrived despite the existence of a newly promulgated national language.

Another aspect of the ambiguity toward nationalism in Shanghai is that national identity is anchored in the imposed national language. The relation between the Chinese state's vision of a strong and rising China and a standard national language appears straightforward in light of the need for unity and conformity under nationalism. But it becomes muddled if we take into consideration the two modern senses of "nation." As Eric Hobsbawm points out, one is a cultural relation between state and people based on political participation and is known as citizenship; the other is based on some imagined, shared cultural identity.[73] In the case of national language, the question becomes, is it mandatory for every citizen to speak it or only those who identify with the cultural identity regardless of citizenship?

Hobsbawm's first sense of nation can be applied smoothly in terms of the connection between nation, citizenship, and national language; while it is his second sense of nation that proves most useful to understand the collapse of an imagined, internalized Chinese identity. As detailed in chapter 2, the entire Chinese legal structure, from the Constitution down to local regulations, requires citizens to speak Putonghua, abiding to the first sense of the nation, in terms of political and social obligations. However, the idea of Chinese as a unified ethnicity is problematic. Within China, Chinese is more an imposed political identity than a historically rooted cultural identity. There was never an agreed-upon national cuisine or a nationwide shared mother tongue with which to identify a uniform Chinese identity, not to mention the expansion and shrinkage of the geographical area historically occupied by Han Chinese and ruled by feudal China. When Chinese as citizenship is invoked, it includes the fifty-five officially recognized ethnic minorities with their distinctive languages, cultural traditions, histories, and in some cases religions; together they account for roughly 8.4 percent of the country's population, according to the 2010 census.[74] However, if understood as an ethnic identity, the category Chinese would be restricted to Han Chinese, the dominant ethnicity. Such is the ethnic background of my discussion of Shanghairen as a regional identity when native Shanghairen could be of a non-Han Chinese background.

Susan Gal's insight on national languages coincides with Hobsbawm's second sense of nation that "the uniformity of language is . . . proof that the speaking subject is an authentic member of the nation, linking speaker and language to the past and its (invented) traditions."[75] Therefore, speaking a national language holds the significance of an internalized national history and ready identification with that nation. In this sense, the Chinese state treats Putonghua as a uniting force to synthesize a united history of the Chinese people, to blanket over ethnic and linguistic diversity and to mitigate the internal tensions resulting from rising inequality in the economic reform era. The imposed happy fusion between the Chinese nation and Putonghua exemplifies an illusion Gal identifies elsewhere, which is "a circumscribed and internally homogeneous language with a similarly configured nation."[76]

Earlier studies on the imposition of Putonghua published shortly after the implementation of the *Law of the People's Republic of China on the Standard Spoken and Written Chinese Language* in 2001 point out the underlying agenda of political control. In deciphering China's language policies, Minglang Zhou and Heidi Ross argue that the nationwide advocacy for a single, standardized language reflects the cultural and political elites' agenda of building up national unity, on the one hand, and political controllability, on the other.[77] Writing about the imposition of a national identity anchored on language in ethnic minority regions, Longsheng Guo stresses that Putonghua "serves as a tool for both political control of the country's periphery and the construction of a homogenous identity of Chinese-ness."[78] By presenting Putonghua as the shared ancestral language of Han Chinese—when, in fact, many mutually unintelligible non-Mandarin dialects persisted in use until recently—and by binding Putonghua with a national identity, the Chinese state deliberately conflates the two senses of nation, to forge a sense of unity and uniformity.

Over the course of Shanghai's relatively short history, nationalism took on different meanings. The anti-colonial and anti-capitalist labor protests in Shanghai during the turbulent years of the early twentieth century epitomize Gellner's argument that "the age of transition to industrialism was bound to be an age of nationalism."[79] Nationalist sentiment a century ago was anchored on political independence from imperialist and capitalist powers. More recently, nationalism is used as a powerful ideological tool for population control at a moment when the authoritarian state, practicing a socialist market economy, opens itself to the world. This nationalist agenda channeled through the imposition of Putonghua is enforced at the frontier of China's participation in economic globalization.

Other post-socialist cities, such as Budapest, have experienced this transition differently. In Budapest, there is an increasing degree of social and cultural heterogeneity within the city, a proliferation of difference, as people from varied places, speaking varied dialects and languages, plying varied trades, and worshipping in varied ways converge.[80] In sharp contrast, Shanghai's reconnection to the world or its re-globalization was *not* brought about by the collapse of the Communist Party's power.[81] Rather, all the redevelopment, reconnection, and reclamation of global city status are cautiously initiated, closely monitored, and strategically enabled by the state. The uniformity and cultural homogeneity required by the nationalist vision clashes with the diversity inherited from Shanghai's semi-colonial history, its landscape, urban culture, and population, which I will elaborate on in the next chapter about Shanghai's cosmopolitan past. To resolve the tension, the Shanghairen identity must be weakened and the unique dialect silenced, so that the invented, single Chinese-ness can prevail.

FIELD RESEARCH

Born and raised in Shanghai with the Shanghai dialect as mother tongue, I have experienced first-hand the urban redevelopments and overwhelming cultural and demographic changes in Shanghai since the 1980s. After relocating to North America in 2007, I have continued to be a keen observer of social, cultural, and linguistic changes in Shanghai. To capture the multiple social processes Shanghairen utilized to make sense of and to come to terms with this urban transformation, I incorporated quantitative surveys, in-depth interviews, and qualitative observation in public spaces into my research.

In the summer of 2013, I collected state language policies and documents from the Ministry of Education regarding the promotion of Putonghua from corresponding governmental agencies' websites. Also, through Weibo, the so-called Chinese Twitter, and WeChat, another Chinese social media platform, I established contacts with dialect preservation activists and public intellectuals in Shanghai. Many of them became gatekeepers essential for my fieldwork later that year.

The first phase of my field research in Shanghai took place in the fall and winter of 2013. I conducted twenty-two in-depth interviews with members of the following groups: activists in the Shanghai dialect preservation movement, public intellectuals, schoolteachers and principals, vernacular novelists and comedians, journalists, college language organization leaders, and entre-preneurs in the language training business. The majority of them were born and spent most, if not all, of their lives in Shanghai and regarded the Shanghai dialect as their native language. The only exceptions were a publisher from Anhui province and three entrepreneurs in the language training business from Zhejiang province adjacent to Shanghai. The publisher attended college and has lived in Shanghai for more than twenty years. He spoke the Shanghai dialect with a Mandarin accent and was a leading figure in publishing dialect-related works. The three entrepreneurs spoke another variation of the Wu language—very similar to the Shanghai dialect—as their mother tongue and had lived in Shanghai for more than a decade. Interview questions ranged from their personal experiences using the dialect privately and professionally to opinions on its fate .

Apart from interviewing experts and those who have a personal stake in the fate of the Shanghai dialect, I also investigated changes in the language attitudes and practices of ordinary Shanghairen, of various backgrounds. The interview guide covers areas of language practices in private and in public, attitudes about mass media products using the dialect, and social encounters with non-speakers. Using purposive sampling to cover multiple generations of Shanghairen who had lived in different parts of the urban center, I con-ducted twenty-eight interviews with a wide variety of participants, ranging from college students in their early twenties, middle-class parents in their thirties and forties, to middle-school educated seniors laid off from their work units in the 1990s. Every native Shanghairen I interviewed had experienced relocation from the overcrowded urban residences of their childhood or youth to their current single-family apartments or condos in the city's periphery. Conversations about language practices invariably led to reminiscences about their old neighborhoods, feelings of alienation, and descriptions of new urban areas and public transportation systems which did not exist ten or even five years ago. Their ready association of changes in language practices and changes to the city's demography and landscape demonstrate the inextricable relations between individual identity, sense of place, and language.

All my fifty interviewees provided consent and allowed me to use their real names in the publications of this study, feeling they had nothing to hide about their language practices and opinions on urban transformation. However, due to the uncertainty of the political atmosphere within China in recent years, I decided to use pseudonyms, and altered details about their affiliation to protect their identity in this book. The only exceptions are a few public intel-lectuals who had already published works on the Shanghai dialect or the pres-ervation of it at the time of our interviews in 2013. They were eager for more publicity or international attention, academic or not, and were particularly excited about the prospect of being quoted or mentioned in my work outside of China. Anonymity was less an issue for my survey research. Modeled after Kathryn Woolard's study on Catalan speakers in Barcelona in the 1980s, my survey questionnaire focused on the Shanghai dialect proficiency and language choices at home, in school, at work, and in public, with different audiences, and covering decades of private and public life. The respondents' names and contact information were not collected.

Using snowball sampling, I recruited native Shanghairen survey respondents both offline, through my personal network and in public gathering spaces, and online via Weibo and WeChat. The survey questionnaire was set up on Surveymonkey.com. It allowed my initial respondents to send the web link to their family members, coworkers, friends, and acquaintances. Offline recruitment mostly targeted seniors who were unfamiliar or uncomfortable with using computers or smartphones to fill out the online questionnaire. To collect data from that demographic group, I developed two strategies. First, I encouraged young and middle-aged survey participants to recruit their parents into the study and help them to fill out the online survey questionnaire.

Next, I established contact with Minmin Ge, who retired in the early 2010s after twenty-five years producing the well-known dialect radio show "Humorous Wang Xiaomao" (*huaji wang xiaomao*). Since April 2012, he has produced and organized a biweekly vernacular standup comedy and variety show called Shanghai Storytelling Gathering (*shanghai gushi hui*). This free event has been sponsored and hosted at the Shanghai Mass Art Center (*shanghaishi qunzhong yishuguan*) and has attracted a loyal following among Shanghairen retirees. To me, they were a hard group to reach: often suspicious of strangers and fearful of trickery. An introduction from their beloved host, Ge, smoothed the way to recruit many Shanghairen seniors into my survey research. From four consecutive biweekly events in the fall of 2013, I was able to collect survey responses from audience members ranging in age from sixty to nearly ninety, who were either children of or themselves early migrants to Shanghai. For those without their reading glasses handy, I read aloud survey questions and response categories in either the Shanghai dialect or a mix of the dialect and Putonghua to collect responses.

Out of the 248 survey responses, the majority are in the 19–44 age range (85.1 percent) with the largest age group being 25–34 years (47.6 percent). 61.1 percent of the respondents are female. By education level, more than half have a bachelor's degree from a domestic university (57.7 percent), and the proportion of bachelor's degree and higher, including both domestic and foreign postgraduate institutions, is 74.2 percent. And if we count associate degrees, then only 35 individuals in the sample do not have any college education. Thus, this is a highly educated sample, which does not represent the overall population in urban Shanghai. However, we can safely say this is the group, both economically mobile and intellectually curious, that the state intends to shape into loyal and obedient citizenry with the promise of achieving the "China Dream." Statistical analysis was performed to generate frequencies and cross-tabulations of language practices at home and in public in correlation with gender, age group, and educational level.

Supplementing interview and survey data, I conducted participant observations about language practices, namely, which language(s) ordinary Shanghairen used to communicate with family members, friends, acquaintances, shopkeepers, bank cashiers, or staff at government agencies in public. This provided me with opportunities to cross-validate language proficiency and choice data, as well as to capture how social dynamics played out through linguistic practices. Those dynamics mostly involved demonstrations of educational level, social status, and, most importantly, Shanghairen identity, a fascinating category I explore throughout this work. Qualitative observations in public spaces, such as public transit hubs, shopping malls, hospital lobbies, restaurants, or parks, also expanded the scope of my data collection to include non-native Shanghairen who do not speak the Shanghai dialect. To communicate with them, multilingual native Shanghairen had no choice but to switch to Putonghua. The subtle but significant tension and hesitation in the split second required to judge the circumstance and decide which language to use to initiate a conversation with a stranger in public was crucial for a better understanding of social inclusion and exclusion in Shanghai.

The story of urban transformation in Shanghai is incomplete without the voices from recent internal migrants. I travelled to Shanghai in the summer of 2017 to conduct follow-up research that explored their integration into Shanghainese society. I specifically investigated whether and to what extent they acquired dialect proficiency, whether the dominance of Putonghua in Shanghai eased their integration, and whether language remained an obstacle for them to identify as Shanghairen. From my earlier findings of the increasing social integration of non-natives, I hypothesized that the bilingual capacity of native Shanghairen facilitated migrants' integration but reduced the incentives for migrants to acquire the dialect. In total, I interviewed twenty highly educated non-natives who migrated to Shanghai at different times, from the late 1990s to mid-2010s. I also observed language practices in public spaces from urban center subway transfer hubs and public parks to shopping centers. The new data help me to illustrate a fuller image of the language attitudes and practices in the city and provide a systematic examination of the connections between language, place identity, and social integration in Shanghai. The interview guides for my 2013 field research with native Shanghairen and the 2017 one with non-natives, as well as the 2013 survey questionnaire can be found in the Appendix.

CHAPTER OVERVIEW

Chapter 1 synthesizes the multilayered history of Shanghai around three central themes that contribute to Shanghai's sense of exceptionalism and correspond to the later empirical chapters. First, Shanghai is a migrant city, where hardly anyone can make nativist claims. Each of the four waves of internal migration into Shanghai since the mid-nineteenth century took place at a particular junction of local, national, and global forces. Migrant origins also contributed to the formation of the Shanghai dialect. Second, the divided urban landscape inherited from the semi-colonial era bears cultural and class significance for native Shanghairen. The issue of boundaries has always been important in Shanghai; from the city wall separating the territory controlled by the Qing Dynasty from the settlements and concessions under Western imperialist rule, to an upper/lower corner distinction based on the quality of housing and inhabitants' socioeconomic status, and to the Huangpu River which separates the west bank, once the heart of urban Shanghai, from the formerly rural east bank, and traverses the city before reaching the East China Sea. Lastly, this chapter briefly explains the origin and development of the Shanghai dialect, highlighting its hybrid, modern, and urban nature. Its continuous change reflects the vicissitude of various forces in the city since its formation a little more than a century ago.

In chapter 2, I examine the Chinese Communist Party's language policies, from the Constitution down to municipal guidelines, and how they have marginalized the Shanghai dialect. As demonstrated by my survey and interview data on language practices at home and in public across three generations of native Shanghairen, dialect proficiency has drastically declined over the last two decades among native Shanghairen. This confirms existing literature on language shift but goes beyond the surface phenomena to investigate deeper motivations. In the context of China's economic reforms, top-down promotion of the national language has successfully tapped into pragmatic locals' yearning for upward mobility, preventing them from passing the Shanghai dialect down to their children, and has dissuaded newcomers from learning the city's former *lingua franca*. The language attitudes and practices appear to be gendered as well as divided by social class. The lower social status of women and those of working-class background makes those groups more likely to comply with the dominant language ideology by using Putonghua in public and in private. Furthermore, class difference not only contributes to differentiated adoption of the dominant language ideology but also sheds light on an alternative language ideology. This alternative highlights the dialect's cultural values and may ensure that it will be preserved. I describe the major strategy of the Shanghai dialect preservation movement at the end of this chapter. Despite their efforts, it is nearly impossible to fight against both the state propaganda machine and the general public's mindset.

Urban redevelopment and geographical displacement also contribute to the endangerment of the Shanghai dialect. This was accomplished by destroying the material basis for everyday linguistic expressions and the dispersal of dialect speakers to linguistically mixed communities, respectively. Chapter 3 tells a multifaceted displacement story with many layers of loss and alienation. The abrupt disruption of a lifestyle closely associated with those old residential architectures threatens the language used to describe and inhabit them. Furthermore, the new residential housing pattern echoes a class-based hierarchy, resulting in a Shanghairen insider membership no longer obtained or recognized along the city's historical-geographical divide. In response, the displaced create a new mental mapping of the city. They reject the newly developed Pudong as their Shanghai and are nostalgic for the lifestyle in the urban core that they can no longer afford.

Chapter 4 examines how demographic changes have contributed to the decline of the dialect. In the twenty years since the reforms to the household registration system that once prohibited geographical mobility within the country, non-natives now make up 40 percent of Shanghai's urban population. Under this overarching structural change, my closer look at the social integration of recent internal migrants reveals that the acceptance of non-natives into Shanghairen's social circles and families is based less on dialect competence and more on educational level and socioeconomic status. Migrants to China's economically vibrant coastal cities at the beginning of economic reforms were mostly from rural areas and less educated. In contrast, many new arrivals since are of high educational level and some even with considerable personal wealth. However, the institutional (and selective) social acceptance of this new generation of migrants backfires in the debate over who counts as a Shanghairen. Insights from my in-depth interviews with native Shanghairen suggest dialect proficiency continues to serve its boundary maintenance function for a Shanghairen identity.

The last empirical chapter is predominantly based on new data collected in 2017. It focuses on non-natives' place attachment to the city. Despite the diminished power of the household registration system in creating legal obstacles for highly educated and well-off non-native Shanghairen, a Shanghai *hukou* still matters for their sense of belonging and identification with the city. Multiple secondary factors act as pull or push forces to generate this new generation of migrants' decision to settle down in Shanghai, but it does not necessarily mean they identify as Shanghairen. The Shanghai dialect remains the ultimate obstacle for them to either recognize themselves or be recognized by native Shanghairen as genuine insiders. In response, those migrants who are embodied with human capitals in the form of educational credentials, highly sought-after skills, or personal wealth develop what I call flexible resident identity. This affords a sense of fluidity and mobility that circumvents undesirable aspects of a fixed place identity associated either with their hometown, or Shanghai, or abroad. Unfortunately, such flexibility further diminishes the incentive for them to learn the dialect.

The conclusion summarizes the negative impact of the three sets of state policies on the linguistic space and future for the Shanghai dialect. The urban landscape in Shanghai has become increasingly uniform as it takes on a global city look. The linguistic environment no longer privileges the Shanghai dialect in the social integration of non-natives, which instead depends mostly on social class. Though extreme caution must be taken when predicting the death of a language, the Shanghai dialect nonetheless has a dim future. Since the beginning of this research, the dialect has mostly disappeared from the city's audible landscape. As the city becomes China's showcase to the world, and in doing so revives its cosmopolitan, migrant city identity, its own vernacular is overshadowed, if not silenced altogether. In this transient historical moment, when Shanghai embraces a status as a truly global city, the notion of an authentic Shanghairen identity is challenged by multiple forces. Dialect proficiency is rapidly losing its significance and struggles to claim its legitimacy without being seen as xenophobic.

NOTES

1. "On the 'International Mother Tongue Day,' Xu Haoliang, the Assistant General Secretary of the United Nations Gave an Interview in the Shanghai Dialect." February 21, 2014. Kankanews.com. To watch the full length of the video in Shanghai dialect: http://www.kankanews.com/a/2014-02-21/0014269910.shtml.

2. Liang, Sihua. 2015. *Language Attitudes and Identities in Multilingual China: A Linguistic Ethnography*. Heidelberg, New York: Springer. P.11–12.

3. Mair, Victor H., and Victor H. Mair. 1991. "What Is a Chinese 'Dialect/Topolect'? Reflections on Some Key Sino-English Linguistic Terms." *Sino-Platonic Papers* 29: 1–38. P.15.

4. Bourdieu, Pierre. 1991. *Language and Symbolic Power*. Cambridge, MA: Harvard University Press. P. 236.

5. Ferguson, Charles A. 1959. "Diglossia." *WORD* 15 (2): 325–40. P.328, 337–38.

6. Snow, Don. 2010. "Hong Kong and Modern Diglossia." *International Journal of the Sociology of Language* 206: 155–79. P.160.

7. Fuller, Michael Anthony. 1999. *An Introduction to Literary Chinese*. Cambridge, MA: Harvard University Asia Center. P.1.

8. Norman, Jerry. 1988. *Chinese*. Cambridge: Cambridge University Press. P.83.

9. Ramsey, S. Robert. 1989. *The Languages of China*. Princeton, NJ: Princeton University Press. P.4.

10. Ramsey. *The Languages of China*, P.21.

11. The endangerment of languages in ethnic minority regions in China is beyond the scope of this study. If interested, see for example Zhou, Minglang, and Hongkai Sun (eds.) 2004. *Language Policy in the People's Republic of China: Theory and Practice Since 1949*. New York and Boston: Springer Science & Business Media, and Q. Dai, & Y. Dong, 2001. The Historical Evolution of Bilingual Education for China's Ethnic Minorities. *Chinese Education & Society* 34 (2): 7–47.

12. Hudson, Alan. 2002. "Outline of a Theory of Diglossia." *International Journal of the Sociology of Language* 157: 1–48. P.30.

13. Fishman, Joshua A. 1980. "Bilingualism and Biculturism as Individual and as Societal Phenomena." *Journal of Multilingual and Multicultural Development* 1 (1): 3–15. P.8.

Fishman, Joshua A. 1985. "Macrosociolinguistics and the Sociology of Language in the Early Eighties." *Annual Review of Sociology* 11: 113–27.

14. See for example

Bergère, Marie-Claire. 2009. *Shanghai: China's Gateway to Modernity*. Stanford, CA: Stanford University Press.

Lee, Leo Ou-fan. 1999. *Shanghai Modern: The Flowering of a New Urban Culture in China, 1930–1945*. Cambridge, MA: Harvard University Press.

Lu, Hanchao. 1999. *Beyond the Neon Lights: Everyday Shanghai in the Early Twentieth Century*. Berkeley, CA: University of California Press.

Yeh, Wen-hsin. 2007. *Shanghai Splendor: Economic Sentiments and the Making of Modern China, 1843–1949*. Berkeley, CA: University of California Press.

15. Chen, Xiangming. 2009. "A Globalizing City on the Rise: Shanghai's Transformation in Comparative Perspective." In *Shanghai Rising: State Power and Local Transformations in a Global Megacity*, edited by Xiangming Chen, xv–xxxv. Minneapolis: University of Minnesota Press. P.xx.

16. Lu, Hanchao. 2002. "Nostalgia for the Future: The Resurgence of an Alienated Culture in China." *Pacific Affairs* 75 (2): 169–86. P.172.

17. King, Anthony D., and Abidin Kusno. 2000. "On Be(Ij)Ing in the World: 'Postmodernism,' 'Globalization,' and the Making of Transnational Space in China." In *Postmodernism and China*, edited by Xudong Zhang and Arif Dirlik, 41–67. Durham & London: Duke University Press.

18. Sklair, Leslie. 2010. "Iconic Architecture and the Culture-Ideology of Consumerism:" *Theory, Culture & Society* 27 (5): 135–59. P.138–9.

19. Xu, Fang. 2013. "Governance on the Production of Identity: Consuming Western High-Culture in Contemporary Shanghai." In *China and the Humanities: At the Crossroads of the Human and the Humane*, edited by Kang Tchou, 161–88. Champaign, IL: Common Ground Publishing.

20. Sklair. "Iconic Architecture and the Culture-Ideology of Consumerism," 135–59. P.141.

21. Ong, Aihwa. 2006. "Reengineering the 'Chinese Soul' in Shanghai?" In *Neoliberalism as Exception: Mutations in Citizenship and Sovereignty*, 219–40. Durham & London: Duke University Press. P.221.

22. Bunnell, Tim. 2002. "Multimedia Utopia? A Geographical Critique of High-Tech Development in Malaysia's Multimedia Super Corridor." *Antipode* 34 (2): 265–95. P.287.

23. Sassen, Saskia. 2011. *Cities in a World Economy*. 4 edition. Thousand Oaks, CA: SAGE Publications, Inc.

24. Woolard, Kathryn A. 1998. "Introduction: Language Ideology as a Field of Inquiry." In *Language Ideologies: Practice and Theory*, edited by Bambi B. Schieffelin, Kathryn A. Woolard, and Paul V. Kroskrity, 3–47. Oxford Studies in Anthropological Linguistics. Oxford & New York: Oxford University Press. P.3.

25. Irvine, Judith T. 1989. "When Talk Isn't Cheap: Language and Political Economy." *American Ethnologist* 16 (2): 248–67. P.255.

26. Irvine, Judith T., and Susan Gal. 2010. "Language Ideology and Linguistic Differentiation." In *Regimes of Language: Ideologies, Polities, and Identities*, edited by Paul V. Kroskrity, 35–84. Santa Fe: School of American Research Press. P.35.

27. Dorian, Nancy. 1998. "Western Language Ideologies and Small-Language Prospects." In *Endangered Languages: Language Loss and Community Response*, edited by Lenore A. Grenoble and Lindsay J. Whaley, 3–21. Cambridge, MA: Cambridge University Press. P.8.

28. Woolard, Kathryn A. 1985. "Language Variation and Cultural Hegemony: Toward an Integration of Sociolinguistic and Social Theory." *American Ethnologist* 12 (4): 738–48. P.739.

29. Jaffe, Alexandra. 1999. *Ideologies in Action: Language Politics on Corsica*. *Ideologies in Action*. Berlin & Boston: De Gruyter Mouton.

30. Cavanaugh, Jillian R. 2009. *Living Memory: The Social Aesthetics of Language in a Northern Italian Town*. Malden & Oxford: Wiley and Blackwell.

31. Woolard. "Language Variation and Cultural Hegemony," 738–48. P.741.

32. Bourdieu. *Language and Symbolic Power*.

33. Huang, Shuanfan. 2000. "Language, Identity and Conflict: A Taiwanese Study." *International Journal of the Sociology of Language* 143: 139–50.

34. Singapore was under British rule from 1819–1963.

35. Milroy, James, and Lesley Milroy. 1985. *Authority in Language: Investigating Standard English*. London, Boston & Henley: Routledge & Kegan Paul. P.109.

36. Woolard. "Language Variation and Cultural Hegemony," 738–48. P.742.

37. Labov, William. 1972. *Language in the Inner City: Studies in the Black English Vernacular*. Philadelphia: University of Pennsylvania Press.

38. Bourdieu, Pierre. 1986. "The Forms of Capital." In *Handbook of Theory and Research for the Sociology of Education*, edited by John Richardson, 241–58. Westport, CT: Greenwood.

Bourdieu. *Language and Symbolic Power*.

39. Bourdieu. *Language and Symbolic Power*.

40. Bourdieu. *Language and Symbolic Power*. P. 220.

41. Jaffe. *Ideologies in Action*, P.30.

42. Sassen, Saskia. 2001. *The Global City: New York, London, Tokyo*. 2nd edition. Princeton, N.J: Princeton University Press.

43. Lefebvre, Henri. 1991. *The Production of Space*. Oxford: Wiley and Blackwell.

44. Marcuse, Peter. 2012. "Whose Right(s) to What City?" In *Cities for People, Not for Profit: Critical Urban Theory and the Right to the City*, edited by Neil Brenner, Peter Marcuse, and Margit Mayer, 24–41. London & New York: Routledge. P.31.

45. Harvey, David. 2005. "Neoliberalism 'with Chinese Characteristics.'" In *A Brief History of Neoliberalism*, 120–51. Oxford & New York: Oxford University Press. P.120.

46. Harvey, David. 2001. "From Managerialism to Entrepreneurialism: The Transformation in Urban Governance in Late Capitalism." In *Spaces of Capital: Towards a Critical Geography*, 345–68. New York: Routledge. P.348.

47. Harvey. "From Managerialism to Entrepreneurialism," 345–68.

48. Harvey. "From Managerialism to Entrepreneurialism," 345–68, P.358.

49. Sassen. *The Global City.*

50. Hsing, You-tien. 2006. "Land and Territorial Politics in Urban China." *The China Quarterly* 187: 575–91.

51. Fu, Zhengji. 2002. "The State, Capital, and Urban Restructuring in Post-Reform Shanghai." In *The New Chinese City: Globalization and Market Reform*, edited by John Logan, 106–20. Oxford & Malden, Mass: Wiley-Blackwell. P.107.

52. He, Shenjing. 2007. "State-Sponsored Gentrification under Market Transition: The Case of Shanghai." *Urban Affairs Review* 43 (2): 171–98.

Zhang, Li. 2006. "Contesting Spatial Modernity in Late-Socialist China." *Current Anthropology* 47 (3): 461–84.

53. See for example

He, Shenjing, and Fulong Wu. 2005. "Property-Led Redevelopment in Post-Reform China: A Case Study of Xintiandi Redevelopment Project in Shanghai." *Journal of Urban Affairs* 27 (1): 1–23.

Ren, Xuefei. 2011. *Building Globalization: Transnational Architecture Production in Urban China*. Chicago & London: University of Chicago Press. P.110–23.

Wai, Albert Wing Tai. 2006. "Place Promotion and Iconography in Shanghai's Xintiandi." *Habitat International* 30 (2): 245–60.

54. Harvey. "From Managerialism to Entrepreneurialism," 345–68. P.355.

55. Lalli, Marco. 1992. "Urban-Related Identity: Theory, Measurement, and Empirical Findings." *Journal of Environmental Psychology* 12 (4): 285–303.

56. Twigger-Ross, Clare L., and David L. Uzzell. 1996. "Place and Identity Processes." *Journal of Environmental Psychology* 16 (3): 205–20.

57. Ghertner, D Asher. 2011. "Rule by Aesthetics: World-Class City Making in Delhi." In *Worlding Cities: Asian Experiments and the Art of Being Global*, edited by Ananya Roy and Aihwa Ong, 279–306. Malden & Oxford: Wiley and Blackwell.

58. Tuan, Yi-Fu. 1977. *Space and Place: The Perspective of Experience*. Minneapolis & London: University of Minnesota Press. P.154.

59. Tuan. *Space and Place*. P.159.

60. Proshansky, Harold M. 1978. "The City and Self-Identity." *Environment and Behavior* 10 (2): 147–69. P.155.

61. Tuan. *Space and Place,* P.187.

62. Proshansky. "The City and Self-Identity," 147–69.

63. Chart 2.1 Total Households, Population, Density of Registered Population and Life Expectancy (1978–2018). Shanghai Statistical Yearbook 2019. http://tjj.sh.gov .cn/tjnj/nj19.htm?d1=2019tjnje/E0201.htm retrieved August 9, 2020.

64. Marcuse. "Whose Right(s) to What City?" 24–41, P.31.

65. Tuan. *Space and Place*, P.188.

66. Gellner, Ernest. 1983. *Nations and Nationalism*. Ithaca: Cornell University Press. P.1.

67. Gellner. *Nations and Nationalism*, P.45.

68. Under "One country, two systems," Hong Kong and Macau enjoy a certain level of autonomy, which has been rapidly diminishing. The historical and political environments there are too different and complex to be grouped together here.

69. Coulmas, Florian. 1988. "What Is a National Language Good For?" In *With Forked Tongues: What Are National Languages Good For?* edited by Florian Coulmas, 1–24. Ann Arbor, MI: Karoma Publishers. P.10.

70. Gellner. *Nations and Nationalism*, P.34.

71. Coulmas. "What Is a National Language Good For?," 1–24. P.7–8.

72. Gellner. *Nations and Nationalism*, P.42.

73. Hobsbawm, Eric. 1992. "Introduction: Inventing Traditions." In *The Invention of Tradition*, edited by Eric Hobsbawm and Terence O. Ranger, 1–14. Cambridge: Cambridge University Press.

74. Calculated from Table 1.6 Regional Population by Sex and Ethnicity. 2010 Census of the People's Republic of China. http://www.stats.gov.cn/tjsj/pcsj/rkpc/6rp /indexch.htm. Retrieved August 10, 2020.

75. Gal, Susan. 1992. "Multiplicity and Contention among Ideologies: A Commentary." Edited by Bambi B. Schieffelin, Paul V. Kroskrity, and Kathryn A. Woolard. *Pragmatics* 2 (3): 445–9. P.448.

76. Gal. "Multiplicity and Contention among Ideologies," 445–9. P.449.

77. Zhou, Minglang, and Heidi Ross. 2004. "Introduction: The Context of the Theory and Practice of China's Language Policy." In *Language Policy in the People's Republic of China: Theory and Practice Since 1949*, edited by Minglang Zhou and Hongkai Sun, 1–18. New York & Boston: Springer Science & Business Media.

78. Guo, Longsheng. 2004. "The Relationship between Putonghua and Chinese Dialects." In *Language Policy in the People's Republic of China: Theory and Practice Since 1949*, edited by Minglang Zhou and Hongkai Sun, 45–54. New York & Boston: Springer Science & Business Media.

79. Gellner. *Nations and Nationalism*, P.40.

80. Szelenyi, Ivan. 1996. "Cities under Socialism: And After." In *Cities After Socialism: Urban and Regional Change and Conflict in Post-Socialist Societies*, edited by Gregory Andrusz, Michael Harloe, and Ivan Szelenyi, 286–317. Oxford & Cambridge, MA: Wiley-Blackwell.

81. Wasserstrom, Jeffrey N. 2009. *Global Shanghai, 1850–2010*. London & New York: Routledge. P.135–8.

Chapter 1

A Cosmopolitan Past

To contextualize the current situation in Shanghai, I will briefly trace the city's history of migration, the expansion and redevelopment of the urban landscape, and the origin of the vernacular. This will illustrate how the Shanghai dialect has always been entwined with and enriched by Shanghai's cosmopolitan past and quotidian present. Earlier migrants, who mostly came from neighboring provinces starting in the mid-nineteenth century, lived on land leased to Western colonial powers by the feudal Qing government. In the everyday mingling of so many migrants of diverse origins, a *lingua franca* was born, and a unique urban culture arose. Much has changed since the recent economic reforms, and currently migrants account for roughly 40% of the urban population, and Shanghai again enjoys a reputation as a cosmopolitan metropolis. In brief, this is *not* a story about a native population losing their indigenous language or territory. Instead, it is about power struggles between earlier and more recent migrants over who has the right to the city, whose interests dominate the city and the urban language scene they jointly produce and reproduce in the era of neoliberalism with Chinese characteristics.

A MIGRANT CITY

To understand Shanghai's cosmopolitan character, we first need to look at the city's contested beginnings. There are two competing narratives of Shanghai's origin. The one recognized and promoted by the central and the municipal governments stress that Shanghai has a relatively long history, reaching back 700 years as a coastal town. When Shanghai became a cosmopolitan metropolis in the early twentieth century, it was invaded, occupied, and exploited by the West. Western settlers, as Jeffrey Wasserstrom points out, favored a counternarrative. These settlers declared 1843 as the year the city was founded, and thus their presence was natural and beneficial to the land and to its native people, typical of imperialist rhetoric.[1]

There is merit and fault in both narratives. On the one hand, when Shanghai Township first appeared in Chinese historical records, it was not located where urban Shanghai is now. This fact disputes the official narrative recounting 700 years of local history. On the other hand, to argue that Shanghai did not exist at all until 1843 disregards all previous history and the significant Chinese population that lived on the land currently recognized as metropolitan Shanghai. Therefore, for the central and local governments to insist on the rich history of Shanghai Township before the Treaty of Nanking is to claim the city's Chinese origin. This narrative undermines the role played by foreign forces in building the city's rich cosmopolitanism. Naturally, this version is vital to the current state-led global city–building process. This time, Shanghai will become a bigger, stronger, and distinctly Chinese global city, under the Chinese Communist Party's leadership.

Interestingly, the Western-dominated narrative has supporters among the so-called native Shanghairen, whose ancestors mostly came to Shanghai in the late nineteenth or early twentieth centuries from nearby towns or villages in the Yangtze River Delta. Compared to recent internal migrants to Shanghai, these so-called native Shanghairen are the earlier migrants or their descendants, who contributed to the formation of cosmopolitan Shanghai in the early twentieth century. By insisting on 1843 as the beginning of the city of Shanghai, these Shanghairen assert their birthright to the city. This migration history is crucial for understanding the cosmopolitan identity of Shanghai and the conflicts between so-called native Shanghairen and recent migrants, regarding their claims to the city in various spheres. Fundamentally, the two competing narratives about Shanghai's history represent tensions between nationalism and local pride flavored with nativism.

According to the official record and history textbooks certified by the Chinese Communist Party, 1291 was the year when a place called "Shanghai" first appeared in written documents. The predecessor of the city was a fishing village in the tenth century called Hu Du, named after *hu* (bamboo stakes), which fisherman sank into the mud to anchor their nets. In 1291, Shanghai County was established with Shanghai Town as the county seat. This official record established the starting point of Shanghai's history. The town was located at the tip of the Yangtze River Delta on the East China Sea and sat at the midpoint of China's coastline. When Huating County—later renamed Songjiang County, and which Shanghai Township once belonged to—was established in the prosperous Tang Dynasty (AD 751), the current urban area of Shanghai was still under water. Therefore, no group can claim themselves indigenous to the city.[2] The population grew gradually after the establishment of the county seat. Denison and Ren note that toward the end of the fifteenth century, Shanghai was already a large town, celebrated for its economic strength and rich culture, with poets, musicians, eminent scholars, and politicians making it a place of renown.[3]

Before the outbreak of the Opium War (1839–1842), the population of Shanghai was estimated to be 120,000.[4] On August 29, 1842, the defeated Qing Dynasty signed the Treaty of Nanking to end the Opium War. The treaty made Shanghai one of five treaty ports opened to British residence and trade. The treaty granted the British a vast amount of land west and north of the walled county seat in 1843. At that time, the county seat was merely nine square li, approximately 556 acres.[5] In that year of opening treaty ports, or *kaibu*, the population in Shanghai was less than two hundred thousand.[6]

Western settlers tell a different story. They declared 1843 as the year the city was founded. Before, they said, it was merely a fishing village. To demystify the fishing village myth, Wasserstrom asks whether a village could have a population of a quarter million, city walls, elaborate gardens, temples, trade guilds, and governmental bodies.[7] Official records show that by 1852, the population had reached 544,413, largely due to internal migration.[8] Wasserstrom further points out that origin stories are always important to the identity of a city.[9] Embracing the Western imperialists' narrative, current native Shanghairen challenge the Communist Party's nationalist agenda. The fact that so-called native Shanghairen embrace the story of the city's origin based on where the current urban center of Shanghai is, rather than the historical record of feudal jurisdiction, appears to be an ideological choice. Their chosen origin story portrays Shanghai as a modern hybrid that Western power and influence brought into being and their ancestors contributed to its growth and prosperity.

The tension between the two narratives of Shanghai's origin reveals how the state-driven nationalist rhetoric tries to downplay and even demonize Western influence on Shanghai in the early twentieth century. Although it predates the founding of the People's Republic of China in 1949, the city's semi-colonial history inevitably exposes the weakness of the Chinese state. Therefore, to insist on the rich history of Shanghai Township before the treaty is to claim a Chinese origin for Shanghai and envision its future prosperity as China's global city. This tension is illustrated by an incident described to me by a producer at the Shanghai People's Radio Station. In 2013, the Culture and Propaganda Bureau in Shanghai shut down a planned celebration of the 170th anniversary of *kaibu* organized by local state-owned TV and radio stations. According to the producer, *kaibu* was a humiliating event for the Chinese nation in the eyes of the government so that it should not be celebrated. In contrast, my interviewee and his team, all native Shanghairen, perceived it as the moment when the modern and cosmopolitan Shanghai was born, emerging as a city beyond the bounds of the feudal Qing Dynasty (AD 1644–1911). To a certain extent, native Shanghairen embrace the idea that colonial Shanghai was not fully Chinese. In this view, Shanghai under Western imperialism was modern and progressive, in contrast to most of the rest of the country that was perceived as backward and traditional.

Waves of Early Migration

Shanghai quickly turned into a migrant city after *kaibu*. Chunlan Zhao, studying urban Shanghai residential patterns, points out that historically the Chinese elite and literati were rooted in rural areas, where they kept their permanent property, family tombs, and lineage temples. Urban living was mostly for officials to fulfill their duties or for merchants. Little evidence indicates any large-scale rural-to-urban migration in Shanghai before 1843.[10] In his research on population changes during the treaty port period (1843–1943), Yiren Zou documents that the population of Shanghai grew almost threefold from almost 1.3 million in 1900 to 3.7 million by 1935. The population in 1949, when the Chinese Communist Party took over and most foreigners left the city, was roughly 5.46 million.[11] The main reason for such rapid population growth was waves of internal migration, driven mostly by wars.

The population in urban Shanghai after *kaibu* was not the result of rural-to-urban migration within Shanghai County. Residents from rural parts of the county were always a minority in urban Shanghai, especially in the more prestigious and modern urban central districts. When the British and the United States jointly ruled International Settlement and the French Concession both ceased to exist in 1943, rural-origin Shanghai Bendiren (locals) accounted for 20.7% of Shanghai's urban population within Chinese jurisdiction and only 5.9% in the most prosperous urban central Huangpu District, which was part of the International Settlement.[12]

The low percentage of Shanghai Bendiren proves urban Shanghai's migrant city origin and reveals that the now so-called native Shanghairen are themselves descendants of migrants from only a century ago. In the last century and a half, Shanghai has experienced four huge waves of internal migration. The urban population first started to increase rapidly during the Taiping Rebellion (1851–1864), a peasant-led revolt against the Qing Dynasty that originated in Guangxi province in southern China. Shanghai itself came under threat when the rebel army established the Heavenly Kingdom and set the capital in Nanking, only 200 miles to the northwest. Twice the army of Taiping appeared outside of the walls of Shanghai, in 1860 and 1862, and twice were defeated by joint French, British, and Qing Dynasty forces, as Marie-Claire Bergère records.[13] During that period, hundreds of thousands fled their homes in the Yangtze River Delta to seek refuge in Shanghai's foreign concessions, which quickly changed these areas from "quarters reserved for Westerners into Sino-foreign towns."[14]

It is from the influx of war refugees during the Taiping Rebellion that a socioeconomic hierarchy based on regional origins began to emerge among Chinese residents of the city, in both the walled Chinese City and the foreign concessions. The wealthy gentry, merchant, and literati families that sought refuge in the treaty port during the Taiping Rebellion came predominantly from the adjacent Suzhou-Wuxi area of southern Jiangsu province, the Ningbo-Shaoxing region of northern Zhejiang province, and Canton. After the unrest, they largely remained in Shanghai, and, often in partnership with foreigners began investing in trade and commerce, shifting native capital from the countryside into the city.[15] The other group arriving in the city was laborers, mostly from northern Jiangsu province, as Emily Honig notes.[16]

The second wave of migration was caused by the Boxer Rebellion (1898– 1900), when war refugees again poured into the settlement and concessions to escape the unrest and revolts in the nearby countryside. Among this influx, class differentiation based on origin echoed that of the first wave. The gentry and merchants from southern Jiangsu and northern Zhejiang joined their earlier fellow villagers to form the Chinese elites in Shanghai. Those from northern Jiangsu of poor rural origin and with limited education primarily occupied the unskilled service sector as coolies and sanitation workers, if they did not become beggars.

After these first two waves, the population in Shanghai was 3.7 million in 1935, among which there were many foreign residents, making the city truly cosmopolitan. Great Britain, the United States, France, and the Chinese Republic all had some jurisdiction over certain parts of the city, a hybrid government overseeing a globalized population. Just as Chinese migrants from various parts of the country found their way to the city, by 1932, some 48,000 foreigners representing 50 different nationalities lived in Shanghai. In addition, there were anywhere from 15,000 to 20,000 Russian refugees, who fled the Bolshevik Revolution. They were singled out in the official category due to the fact that they did not enjoy the extraterritoriality granted to other foreigners through treaties between the Chinese state and Western imperialist powers. Their presence in Shanghai is still evident today, with two onion-dome orthodox churches and a statue of Pushkin located in the former French Concession.

The urban population swelled again during the Anti-Japanese War (1937–1945), which the West knows as World War II. During this third wave, on August 14, 1937, remembered ominously in the annals of Shanghai as "Bloody Saturday," hundreds of thousands of residents from urban areas controlled by the Republic of China and Shanghai's outlying countryside poured into the foreign concessions, and this wave continued in the next two months. That resulted in a combined population increase for the International Settlement and the French Concession of 780,000.[17] Shortly after, the fourth wave occurred during the Chinese Civil War between Kuomintang (the Chinese Nationalist Party) and the Chinese Communist Party (1946–1949). This wave brought more than two million people to Shanghai.

In less than a century, the migrant city of Shanghai grew from a node in the network of towns in the Yangtze River Delta to a globalized treaty port and haven for those seeking refuge both from home and abroad. Shanghai was geographically, politically, economically, and culturally significant in China's recent history, but was stripped of its migrant city identity by the Communist Party's population control policies enacted shortly after the founding of the People's Republic in 1949. The halt of geographical mobility facilitated the birth of the notion of native-ness in Shanghai.

During the Maoist Era

Restrictions on internal migration in accordance with the planned economy during the Maoist era altered the migrant city nature of Shanghai. Beginning in the early 1950s, regulations adopted to control rural-to-urban population flows reestablished public order after years of warfare, facilitated agricultural production, and regulated resource allocation.[18] The household registration system, or *hukou* system, was implemented in 1958 and classified all citizens of the People's Republic into two groups, "agricultural" for residents of rural areas and "non-agricultural" for urbanites.[19] The system later became the legal basis for restriction and control of geographical mobility, as well as for monitoring and limiting an individual's claim to social resources.

This regulation was intended to stabilize population movement, with the effect of strictly limiting the ability of rural workers to find non-agricultural work in cities.[20] *Hukou* status defined individual entitlement to an array of state-provided welfare measures under the planned economy until the late 1980s.[21] A further designation of *hukou* status indicates the location of an individual's claim to social resources;[22] for example, the municipality of Shanghai was only responsible for providing public services such as food rations or health care to those with Shanghai *hukou*, thus making relocation to Shanghai without official approval nearly impossible.

In most cases, *hukou* status is tied with one's birthplace and recorded in a booklet associated with one's residential address. Thus, in the era before *hukou* reforms, it functioned as an ascribed status with implications for one's life chances.[23] The entitlement to social resources associated with *hukou* and the disparity of social resources between coastal cities and inland rural regions sharply divided Chinese citizens into two tiers. In the upper tier, a non-agricultural (urban) *hukou* status granted superior economic and social opportunities in contrast to an agricultural (rural) one in terms of education, health care, employment, and pension. This system "created a chasm in Chinese society and produced and reproduced social segregation and social disparity."[24] It was, essentially, a de facto internal passport system.[25]

The *hukou* system strictly implemented nationwide remained essential for a Chinese citizen's everyday life during the Maoist era's cradle-to-grave socialist system. The passing of the Household Registration (*Hukou*) Regulation in 1958 led to a decline in numbers both entering and leaving Shanghai until 1967. The Up to the Mountains and Down to the Countryside Movement during the Great Proletarian Cultural Revolution sent more than 1.1 million urban youth in Shanghai to other provinces and another nearly half million to rural Shanghai counties between 1968 and 1978, according to the Office of Shanghai Chronicles.[26] Though essentially a struggle within the party for the next generation of leadership after Mao, that period resulted in a nationwide movement to forcefully relocate high-school and middle-school students to rural areas to work on collective farms, instead of advancing academically. Nationwide, 40 million youth participated, most involuntarily, in this political movement. When this group returned, many of them took over their parents' jobs, and a select few were admitted into universities. The higher education system, halted during the Cultural Revolution period, reopened for the first post-revolution cohort in 1977. That generation of Shanghairen was driven out of their home city by fanatic state policies during their formative years. Many sought tirelessly for years, if not decades, to return to Shanghai, both physically and legally by having their *hukou* reassigned back to Shanghai, even after retirement in other provinces. The population change from the late 1960s to the end of 1970s tells the story of a generation of native Shanghairen traumatized by ideologically driven policies and serves as the background of their eagerness to claim nativeness and right to the city. Over the course of the contemporary migration history of Shanghai, that period can be seen as a hiatus, with little *voluntary* migration in or out of the city.

Migrants in the Economic Reform Era

The migration situation in Shanghai started to change gradually after the 1992 Southern Tour (*nanxun*) of Deng Xiaoping, then the Chinese Communist Party Secretary. Despite the Open Door Policy issued in 1978, economic reforms did not reach Shanghai in large measure until after that tour. Yilong Lu notes that the central government saw social stability, built through household registration system, as a prerequisite for economic developments in the early years of economic reforms.[27] As a result, the divide between urban and rural *hukou* was deepened. It was not until 1992, when state power related to resource allocation and population mobility control was decentralized, that reforms emerged in more coastal regions including the Yangtze River Delta.[28] This was when Shanghai adopted an investment-based internal migration measure, called the Shanghai Blue-stamp *Hukou* Temporary Management Regulation (*shanghaishi lanyin hukou guanli zanxing guiding*), which went into effect on February 1, 1994, bypassing the national *hukou* system, and granting non-natives' the right to reside and work in the city.

Economic developments in Shanghai and further local amendment of the *hukou* system are inextricably linked from this point forward. The first clause of the 1994 regulation explains that its purpose is to fulfill the needs of establishing a socialist market economy and to manage temporary residents from outside Shanghai. The lack of a significant increase in the migrant population in Shanghai after this new regulation was due to the application process being difficult and expensive. Between 1994 and 2002, internal migrants received a blue stamp in their *hukou* booklet, which listed their birthplace, instead of the red stamp used in native Shanghairen's *hukou* booklets. For each blue-stamp *hukou*, applicants from foreign countries, or Hong Kong, Macau, and Taiwan were required to invest at least U.S. $200,000, and internal migrants at least RMB 1 million. In addition, private investors were required to establish lawful long-term residence in Shanghai before submitting the application. The costs were the same for each additional blue-stamp *hukou*, for example, for spouse or children.

According to the Shanghai Statistical Yearbook 2004, per capita disposable income in urban households for 1994 was RMB 5,868, and the highest quantile was RMB 11,608.[29] This makes the RMB 1 million astronomical even for the wealthy in Shanghai, not to mention capital investment is different from disposable income. Other ways to apply for a blue-stamp *hukou* included applying through one's employer or the purchase of market-rate housing of more than 70 square meters in Puxi, the west bank of Huangpu River or more than 65 square meters in Pudong, the newly urbanized and developed east bank.[30] Simply put, those able to acquire a blue-stamp *hukou* in Shanghai belonged to the newly rising elites, comprised of expatriates, domestic entrepreneurs, and the highly educated and skilled. However, they represent only a small portion of internal migrants in Shanghai.

The majority of internal migrants were from rural areas with little education, arriving to work as low-skill temporary laborers. Their status as wage labor echoed that of migrants arriving in the first half of the twentieth century. To manage them, the Shanghai Municipal Government enacted the Shanghai Floating Population Management Regulation (*shanghaishi wailai liudong renyuan guanli tiaoli*) on January 1, 1997. The first clause of this regulation emphasizes the need to maintain social order, a significant difference from the measures for blue-stamp *hukou* that targeted the privileged. Unsurprisingly, the 1997 regulation contains no clause about housing purchases; rather, it has detailed procedures for finding apartments and rental properties. On top of the temporary residency card, these floating migrants were required to apply for a work permit to obtain employment in Shanghai. One detail in the 1997 regulation stands out as illustrative of the type of jobs many migrants found: a clause explaining how to obtain a work permit as a domestic worker. This is in sharp contrast to those non-natives eligible for a blue-stamp *hukou*, who were capable of investing at least RMB 1 million.

Both the 1994 and 1997 regulations were adjusted and updated in the early 2000s. It indicates the Shanghai Municipal Government was carefully monitoring the population flow to aid the building of a global city with the help of migrant capital and labor. The rhetoric used to describe the purposes of the two regulations changed in the new versions, from the hesitant openness that characterized the 1994 and 1997 regulations to a full embrace of a migrant influx, though that welcoming tone remains contingent upon social class. That is to say, to highly educated, skilled, and wealthy migrants, the purpose of the regulation focused on their rights and potential contribution to the city while to those less educated migrants from rural areas, the tone of the regulation suggests more control.

The blue-stamp *hukou* system poured much-needed outside capital into Shanghai's housing market but had limited impact in attracting talents. When it expired in April 2002, the temporary regulation on the Shanghai Resident Permit for imported talents (*yinjin rencai shixing "shanghaishi juzhuzheng" zhidu zanxing guiding*) went into effect.[31] This temporary regulation explicitly aims to facilitate the flow of talents to encourage employment, investment, and enhance the city's overall competitiveness. It makes a bachelor's degree the minimum educational requirement for a Shanghai Resident Permit. Two years later, on August 30, 2004, the Shanghai Resident Permit Temporary Regulation (*shanghaishi juzhuzheng zanxing guiding*) went into effect. This regulation expands on the previous one to include less educated migrants. The stated purpose of this updated regulation differs from its antecedent. Rather than claiming to bolster the city's competitiveness or to enhance Shanghai's status as a global city, this regulation declares in Clause 1 its intention to "protect the legal rights of those coming to Shanghai, to standardize and digitalize population management, and to improve governmental services."[32] This regulation allows legal residency and employment for working-class migrants (79.4 percent of the newcomers according to the 2010 census) who come to Shanghai to seek a better life. Two surveys conducted by the Shanghai Statistical Bureau in 2000 and 2003 show that more than half of the non-*hukou* population in Shanghai had a middle-school education or lower, and only 10 percent had completed high school.[33]

The blue-stamp *hukou* and later residency permit system bypassed the national *hukou* system and brought an influx of internal migrants to Shanghai vital for globalizing the city, both on construction sites building infrastructure and in office towers growing the tertiary sector. A close reading of the four regulations reveals that non-natives entering Shanghai were allotted very different levels of governmental support and service based on their initial socioeconomic status. Less-educated migrants are called job seekers (*jiuye renyuan*) while those who are highly educated, skilled, and wealthy belong to a category called imported talents (*yinjin rencai*). The latter either obtain blue-stamp *hukou* or fall under the talent category in their official dossier. These are similar to the two groups Saskia Sassen identifies in the migrant labor force of global cities: the highly educated and wealthy who work predominantly in Fortune 500 companies and tertiary industries and laborers with limited education who work in the service sector.[34]

These measures turned out to be very effective in attracting migrants from across the country, reviving Shanghai's character as a migrant city. Looking at the fifth and the sixth censuses, conducted in 2000 and 2010, respectively, the *hukou* population and long-term non-*hukou* residents together have increased from 16.7 to 23 million in just ten years.[35] Among them, the migrant population rose from 3.5 to 9 million.[36] This indicates that of the 6.3 million new residents over ten years, roughly 5.5 million, or 87 percent, were internal migrants.

Sharp population increase in such a short period of time posed challenges to the provision of public services, such as public transportation, schools, and hospitals. When new policies extended to migrants material privileges once associated exclusively with Shanghai *hukou* without a corresponding increase in supply, tensions between the two groups inevitably erupted. Conflicts around material resources since have had a lasting impact on the debate about who counts as Shanghairen, and thus is entitled to its associated access to public resources.

After twenty years of using local regulations to circumvent the national *hukou* system under neoliberalism with Chinese characteristics,[37] the municipal government of Shanghai eventually replaced the 2002 and 2004 regulations with Regulations on Shanghai Resident Permit, which came into effect on July 1, 2013. This law continues the rhetoric of protecting internal migrants' legal rights. It promotes the standardization of population management, improvement of governmental services, and facilitation of economic, social, and environmental developments. In addition, the criteria for application are streamlined, only requiring legal employment, lawful residence, and more than six months' contribution to social security.

Compared to the rigid requirements for a blue-stamp *hukou* in 1994, the requirements to apply for a resident permit in 2013 are significantly less. Moreover, the Experimental Measure for Resident Permit Holders to Apply for Shanghai *Hukou*, issued on February 12, 2009, officially offers a way for Resident Permit holders to become legally a Shanghairen with a Shanghai *hukou*. This new measure allows those who have held a resident permit for seven years, during which time they continuously contributed to social security and paid income tax, to obtain a Shanghai *hukou*. On the one hand, this rewards migrants who contributed to building a globalized Shanghai with legal status; on the other hand, it shakes the legal pillar of Shanghairen identity. The gradual erosion of the Maoist era boundary between urban and rural, and between Shanghairen and outsiders, further indicates Shanghai's transition back to a migrant city.

Those who lived through the Maoist era in Shanghai, when the *hukou* system rigidly controlled geographical mobility and resource allocation, have witnessed the diminishment of their privileges while Shanghai regains its cosmopolitan status. Despite the fact that native Shanghairen are themselves children of earlier migrants, the *hukou* system has fostered a sense of territoriality since the 1950s. Along with the erosion of *hukou* status and its associated exclusive access to legal residence, employment, and public services in Shanghai, changes have also come to the city's built environment. Imprinted in the contours of the city and the built environment is the sociospatial hierarchy of urban neighborhoods inherited from the semi-colonial era. The mental mapping of the city among native Shanghairen has always been marked by socioeconomic and cultural boundaries.

A DIVIDED LANDSCAPE

The divided urban landscape of Shanghai is a story of East-meets-West. But more importantly, it is a story of rezoning and urban expansion, starting from the previously rural land outside the walled county seat after *kaibu* in 1843. The International Settlement, which occupied the area surrounding the walled county seat on northeastern waterfront, was under British and the United States' rule, with street names such as Avenue Edward VII. The settlement also celebrated Queen Victoria's Diamond Jubilee in June 1897. Located southwest of the county seat was the French Concession, with street names such as Avenue Joffre, named after Joseph Joffre, who served as Commander-in-Chief of the French forces on the western front during World War I. These divided jurisdictions transformed Shanghai into a cosmopolitan metropolis with a diverse built environment and urban culture.

The settlement boundaries functioned as means of social segregation from the time of their establishment, and the divide later translated into what was called an upper/lower corner distinction. Neighborhoods with modern, upscale, Western-looking housing in central and southwestern areas of the city were called *shangzhijiao* (upper corner), while those shantytowns and low-end alleyway housing in the working-class north and northeastern part of the city were deemed *xiazhijiao* (lower corner). Not even the founding of the People's Republic in 1949 and the Communist Party's condemnation of capitalist consumption and lifestyle and promotion of socialist values could alter this distinction in the minds of millions of Shanghairen. As Lei Ping argues from her archival research on Shanghai's urban culture in the Maoist era, a fetishized bourgeoisie materialism was preserved among petty urbanites' quotidian lives in Shanghai.[38] And one of the most important elements of this class-conscious boundary-drawing among Shanghairen was the upper/lower corner divide.

This dichotomy inherited from the colonial era influenced Shanghairen's housing choices, geosocial mobility and place identity throughout the twentieth century, until a new divide emerged in the economic reform era. Pudong, rural land located east of the Huangpu River, was rezoned as part of urban Shanghai in 1993. Since then, urban Shanghai has been divided by the Huangpu River ideologically. Puxi, the west bank remains the city imbued with the vicissitudes of a century and a half of colonial occupation, civil war, cosmopolitan culture, waves of internal migration and class struggles under Communist Party rule; while Pudong, which was rural three decades ago is now crowded with skyscrapers of a twenty-first-century global city. The divided landscape in Shanghai tells a story of power and capital on a global scale.

Semi-Colonial Era

Under the 1843 Treaty of Nanking, Britain, France, and the United States—each employing a different strategy and of varying appetite—carved up thousands of acres of farmland outside Shanghai's county wall. On November 29, 1845, the British Consul George Balfour and Shanghai Circuit Intendant (*daotai*) Gong Mujiu ratified the first Land Regulations abiding by the treaty. This ratification expedited the creation of a British Settlement officially recognized by the Qing Dynasty in 1846. The settlement was established on a rectangular plot of land at the intersection of Huangpu River, Suzhou Creek, and Yang Jin Bang Creek. Yang Jin Bang Creek would later become a border with the French Concession, which came into being in 1849 when negotiations between French Consul Louis Montigny and Shanghai *daotai* Lin Gui led to the French acquiring land for the exclusive use of French nationals.[39] The 164-acre French Concession was bound to the south by the moat of the "Chinese City," to the north by Yang Jin Bang Creek, and to the east by Huangpu River. Later, the name Yang Jin Bang was added to the Shanghai dialect's vocabulary to mean non-standard, bordering, or neither fish nor fowl, originating from its geographical in-betweenness. This is just one of many ways the Shanghai dialect encodes the city's history and landscape.

Over the years, both the International Settlement and the French Concession expanded drastically. In 1900, the French Concession more than doubled in size to 358 acres. Then, on April 8, 1914, French authorities obtained a 2,470 acres expansion.[40] The United States entered the scene shortly after the French and accelerated the expansion of settlements. The American Settlement grew from American consul John N. Alsop Griswold's protest against the creation of the French Concession and the existence of the French's exclusive privileges and rights.[41] Without any formal designation, the American Settlement started to grow near the small port where Suzhou Creek joined Huangpu River. In 1863, that area was combined with the British Settlement to become the International Settlement.[42] With ever-increasing business opportunities and an increasing number of both foreign and Chinese residents, the foreign community required an extension of settlements from Chinese authorities. In May 1899, the International Settlement was expanded from 1,779 acres to 5,583 acres.[43] When the Qing Dynasty collapsed in 1911, the total area of Shanghai's foreign settlements was more than 8,043 acres, almost fifty-eight times larger than the first British Settlement established in 1846, and twelve times larger than the original walled Chinese City.[44] Figure 1.1 shows the location and expansion of the foreign settlements in Shanghai. In this Plan of Shanghai 1919 map, which was compiled from surveys made by the Shanghai Municipal Council, place names such as Hwangpoo River, Soochow Creek, or Chapei district under the Chinese rule were spelled by using the Wade–Giles system. It is a different romanization system from the *pinyin* system which was developed in China in the 1950s and has been adopted nationwide since. Forms of languages have documented power dynamics in Shanghai everywhere you look. It was the same

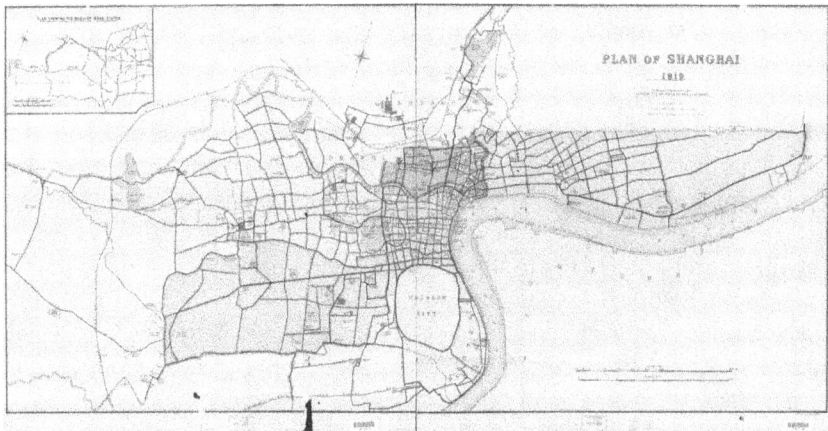

Figure 1.1   Plan of Shanghai 1919. *Source:* Courtesy to the Earth Science Library, UC Berkeley.

time period that Putonghua was designated as the national language and started to be promoted across the country, which I will elaborate in the next chapter.

Upon the establishment of foreign settlements, the landscape of Shanghai was not only divided but also segregated. The first Land Regulation of 1845 signed by the Qing Dynasty and British officials stated that the special international territories were reserved for foreigners only. The pool of foreigners was comprised mainly of diplomats, traders, and missionaries, their servants and families.[45] Chinese citizens were forbidden to live there, and along with foreigners were prohibited from building houses to rent to the Chinese.[46] However, economic incentives quickly eroded this segregation when migration waves hit. The force of urban political economy to reshape the urban landscape was omnipresent from the beginning of the history of Shanghai. Profit-driven British Shanghailanders[47] convinced settlement authorities to admit refugees from the Taiping Rebellion by appealing to profits and efficiency, even though it was against treaty clauses.[48] Soon the segregation policy was officially abandoned. Shanghai's foreign settlements were transformed from reserves for foreign residents to Western-run municipalities populated predominately by Chinese citizens.

Refugees fleeing wars in the countryside led to building frenzies to accommodate them. Combined with the expansion of foreign settlements, this was the beginning of the upper/lower corner distinction in the city. The distinction overlapped the settlement borders in some places, with the northeastern part of the International Settlement and lands under Chinese rule being *xiazhijiao*, the lower corner; the southwestern and central areas of both settlements being *shangzhijiao*, the upper corner. Housing quality, social environment, and the socioeconomic status of inhabitants all contributed to this socially constructed distinction.

First, housing quality differentiates quality of life and lifestyle in the two corners. Beginning in the 1870s, two kinds of *lilong* housing were built to accommodate groups of different socioeconomic status. The name *lilong* (*longdhang* in the Shanghai dialect) means neighborhood lanes or alleyways. The lower quality alleyway housing was *shikumen*. Its defining feature was a courtyard behind a heavy wooden gate (*kumen*) wrapped in stone (*shi*) (see figure 1.2). The other was the new style *lilong* housing with relatively modern amenities. From the 1910s to the 1930s, a period of westward expansion of both the International Settlement and the French Concession, the new-style *lilong* housing, with electricity and other modern amenities such as steel-framed windows and waxed floors, experienced rapid growth. Compared to its antecedent *shikumen* housing, which lacked indoor plumbing, *lilong* housing added an attic, an additional floor above the kitchen, and service rooms.[49] Both kinds of alleyway housing reached their greatest numbers between the 1920s and 1940s in the development of modern Shanghai.[50] Their dominance of the urban landscape continued until the massive demolition and redevelopment brought about by economic reforms starting in the 1990s.

For those unable to afford *shikumen* housing, straw and bamboo shacks were erected on land beyond the northern border of the International Settlement in Zhabei and Baoshan County under Chinese control (see "Chapei" and "Paoshan," respectively, in figure 1.1). In 1929, Shanghai had an estimated 21,000 of these makeshift hovels housing the most desperate classes.[51] In the eastern part of the International Settlement also had factories and mills that drew a constant flow of rural migrants, who lived in shantytowns and *shikumen* housing nearby. This concentration of low-end housing and working-class and urban-poor inhabitants gave the area the name lower corner.

In contrast, better quality housing such as new-style *lilong* and villas were more commonly seen in the upper corner, comprised of the central parts of the International Settlement and the French Concession. For the middle-class population and clerks of higher ranks, garden *lilongs* and apartment *lilongs* were built.[52] Improvements in living standards were achieved in a number of ways, including the incorporation of bathrooms with toilets, utility rooms, and the introduction of electricity, hot water, and gas. Instead of a courtyard behind a heavy wooden gate, most new-style *lilong* housing enjoyed an open

Figure 1.2 For an Example of a Typical *shikumen* Housing Complex in Shanghai.
Source: Photo by the author.

or semi-open green space in the front. These garden *lilong* houses already bore the appearance of a terraced townhouse (see figure 1.3).[53]

The upper corner was also the home of the local and national elites. Wealthy foreign residents and Chinese businessmen acquired land and built magnificent villas and mansions with exquisite gardens in the expanded western part of the International Settlement and the French Concession. The western section was famous for its prestigious inhabitants, for example, from 1918 to 1924, the provisional first president of the Republic of China (1911–1949) and of Kuomintang, Sun Yat-sen, along with his wife Song Qingling maintained a residence on 29 Rue Molière in the French Concession. The western district of the International Settlement, similar to the western part of the French Concession, was known for its sumptuous Western-style garden houses (*xishi yangfang*).[54] The largest and most luxurious of these, Aili Garden, belonged to Silas Hardoon, a Sephardic Jew from Iraq who moved to Shanghai to seek his fortune and was once the richest man in Asia.

In general, housing types and the socioeconomic status of their inhabitants explain the upper/lower corner divide in Shanghai over the first half of the twentieth century. The best housing (Western-style villas, modern apartments, and new-style *lilong* houses) was located in the western and

Figure 1.3   For an Example of a Gated Garden *lilong* Housing Complex on Changle Road in the Former French Concession. *Source:* Photo by the author.

southwestern part of the city, while the worst housing (single-story houses and straw huts/shacks) gathered in the north and northeast. And housing in between these two extremes (*shikumen*) was scattered all over.[55] Furthermore, the divide also indicates the differentiation between the designated function and social environment of the two corners. Those areas representing industrial production and its impoverished labor force were grouped together as the lower corner, which was hidden behind the glistering surface of Shanghai; the upper corner flaunted its conspicuous consumption, luxury, and leisure. The upper corner of Old Shanghai in the early twentieth century was the Shanghai synonymous with modernity and glamour.

Use of urban space for industrial production or for conspicuous consumption, residential housing types, and the socioeconomic status of the inhabitants and their lifestyles sustained these divisions. The upper/lower corner divide would remain in place even when official divisions between foreign settlements and Chinese areas ceased to exist in 1943 during World War II, or upon the founding of the People's Republic in 1949. Even when Mao established a People's Democratic Dictatorship (*renmin mingzhu zhuanzheng*) under the leadership of the proletariat, the predominantly working-class neighborhoods were still referred to as the lower corner.

This upper/lower corner distinction constitutes an integral part of Shanghairen identity, as in the way they understand their place in the city geographically and socioeconomically. In this way, Shanghairen associated their place identity with the symbolic value of the corner they inhabited until the end of the twentieth century. It defines the desired path of their geo-economic mobility and explains the grief of displacement from the prestigious upper corner. Up until the 1990s, if a Shanghairen family occupied only one single room in a *shikumen* housing unit in the upper corner, they would have enough pride and confidence to look down on people of the lower corner, even if the latter enjoyed a more spacious dwelling.

Transition of the Upper/Lower Corner Divide

The nationalization and redistribution of urban housing soon after the liberation in May 1949 did not disturb the upper/lower corner divide. Over time, it rather strengthened its symbolic power. During the Maoist era, the nationalization of housing ownership was carried out through confiscation, coercion, and forced revocation of property rights, as proof of the owners' allegiance to the new Communist government.[56] As a result, most houses built before 1949 were taken over by local housing authorities, in effect rendering all residents in the city tenants of the state.

In the process of housing redistribution, some working-class families were relocated into pre-liberation era middle- or upper-class neighborhoods. These initiatives were intended to better the living conditions of the working class. Consequentially, they created more socioeconomically heterogeneous neighborhoods in Shanghai, though these measures ultimately failed to alter the upper/lower corner distinction. The strength of the divide is especially notable when we consider that the finest residences, previously occupied by the upper- or upper-middle class of both foreign and Chinese origin in the upper corner, were taken over by high-ranking government officials and party bureaucrats.

Residential housing in Shanghai saw limited new development and a significant lack of maintenance in the Maoist era. It further contributed to the distinction for three decades after 1949 even when over-crowding and dilapidation plagued the two corners indiscriminately. At the time of the liberation in May 1949, Shanghai's housing stock was comprised of 52.7 percent old *lilong* houses (*shikumen* housing, which does not have indoor plumbing), 19.8 percent new-style *lilong* houses, 13.7 percent temporary shacks, 9.5 percent garden villas, and 4.3 percent apartments.[57] That the majority of residential housing was *lilong* housing of either the old or new type serves as the best example to illustrate the importance of the *lilong* lifestyle in Shanghai. It also explains how it serves as the material basis and background for Shanghairen identity.

Initially, a *lilong* housing complex was planned to occupy one acre of land, and 120 units would house 600 residents. But in reality, the density was much higher. During the Treaty Port era, only in rare cases could one family afford to occupy one entire two-story *lilong* unit. Instead, the tenant family, almost without exception, would sublet the extra space to poorer families, artists, and students, to supplement household income.[58] Families of lower financial means had little choice but to cram into one room, with a shared kitchen and bathroom (if there was one at all) under the secondary rental system, sometimes for decades. According to the 1937 Shanghai Municipal Council Report, in the International Settlement where most *lilong* housing neighborhoods were located, more than 86 percent of families lived in this way in one house, with family numbers ranging from two to nine. A concentration of four families, or twenty-four persons, per house was the norm in those neighborhoods. When calculated at the individual level, each person was allotted an average 2.8 square meters or 9.5 cubic meters.[59] Those numbers further prove that residency in the upper corner did not necessarily mean spacious dwellings or upscale housing. The appeal of the upper corner lies predominantly in the proximity to the urban center, cultural venues, and the symbolic value of the location's earlier status.

The lifestyle of overcrowded *lilong* housing dominated the Maoist era. As Lei Ping documents, a common saying used to characterize Shanghai petty urbanites' living conditions is "practice Daoist rites in a snail shell" (*luosi ke li zuo daochang*).[60] According to Zhang Hongmin at the Shanghai Academy of Social Sciences, by 1980, the per capita living space in Shanghai was merely 4.4 square meters, a miniscule 0.4 square meters' increase over the previous thirty years. The first decade of economic reforms saw the number rise to 6.6 square meters by 1990, but housing shortages were still severe.[61] New construction and urban redevelopment increased in the 1990s; however, this did not alter the upper/lower corner distinction either, even though most *lilong* and villa housing units were demolished in central Shanghai, making space for urban infrastructure, such as subways, elevated expressways, high-rise apartment buildings, and office towers.

The relocation of Shanghairen from the urban core in the 1990s, especially with the demolition of *lilong* housing, was a story of the rebirth of the urban political economy in the reform era. Once again individuals became property owners. Redevelopment in the 1990s treated sitting tenants quite differently from earlier periods. Sitting tenants affected by redevelopment projects between the 1950s and 1980s were offered new rental housing units in the old neighborhood after a temporary relocation or new rental housing in another area, if they preferred not to wait. The terms of their relocation were mediated and arranged through their work units and local housing administration bureaus, which owned and managed the housing through property nationalization in the 1950s. To quicken the redevelopment of the city in the 1990s however, four alternative funding mechanisms arose, all inviting the participation of private developers.

Of the four alternatives, three allowed displaced tenants to move into a new property in their old neighborhood. The funding pool for these three approaches was a combination of funds from private developers, district governments, displaced tenants, and the work units the majority of the tenants in a particular neighborhood belonged to. While these approaches abided by the intentions of the initial contracts that allowed relocation, the fourth, which did not, was more popular. This fourth approach, fittingly called "Commercial Housing Operation" (*shangpingfang jingying*), was a process by which developers leased land in central districts from the municipal government, upon which stood straw and mud shacks or *lilong* housing. In the redevelopment of these areas, all sitting tenants would be relocated with no prospect of moving back, and the whole neighborhood would be demolished.[62]

While the 1991 housing policy required developers to provide ready permanent housing to those displaced,[63] the 1997 relocation and compensation policy suggested two options to handle those who lost their homes. Besides providing permanent housing, the new option was to provide monetary compensation to allow the displaced to purchase housing on the market.[64] The tiers of monetary compensation were defined by the Shanghai Municipal Housing Management Bureau (*shanghaishi fangwu guanli ju*) and paid to the displaced by developers. The sum was usually not enough for units in apartment buildings in the same neighborhood and represented only a fraction of the market price of the new units built where the demolished buildings once stood, in the more desirable central city districts.

As a result, former tenants were mostly relocated to less valuable property in the less desirable lower corner or even Pudong New District, across the Huangpu River. For example, the Songbai Alley neighborhood in central Huangpu District was categorized as "dangerous housing" (*wei fang*) and "ripe" for redevelopment. Eighty percent of former residents were relocated to Pudong New District.[65] The depopulation of the urban core was intensified in a new round of *lilong* neighborhood redevelopment projects from 2001 to 2004. The overall rate of return among previous residents in that round of redevelopment remained around 10 percent, about the city average.[66]

Redevelopment of *lilong* housing neighborhoods in central Shanghai was only part of the story of massive urban renewal and displacement rippling through the city. The revenue generated by leasing land occupied by *lilong* housing or shacks in central districts, such as Luwan or Huangpu to real estate developers, was later used to modernize the decaying urban infrastructure of the city. The building frenzy of the 1990s changed the city at a rate rarely seen in urban history. The authorities, on average, had to print a new version of the city map every three months.[67] Within ten years, elevated expressways were erected, cutting through the heart of central Shanghai and destroyed *lilong* neighborhoods that once housed tens of thousands of Shanghairen households.

Those drastic changes to the urban built environment disrupted the upper/lower corner divide, as residential neighborhoods in either corner simply disappeared or were rezoned for commercial use. Furthermore, upscale condominiums were built in previous *shikumen* housing neighborhoods in the lower corner, and previously rural counties were rezoned urban, which I will elaborate on in chapter 3. This reconfiguration of the urban landscape resulted in many Shanghairen no longer living in either corner but instead in entirely new parts of the city. A new mental mapping of the city emerged when Pudong was established across Huangpu River in 1993. Prior to the urbanization and redevelopment of the 1990s, it was simply farmland. In the 2010 census, Pudong New District housed more than 5 million long-term residents, roughly a quarter of the urban population.[68]

Huangpu River once defined the border of urban Shanghai. But since the 1990s, the river has served as a different kind of border within the city. Unlike the earlier borders, between foreign settlements and the Chinese City, and the distinction between the upper and the lower corners, this new divide separates the Shanghai of the twentieth century from that of the twenty-first. What remains the same is the power of capital to define, transform, and strengthen the divided landscape of urban Shanghai. It also transformed the city's dialect, which is a hybrid in much the same way as Shanghai's population and built environment.

A HYBRID LANGUAGE

The dialect spoken in urban Shanghai is another contested part of Shanghai's cosmopolitan past. Similar to the way that Shanghai grew from an insignificant trading post in the Yangtze River Delta, the Shanghai dialect, once a small branch of the Wu language family, grew to be the mother tongue for millions of Shanghairen. From *kaibu* in 1843 until the mid-twentieth century, its expansion in vocabulary and cultural influence coincided with the city's growth into a cosmopolitan metropolis embracing a diverse migrant population. Before delving into the recent changes and endangerment of the Shanghai dialect, I will first trace the origin and development of the dialect over the last century and half. In many ways, the Shanghai dialect is at the core of the history of the city and its people.

The Shanghai dialect has been a particular point of tension in the recent transformations of the city. When native Shanghairen stress their place identity through their fluency in the dialect, they unavoidably confront the fact that the dialect itself is not indigenous, but urban and hybrid. In this sense, the Shanghai dialect has always been in the making, constantly reshaped through the contemporary history of Shanghai, by multiple waves of migrants and power struggles between them in the early twentieth century.

The origins of the Shanghai dialect are as modest as the beginning of the town itself. Its significance in the region did not emerge until the late nineteenth century. The dialect dates back to a language spoken in Huating County during the Song and Yuan Dynasties (AD 960–1368)—later Huating County was renamed Songjiang County.[69] In the Songjiang County Record published in 1512, the Jiaxing dialect was the most respected and authoritative tongue within the county. At that time, the native tongue of Songjiang County was very similar in pronunciation to the Jiaxing dialect. One hundred and fifty years later, in 1663, the early period of the Qing Dynasty, the Songjiang County Record suggests that the Suzhou dialect occupied the leading position within the county. Its dominance continued for another 150 years, as the 1817 Songjiang County Record indicates.[70]

It was not until late nineteenth century—nearly half-century after *kaibu*—that the prestige of the Shanghai dialect started to rise.[71] The ancient dialect spoken in Songjiang County, to which the Shanghai Township historically belonged, is part of the northern Wu linguistic cluster. The Wu linguistic cluster dominates most of the Yangtze River Delta region and is one of the ten dialect clusters most spoken by Han Chinese. The linguistic characteristics of what is referred to today as the Shanghai dialect suggest it is part of the Su (Suzhou)-Hu (Shanghai)-Jia (Jiaxing) division of the Tai Lake sub-cluster of the northern Wu language.[72] The ancient tongue, based on the Songjiang dialect and spoken in the rural county for hundreds of years before Shanghai Township came into existence, is not the same Shanghai dialect that has been spoken in the city in the last hundred years. The contemporary Shanghai dialect is a young and urban dialect—formed about 100 years ago, around the 1920s.[73]

Though the historical origin is agreed upon, the composition of the current Shanghai dialect differs according to what linguistic facet that linguists focus on: vocabulary (lexicon) or accent (phonology). Linguists parse the minute variations to determine the Shanghai dialect's similarities to, and diversions from its cousins in the Wu language family. These studies allow a more nuanced understanding of Shanghai's cosmopolitan past, when migrants of various geographic origins shaped this urban dialect.

One thread of argument suggests that the dialect is primarily a conglomeration of dialects spoken by internal migrants pouring into the city after *kaibu* in 1843. Among Chinese linguists, the current Shanghai dialect is defined as a mixed urban dialect, with the Songjiang dialect as a basic tongue supplemented by words and phrases from variations of the Wu language spoken in southern Jiangsu province to the north of Shanghai and northern Zhejiang province to Shanghai's south.[74] This identification was already present in writings about the Shanghai dialect in the early twentieth century. In a study first published in 1917, Yao categorized the origins of the Shanghai dialect under five headings: Cantonese, the Ningpo dialect, the Su cluster dialect (which he identified as spoken by the gentry and landowners from Suzhou and southern Jiangsu), northern tongue (which he identified as spoken in northeastern China), and the Shanghai native tongue. The Shanghai native tongue was spoken by the rural population living in the southern and western areas of the county seat prior to *kaibu*. According to Yao, the Shanghai dialect spoken commonly in the early twentieth century was a mixture of the Ningpo and the Suzhou dialects, both of which were very different from the native tongue spoken before the 1843 treaty port opening.[75]

Tellingly, this breakdown of linguistic influences on the current Shanghai dialect corresponds to the socioeconomic status of the various migrants flowing into the city. As linguistic anthropologists argue, languages take up the status of that of their speakers. Wealthy war refugees, whether merchants or gentry, were predominantly from the southern Jiangsu and northern Zhejiang provinces, representing the cities of Suzhou and Ningbo, respectively. The Suzhou dialect's dominance over the Shanghai dialect grew from its speakers' strong cultural influences, while the Ningbo tongue's influence was a product of its speakers' economic strength. Conversely, the languages of the peasant refugees fleeing northern Jiangsu due to drought and war, who lacked both the cultural and economic stature of Suzhou and Ningbo refugees, were, despite a sizable migrant population, unable to exert much influence in the formation of the Shanghai dialect.[76] Furthermore, people in southern Jiangsu and northern Zhejiang province spoke variations of the Wu language, while those peasant refugees spoke northern Jiangsu dialects, which belong to an entirely different linguistic family, and are mutually incomprehensible.[77] Various scholars who emphasize the hybrid character of the Shanghai dialect recognize the role played by waves of migrants of various origins in shaping its early form.

A counterargument stresses that the dialect is unquestionably rooted in the Songjiang dialect, arguing that other dialects accompanying migrants into the city after 1843 canceled out each other's influences.[78] Qian Nairong acknowledges the influences of Suzhou, Ningbo, and northern Jiangsu dialects, since each is represented by a substantial vocabulary, but rejects the notion that any of them could challenge the dominance of the Songjiang dialect.[79] As a renowned Shanghai dialect scholar and an outspoken Shanghai dialect preservation activist, Qian further suggests that earlier migrants were eager to learn the Shanghai dialect, and their offspring regarded it as their mother tongue and themselves as Shanghairen.[80] Despite his disagreement with other scholars on the early formation of the Shanghai dialect, Qian admits that current dialects closely related to the Songjiang dialect are incomprehensible to contemporary Shanghai dialect speakers. Thus, it is an undeniable fact that the Shanghai dialect is urban and hybrid.

The desire to read the migration history in Shanghai in certain ways often underlines the debate about the composition of the dialect. Shanghai's turbulent political, social, and cultural history in the early twentieth century had a profound effect. Many new words emerged during that period to accommodate social changes and to describe phenomena and goods new to the city.[81] The Shanghai dialect was not itself sufficient for a cosmopolitan population to maneuver through a city with separated jurisdictions and colonial dominance. It has constantly changed and adapted, keeping pace with its shifting social milieu. A hybrid language known as Pidgin English originating in Canton, composed of English, Chinese, Indian, and Portuguese words strongly influenced the fast-forming Shanghai dialect in the early twentieth century.[82]

Neologisms ranging from the business world to the underworld flourished. For example, steamer bus got its name in the Shanghai dialect as "si-ding-ba," on sale became "ang-san," porter is "pao-tuo," sofa "su-fa," and the dialect word for prostitute was taken from lassie, "lah-sey."[83] More relevant to this study is the word for the Western architectural feature, loft window. It was a feature adopted in *shikumen* housing, and its name in the Shanghai dialect is "laofu-cang." It borrows the half phonological and half semantic way of composing Mandarin characters, combining the pronunciation of "laofu," mimicking the English pronunciation of "loft," with "cang," meaning window in the Shanghai dialect. When written down in Mandarin Chinese characters, it becomes *laohu chuang*. The characters mean tiger window, which would be incomprehensible if one doesn't speak the Shanghai dialect.

In general, Chinese linguists argue that the absorption of words or lexical items from Western languages, and the continuous creation of new words to accommodate dynamic treaty-port business, signified the city's open-mindedness and indiscriminate cosmopolitanism.[84] However, shifts and changes to a language do not occur in a political or ideological vacuum. Since the political environment is central to my study of the Shanghai dialect's endangerment, especially as related to the city's transformation over the last two decades, I feel the need to stress the hybridity of the dialect. It encodes and represents the city's semi-colonial history, waves of internal migration, locals' business-minded pragmatism, and a continuation of Shanghai's East-meets-West identity, among other factors. Which part of the dialect's history is highlighted depends on the speaker's language ideology and agenda to shape the future of the dialect.

Changes to the Shanghai dialect since the founding of the People's Republic have taken a slightly different form. The close association between internal migration and changes in the dialect in early twentieth century explains the dialect's period of stability and stagnation in the Maoist era,[85] when the household registration system halted migration flows. Due to the ending of Western influences under Mao, neologisms of that era instead stemmed from political turmoil and practices in the planned economy. New words such as "jia-ji-dou-zeng" (class struggle, *jieji douzheng* in Putonghua), or "che-da-gu-fae" (eating rice from the big wok, *chi daguofan* in Putonghua), record the collective mode of production and socialist redistribution. What differentiates this period's neologisms from those in the first half of the twentieth century is that the source language shifted from English or Pidgin English to Putonghua, the official language. What remains the same is the vitality and wide use of the Shanghai dialect until the late twentieth century. While the flow of internal migration resumed in the 2000s, and the city again opens to the world, the Shanghai dialect's place in the city's linguistic scene has shrunk. In the next chapter, I will delve into language policies since the 1950s and their ramifications for everyday life in Shanghai. Native Shanghairen's ideas about both the official language and their dialect have since changed and resulted in a contested linguistic landscape in Shanghai.

NOTES

1. Wasserstrom, Jeffrey N. 2009. *Global Shanghai, 1850–2010*. London & New York: Routledge. P.120.

2. Zhu, Guodong; Liu, Hong; Chen, Zhiqiang. 2008. "Go to Shanghai [*Dao Shanghai Qu*]." In *Shanghai Migration [Shanghai Yimin]*, 3–23. Shanghai: Shanghai University of Finance & Economics Press.

3. Denison, Edward; Ren, Guangyu. 2013. *Building Shanghai: The Story of China's Gateway*. Chichester, England: Wiley and Academy. P.17–8.

4. Cited from *Shanghai County-Custom* in Zhu; Liu; Chen. "Go to Shanghai [*Dao Shanghai Qu*]," P.7.

5. Zou, Yiren. 1980. *Research on Population Change in Old Shanghai. [Jiu Shanghai renkou bianqian de yanjiu,]*. Shanghai: Shanghai People's Press. P.90–1.

6. Zhu; Liu; Chen. "Go to Shanghai [*Dao Shanghai Qu*]," P.9.

7. Wasserstrom. *Global Shanghai, 1850–2010*. P.2–3.

8. Zou. *Research on Population Change in Old Shanghai*, P.113.

9. Wasserstrom. *Global Shanghai, 1850–2010*. P.3.

10. Zhao, Chunlan. 2004. "From Shikumen to New-Style: A Rereading of Lilong Housing in Modern Shanghai." *The Journal of Architecture* 9 (1): 49–76. P.52.

11. Zou. *Research on Population Change in Old Shanghai*, P.90–1, 113.

12. Zou. *Research on Population Change in Old Shanghai*, P.113.

13. Bergère, Marie-Claire. 2009. *Shanghai: China's Gateway to Modernity*. Stanford, CA: Stanford University Press.P.42–4.

14. Bergère. *Shanghai: China's Gateway*, P.44.

15. Dong, Stella. 2000. *Shanghai: The Rise and Fall of a Decadent City*. New York: Harper Collins. P.75–6.

16. Honig, Emily. 1992. *Creating Chinese Ethnicity: Subei People in Shanghai, 1850–1980*. New Haven: Yale University Press. P.12.

17. Zhu; Liu; Chen. "Go to Shanghai [*Dao Shanghai Qu*]," P.9.

18. Lu, Yilong. 2002. "Structure and Change: The Household Registration System in China after 1949 [1949 *nian hou de zhongguo huji zhidu: jiegou yu bianqian*]." *Journal of Peking University (Humanities and Social Sciences)* 39 (2): 123–30. P.124.

19. Chan, Kam Wing, and Will Buckingham. 2008. "Is China Abolishing the Hukou System?" *The China Quarterly* 195 (September): 582–606. P.587.

20. Lu. "Structure and Change," P.125.

21. Cheng, Tiejun, and Mark Selden. 1994. "The Origins and Social Consequences of China's Hukou System." *The China Quarterly* 139 (September): 644–68.

22. Chan, and Buckingham. "Is China Abolishing the Hukou System?" 582–606. P.588.

Chan, Kam Wing, and Li Zhang. 1999. "The Hukou System and Rural–Urban Migration in China: Processes and Changes." *The China Quarterly* 160 (December): 818–55. P.829.

Solinger, Dorothy J. 1999. *Contesting Citizenship in Urban China: Peasant Migrants, the State, and the Logic of the Market*. Berkeley, CA: University of California Press.

23. Vendryes, Thomas. 2011. "Migration Constraints and Development: Hukou and Capital Accumulation in China." *China Economic Review*, Sustainable Natural Resource Use in Rural China, 22 (4): 669–92. P.680.

24. Chan, and Zhang. "The Hukou System and Rural–Urban Migration in China," 818–55. P.830.

25. Chan, Kam Wing. 1994. *Cities with Invisible Walls: Reinterpreting Urbanization in Post-1949 China*. Hong Kong & New York: Oxford University Press. P.91.

26. Office of Shanghai Chronicles. 2003. "Special Feature II: The Up to the Mountains and Down to the Countryside Movement during the Cultural Revolution (*zhuanji er: 'wenhua da geming' zhong de shangshan xiaxiang yundong*)." November 10, 2003. http://www.shtong.gov.cn/dfz_web/DFZ/Info?idnode=66390&tableName=userobject1a&id=62337.

27. Lu. "Structure and Change," P.127.

28. Chan, and Zhang. "The Hukou System and Rural–Urban Migration in China," 818–55. P.838–9.

29. Chart 4.16 Urban household per capita disposable income (1985–2003). http://tjj.sh.gov.cn/tjnj/nj.htm?d1=2004tjnj/C0415.htm.

30. http://www.shanghai.gov.cn/nw2/nw2314/nw2319/nw2407/nw26170/u26aw27256.html.

31. http://www.shanghai.gov.cn/nw2/nw2314/nw2319/nw2407/nw26170/u26aw27386.html.

32. http://www.shanghai.gov.cn/nw2/nw2314/nw2319/nw2407/nw12938/u26aw2096.html.

33. Zhu; Liu; Chen. "Go to Shanghai [*Dao Shanghai Qu*]," P.18.

34. Sassen, Saskia. 2001. *The Global City: New York, London, Tokyo*. 2nd edition. Princeton, NJ: Princeton University Press.

35. "Data Manual of the Sixth Census of Shanghai." Shanghai Statistic Bureau. http://www.stats- sh.gov.cn/sjfb/201203/239823.html.

36. "Report of Fifth Census – Shanghai." National Bureau of Statistics of People's Republic of China. http://www.stats.gov.cn/tjsj/tjgb/rkpcgb/dfrkpcgb/200203/t20020331_30355.html.

37. Harvey, David. 2007. "Neoliberalism 'with Chinese Characteristics.'" In *A Brief History of Neoliberalism*, 120–51. Oxford & New York: Oxford University Press.

38. Ping, Lei. 2019. "Survival of Shanghai Urbanite Culture in the Mao Era: Bourgeois Aspirations and Practice of Longtang Everyday Life." *Journal of Chinese Architecture and Urbanism* 1 (1): 1–18.

39. Zhao. "From Shikumen to New-Style," 49–76. P.53.

40. Denison; Ren. *Building Shanghai*, P.82, 85.

41. Bergère. *Shanghai: China's Gateway,* P.31–2.

42. Denison; Ren. *Building Shanghai*, P.56.

43. Denison; Ren. *Building Shanghai*, P.75.

44. Zhao. "From Shikumen to New-Style," 49–76. P.53.

45. Zhao. "From Shikumen to New-Style," 49–76. P.54.

46. Denison; Ren. *Building Shanghai*, P.34.

47. A name adopted by British residents themselves.

48. Lu, Hanchao. 1999. *Beyond the Neon Lights: Everyday Shanghai in the Early Twentieth Century*. Berkeley, CA: University of California Press. P.32–35.

49. see Gregory Bracken's 2013 book *The Shanghai Alleyway House: A Vanishing Urban Vernacular* for more architectural details of *lilong* housing.

50. Zhao. "From Shikumen to New-Style," 49–76. P.50.

51. Denison; Ren. *Building Shanghai*, P.165.

52. Lu. *Beyond the Neon Lights*, P.110–12.

53. Denison; Ren. *Building Shanghai*, P.163–64.

54. Denison; Ren. *Building Shanghai*, P.165, 167.

55. Lu. *Beyond the Neon Lights,* P.115

56. Denison; Ren. *Building Shanghai*, P.205.

57. Xu, Mingqian. 2004. *City's Context: Developing Shanghai Urban Central Old Residential Neighborhoods [chengshi de wenmai: Shanghai zhongxin cheng jiu zhuqu fazhan fangshi xin lun]*. Shanghai: Xuelin Publishing. P.128–9.

58. Lu. *Beyond the Neon Lights,* P.20.

59. Zhao. "From Shikumen to New-Style," 49–76. P.67.

60. Ping. "Survival of Shanghai Urbanite Culture in the Mao Era."

61. Wang, Haiyan. 2018. "Shanghai Counselor Zhang Hongmin: '40 Years Ago, How to Solve the Most Difficult Problem in Shanghai- Housing. (*Shanghai canshi Zhang Hongmin: sishi nian qian, shanghai de tyanzi diyihao nanti – zhufang nan shi ruhe jiejue de*'" Shanghai News. October 30, 2018. https://www.shobserver.com/wx/detail.do?id=113215.

62. Xu. *City's Context,* P.167–71.

63. Article 43, in *Shanghai Urban Housing Demolition Management Plan* issued on July 19, 1991. http://www.govyi.com/zhengcefagui/difangfagui/shanghaishifagui/200707/7581.shtml.

64. Article 4, in *Shanghai Dangerous Housing and Shacks Demolition Compensation and Resettlement Trial Measures* issued on December 8, 1997.

65. *Shanghai Construction 1986–1990*, cited in Xu. *City's Context*.

66. Xu. *City's Context,* P.202–04.

67. World Journal. [shijie ribao], November 28, 1999, cited in Lu. *Beyond the Neon Lights,* P.169.

68. Table 2.5 Land Area, Population and Density of Population in Districts and Counties, in Shanghai Statistical Bureau. *Shanghai Statistical Yearbook 2011*. Beijing: China Statistics Press. Accessed August 29, 2020. http://tjj.sh.gov.cn/tjnj/nje11.htm?d1=2011tjnje/E0205.htm.

69. You, Rujie. 2006. "On Classification and Mixed Nature of the Shanghai Dialect [*Shanghai hua zai wuyu fengqu shang de diwei*]." Dialects [*Fangyan*] 1: 72–8. P.75.

70. Xu, Baojie, and You, Rujie. 1988. "Initial Research on the Shanghai Dialect from Regional Gazettes [*fangzhi suo jian shanghai fangyan chu tan*]." In *Collection of Thesis on Wu Language [Wuyu Lun Cong]*, 187–92. Shanghai: Shanghai Education Publishing House. P.188–89.

71. Qian, Nairong. 1998. "On Formation of Urban Central Dialect in Shanghai [*Shanghai chengshi fangyan zhongxin de xingcheng*]." *Journal of Shanghai University (Social Science)* 5 (3): 28–35. P. 33.

72. Chen, Zhongmin. 1992. "Subdivisions of the Shanghai Dialect Region and Its Cultural and Historical Backgrounds [*Shanghai diqu fangyan fenqu jiqi lishi renwen Beijing*]." *Fudan Journal (Social Sciences Edition)* 4: 101–8. P.101.

Qian. "On Formation of Urban Central Dialect in Shanghai," 28–35. P.29.

73. Qian Nairong. 2007. *Shanghai Dialect [Shanghai fangyan]*. Shanghai: Wenhui Publishing. P.72

74. You. "On Classification and Mixed Nature of the Shanghai Dialect," P.72, 75.

75. Yao, Gonghe. 1989 [1917]. *Shanghai Language [Shanghai xianhua* 上海闲话*]*. 2nd ed. Shanghai: Shanghai Classics Publishing House. P.19.

76. Honig, Emily. 1992. *Creating Chinese Ethnicity: Subei People in Shanghai, 1850–1980*. New Haven: Yale University Press. P.55.

77. Honig. *Creating Chinese Ethnicity*, P.24.

78. Qian, Nairong. 2003. *History of the Shanghai Language [Shanghai yuyan fazhan shi]*. Shanghai: Shanghai People's Publishing House.

79. Qian. *Shanghai Dialect [Shanghai fangyan]*, P.275.

80. Qian. *Shanghai Dialect [Shanghai fangyan]*.

81. Qian. "On Formation of Urban Central Dialect in Shanghai," 28–35. P.33.

82. Dong. *Shanghai: The Rise,* P.33.

83. Qian. *Shanghai Dialect [Shanghai fangyan],* P.101–02.

84. Qian, Nairong. 2000. "On Changes to the Shanghai Language [*Shanghai yuyan de bianqian*]." *Social Sciences [Shehui Kexue]* 2: 65–6. P.66.

Qian, Cheng. 2012. *Qian Chen's Shanghai Accent [Qianchen de Shanghai qiangdiao]*. Shanghai: Shanghai Education Publishing House. P.8.

85. Qian. "On Formation of Urban Central Dialect in Shanghai," 28–35. P. 31–2.

Chapter 2

"China Dream" versus the Shanghai Dialect

On the evening of June 16, 2009, I attended a Western classical music concert in the Pudong New District, the showcase of a newly re-globalized Shanghai, located on the east bank of Huangpu River. Though the subway ride took only fifteen minutes, from People's Square in Puxi just across the river, when I got off at the Shanghai Science and Technology Museum station I was immediately lost. Though I am a native Shanghairen and lived in Puxi for twenty-five years before moving to Canada in 2007, recently urbanized Pudong was a totally unfamiliar place. It bore little resemblance to the Shanghai I knew so well. My surprise and disorientation did not end when I arrived at the Shanghai Oriental Art Center. Upon purchasing the playbill for the concert, performed by the United States' National Symphony Orchestra, I said "*xiaxia*" to the staff member ("thank you" in the Shanghai dialect), but was ridiculed and jeered in return, "Seriously, the Shanghai dialect? This is high culture, not standup comedy!" I was utterly shocked. Native Shanghairen like me were raised to speak and treat the dialect as the default language of the city. But now I was shunned for speaking it in public. What had changed?

The Shanghai dialect has been the *lingua franca* of Shanghai since the early twentieth century. The transition from the feudal Qing Dynasty (1644–1911) to the Republic (1911–1949), and then to the People's Republic founded by the Chinese Communist Party, did little to affect Shanghai dialect's primacy. It was not until the late 1990s that the dialect's prestige and wide use in Shanghai were threatened, when the government implemented economic reforms intended to intensify China's participation in globalization, along with a slew of developmental policies meant to put Shanghai on a trajectory to become a global city. The convergence of various forces has led to the near-collapse of the diglossia system in Shanghai. Putonghua is taking over the linguistic space occupied by the Shanghai dialect, resulting in the latter's endangerment.

In order to explain the detrimental impact of state language policies, I will first show how the state has shifted emphasis from linguistic co-existence to domination, in order to cement the hegemony of Putonghua, the national language. Besides formal laws, the annual Putonghua promotion project, started in 1998, associates speaking Putonghua with patriotism, loyalty to the party and the state, allegiance to a national identity, and upward social mobility. More recently, since 2012, speaking Putonghua has been linked to the realization of the "China Dream," which was defined as a "rejuvenation of the Chinese nation" by President Xi Jinping. Though based on studies on national languages in different historical and geographical contexts, the work of Jan Blommaert and Jeff Verschueren on European countries is particularly illuminating. They wrote that the existence of a national language is the primary foundation upon which nationalist ideology is constructed, and national languages are part of the ideological work of nation-building.[1] In the current Chinese context, state language policies that work to establish Putonghua's dominance over regional dialects, such as the Shanghai dialect, reflect the leadership's intention in strengthening nationalism and the promotion of China's soft power through the Belt and Road Initiative.

The legal system, the national language promotion campaigns, and the socialist market economy all work in tandem to establish Putonghua's dominance in Shanghai through influencing native Shanghairen's language ideology. The dominant language ideology imposed by the state identifies Putonghua as modern, sophisticated, and formal, whereas the Shanghai dialect is backward, inadequate, and informal. This ideology is promoted mainly through the school system, where Putonghua is mandated as the medium of instruction. But state guidelines regulating and monitoring language choice in various public spaces also greatly contribute to the wide adoption of Putonghua over the Shanghai dialect among multilingual native Shanghairen.

To analyze the workings of language ideology, Bourdieu's notion of linguistic capital is instructive. Linguistic capital is a form of embodied knowledge accumulated through formal education as well as "inherited" from a class-based family upbringing, and it implies a mastery of language and interactional practices concerning language use.[2] Using Bourdieu's concept as the analytical framework, I treat proficiency in Putonghua and the Shanghai dialect, as well as beliefs about their differentiated aesthetics and functions, as linguistic capital. Over time, language proficiency and proper use are converted from embodied linguistic capital to social, economic, and symbolic capitals.[3] Given the existence of both a dominant language ideology that favors the national language and an alternative, local one that favors the dialect, the conversions of an individual's linguistic capital take place on two different markets. One is defined and sanctioned by the state, while local forces support the other. Similar to Kathryn Woolard's study of the prestige and status of Catalan in Barcelona, versus that of the national language, Castilian, the alternative linguistic market has important ideological support that links dialect speaking with urban identity, especially in encounters with internal migrants speaking the national language.[4]

With Putonghua increasingly pushing the Shanghai dialect to the periphery, language loss is possible. However, as Lenore Grenoble and Lindsay Whaley point out that language loss is rarely if ever a simple process where "speakers across different generations suddenly abandon their mother tongue and completely adopt the imposed or aspired language in every aspect of their lives."[5] Indeed, the adoption of Putonghua in Shanghai is not universal but varies along gender, age group, and social class lines. Lastly, the alternative language ideology in Shanghai remains strong, with Shanghai dialect preservation activists emphasizing the dialect's value as a local cultural heritage, with a long history as part of the ancient Wu language family. With limited resources and local support, however, they are fighting a futile battle to reinstate the diglossia system.

A STATE PROJECT

Upon founding the People's Republic of China, the Chinese Communist Party deployed a wide range of political measures to establish a national language, seeing linguistic uniformity as an essential part of unification and nation-building. The communist regime is not the first political entity to define a national language and standardize pronunciation in modern China, but their effort has been successful in suppressing and endangering regional dialects on the way to instilling the hegemony of Putonghua.[6] The establishment of a modern national language was essential for the founding of a unified and modern Chinese nation, an idea that prompted the Kuomintang to define and promote a national language in the early years of Republic of China (1911–1949). In his historical study on the languages of China, Samuel Ramsey points out that Kuomintang party leaders believed that, even though a written classical language had existed in China for over 2,000 years, only a unified modern vernacular could serve as the linguistic foundation of a modern state.[7] Each province had a vote in the national convention held to decide on the new national language, where representatives from northern provinces speaking Mandarin dialects competed with those from southern provinces speaking non-Mandarin dialects for national language status of their native tongues. Einar Haugen argues in other contexts that, on such an occasion as a national convention, to choose any dialect as a national norm inevitably favors that dialect's native speakers, giving them a head start in the race for power and status.[8] Furthermore, from a Bourdieusian perspective, the imposition of a national language throughout an entire state, used for all official occasions, reinforces the authority and prestige of that language.[9] Thus, the representatives' heated debate about the designation of a national language during the formation of the state was a competition for the status and dominance of their own dialects.

The promotion of a national language with standardized pronunciation in the Republic era served the Kuomintang's agenda for modernization and nationalism but did not fundamentally shake up the diglossia system or sacrifice regional dialects in exchange. With each province having only one vote, the geographically dominant Mandarin dialect, based on Beijing pronunciation, was selected as the national pronunciation (Guoyin) over the three competing non-Mandarin southern dialects Cantonese, Fuzhounese, and Wu (which the Shanghai dialect is a variation of). Guoyin was then promoted nationwide in the school system starting in 1920. Despite these official efforts, in the 1930s, migrants coming to Shanghai from all over the country brought with them different regional pronunciations and vocabularies, creating a polyglot linguistic scene instead of a population unified by a singular national pronunciation. The reasons for this were manifold. The two immediate ones in the sphere of language policy were, on the one hand, the ineffectiveness of promoting Guoyin in schools across the country, and, on the other hand, the separated foreign jurisdictions in semi-colonial Shanghai, which precluded the possibility of enforcing a uniform municipal language policy.

The Chinese Communist Party, having defeated Kuomintang in 1949, shared the latter's agenda of modernization and nationalism represented by national language policies. The Communist Party installed Putonghua (which literally means "common speech") as the national language and retained Guoyin as the official pronunciation. Ping Chen points out, in his study on modern Chinese, that this is a particularly interesting policy choice for the new political rulers, since they themselves had fought so bitterly for the equal status of Cantonese, Fuzhounese, and the Shanghai dialect during the Republic era.[10] While Ramsey sees those former pursuits and concerns of Chinese Communist Party members as either ignored or forgotten when they came into power,[11] I argue that it was actually consistent with the logic of nationalism, since a modern Chinese state speaking a unified language is of paramount importance to the leading party's effort to build up a nation.

This vision of a linguistically unified China gave rise to both Guoyin in the Republic era and Putonghua under the Communist Party's rule. Woolard argues in her study of Catalan speaking in Spain, where Castilian is the national language, that the equation of language and nation is not a natural fact but rather a historical and ideological construct.[12] This construct is usually articulated as a need for clear and accurate communication across a country. This argument makes intuitive sense, because the vernaculars in southern China, such as the Shanghai dialect or Cantonese, belong not only to different linguistic families than Putonghua but also to each other. Thus, for a monolingual Putonghua speaker, those southern tongues are unintelligible. However, as Bourdieu points out, the purpose of the imposition of a national language to replace a diglossia system is the political need to constantly remind and reinforce state authority and the ruling party's dominance.[13] To successfully impose Putonghua and establish its dominance, which, as Ramsey points out is an abstract, standardized language that not a single person at the time spoke as their native idiom,[14] the state deployed nationwide systemic and aggressive legal, administrative, and propaganda measures.

Legal System

The nationwide dominance of Putonghua was a top-down state project, established first and foremost through the legal system. Putonghua's official status is recognized and reinforced at four levels in the country's legal system. At the top are national laws, such as the fourth and current Constitution, and the *Law of People's Republic of China on the Standard Spoken and Written Chinese Language* passed by the People's Congress. These are followed by administrative regulations and policies issued by the State Council at the second tier. The third level is the provisions and documents issued by bureaus under the State Council, such as the "Provisions on the Administration of Putonghua Proficiency Test" issued by the Ministry of Education. The lowest level consists of regional regulations. Together this legal infrastructure has ensured the dominance of Putonghua as the official language of China, guaranteed and reinforced at every level and through various state agencies.

Shortly after the founding of the People's Republic in 1949, meetings of top-level officials were organized to determine an official language. The first state policy concerning the national language was called the "Directive of the State Council on Promoting Putonghua" (*tuiguang Putonghua zhishi*), passed at the State Council's twenty-third National Emblem on January 28, 1956. This directive granted Putonghua the status of an official language, to be used as the common language for all Han Chinese. In terms of Putonghua's relation to other dialects, the most explicit formulation of the official position was published a few months before in *People's Daily*, the state-owned, party-run newspaper, that "[p]romoting Putonghua does not mean intentionally annihilating local dialects, but to gradually limit their scope of use, which is in conformity with the objective rules of societal progress."[15] The 1956 directive also instructed all schools, from first grade through university, to teach students in Putonghua. Through the nationwide public-school system,

Putonghua and its underlying legitimacy and dominance were thus instilled in the minds of future generations. However, the promotion of Putonghua as the language for official settings and as the medium of instruction did not threaten diglossia systems, such as Shanghai's. The Shanghai dialect was still widely used in informal settings and at home until the early 2000s.

The status of Putonghua was further strengthened in the fourth and current Constitution of the People's Republic of China, which was passed on December 4, 1982. This was four years after the adoption of the Open Door Policy used to guide China's economic reforms. The constitutional provision related to Putonghua, Article 19, states that "The state promotes the nationwide use of Putonghua."[16] Thus, it was nearly forty years ago that Putonghua's dominance was established at the highest level of China's legal system. Ever since, the state has been proactive in promoting Putonghua as a unifying force to ensure social stability and every citizen's loyalty to the state and the party.

Under the framework of the Constitution, the Standing Committee of the National People's Congress passed the *Law of the People's Republic of China on the Standard Spoken and Written Chinese Language* at the end of 2000.[17] In effect since January 1, 2001, this measure aids both political control and economic development. Issued shortly after the 1998 Asian Financial Crisis, this law coincides with the beginning of a new phase of China's economic reforms, which include the loosening of the *hukou* (household registration) system to facilitate geographical mobility of labor and further participation in the global economy granted by China's membership in the WTO as of December 2001. The 2001 Language Law effectively gives Putonghua the same significance as state sovereignty, national dignity, and unification. The law describes Putonghua as an essential means to enhance the social construction of the material and ideological infrastructure of the state (*wuzhi jingshen wenming jianshe*). It also makes explicit the breadth and width of the use of Putonghua across the country. It mandates speaking Putonghua within all state organs, at schools of all levels, in mass media, and encourages its use in the service sector. Exceptions are made, though in vague terms, such as in Article 16.1, "local dialects may be used when state functionaries *really need to* use them in the performance of official duties" and in Article 16.4 "where local dialects' use *is really required* in publishing, teaching and research." Exceptions do exist, but subject dialect use to further bureaucratic processes, as in Article 16.2: "Local dialects may be used in broadcasting with the approval of the broadcasting and television administration under the State Council or of the broadcasting and television department at the provincial level." From the top level of the central state's legal system, the linguistic space for regional dialects is sharply reduced and restricted, whereas the linguistic space for Putonghua is clearly defined, guaranteed, and expanded.

Putonghua Promotion as Panopticon

More effective than passing laws is the continual reinforcement of the law. Otherwise, an artificial, standardized language shared across a vast land could only exist on paper or in the imagination. Bourdieu notes that a single "linguistic community" of an invented national language is "endlessly reproduced by state institutions capable of imposing universal recognition of the dominant language."[18] The Chinese state has three main strategies to reinforce Putonghua's prominence. One strategy is the annual nationwide Putonghua Promotion Week. The second is the required Putonghua Proficiency Test for a plethora of occupations. The last, and perhaps the most important, is the everyday surveillance of language use of the populace. All these measures complement each other to create a panopticon-like linguistic sphere of Putonghua speaking.

The Ministry of Education passed the motion creating Putonghua Promotion Week as a national annual event in 1998. The third week of every September is designated as the promotion week, characterized by various promotional and propaganda activities held across the country. Notices guiding the annual promotion are jointly issued by nine central government bureaus including the Ministry of Education, the Ministry of Propaganda, the Ministry of Culture, the Ministry of Personnel, Labor, and Social Security, the State Administration of Radio, Film, and Television, and the General Political Department of the Chinese People's Liberation Army. Every year, the theme for the annual event changes, showing the new political message encoded in the dominance of the national language. Competitions are held, centered on the chosen theme, including poetry recitations, spelling bees, choruses, posters designs, and calligraphy. These competitions are organized by public schools, as well as various cultural institutions and state functionaries across the country.

During the 2013 Promotion Week, Putonghua was integrated into the realization of the "China Dream." The theme of the 2013 Promotion Week was described as "Using Putonghua to describe the 'China Dream,' using standardized simplified Chinese to write the 'China Dream.'"[19] "China Dream" is an idea introduced by President Xi Jinping in a speech in November 2012. In his speech, he used the phrase to mean "the rejuvenation of the Chinese nation," but the exact implications of this political ideal remained vague, without clear parameters.[20] Thus, a practical explanation of what exactly the "China Dream" means for the lives of ordinary citizens remains elusive, aside from the idea of upward mobility similar to former Chinese Communist Party secretary Deng Xiaoping's vision for achieving *Xiaokang*, or middle-class standard of living.

By invoking the "China Dream" in the Promotion Week theme the very next year, the nine top-level ministries and bureaus that jointly issued the notice made it clear that Putonghua was the only linguistic means recognized and encouraged by the state to participate in the Dream. This exclusiveness again reinforces the dominance of Putonghua. Also important to note is that this theme excludes those who use traditional Chinese characters, as in Taiwan or those Chinese diaspora communities established before 1956, when the state passed the directive to simplify Chinese characters.[21] The theme binds together a nationalist vision with the national language, simultaneously excluding other Chinese languages and people not in Mainland China. The undertone of this theme corresponds to the argument about the political component of language ideology; that multiple languages indicate multiple loyalties, and thus "a temperamental flaw, a lack of trustworthiness; . . . and shifting language as evidence of equally shiftable, hence dubious and shallow allegiances."[22] With their chosen theme, the central government made plain that language choice is not a personal linguistic or cultural choice, but an announcement of political affiliation and loyalty.

The 2014 Promotion Week again centered on Xi's political ideal, the "China Dream." The theme reads "Speak Putonghua well, [and] you, I, and he will realize our dream (*shuo hao Putonghua, yuan meng ni wo ta*)." This makes clear that speaking Putonghua is not enough—one must speak it well to make the realization of the "China Dream" possible. This theme combines the wishful thinking of superficial solidarity with the nationalist ideal of an imagined community. It also translates that vision into a linguistic practice of self-governmentality. To borrow from French philosopher Michel Foucault, this means individuals are actively disciplining their linguistic practices to achieve the goal set by the government, which provides the incentives and rationale for them to do so. The state asks its citizens if they want a slice of the pie of China's increasing prosperity, while making explicit that political allegiance, symbolized by using Putonghua, is a prerequisite for participation. The theme's gendered language also merits attention. In the theme, a male third-person pronoun (*ta*, meaning he) is used as a generic to represent everyone other than you and me. This is just one more example of the resurgence of gender inequality in Mainland China during the last two decades.[23] This is in stark contrast to Maoist-era propaganda, which portrayed women holding up half the sky. Later in this chapter, I will show how gender inequality manifests in language practices among native Shanghairen women who favor Putonghua, in the hope of bettering their social status.

From 2015 to 2020, the themes of the annual Putonghua Promotion Weeks revolved around the core message of speaking Putonghua and using standardized characters, tying this rationale to the promotion of traditional Chinese culture, the achievement of a *Xiaokang* society, and progress toward modernization. The nationalist agenda was most apparent in the theme for 2019, the seventieth anniversary of the founding of the People's Republic of China.

The theme reads "Using Putonghua to chant the seventieth anniversary; using standardized characters to write patriotic feelings" (*Putonghua song qishi huadan, guifanzi shu aiguoqinghuai*). The state promotes Putonghua by using both an emotional approach, articulating a unified Chinese people sharing a long and splendid history and culture, and a political one, reinforcing that to love one's country, individuals must celebrate the leadership of the Communist Party. The themes of the last several Putonghua Promotion Weeks also make apparent that the diglossia system, though collapsing, remains the target of these measures, in spite of Putonghua being the mandatory medium of instruction in schools for decades. It is important to remember that since most Mandarin and non-Mandarin dialects do not have a standardized written form, the language conflict takes place in speech. It is everyday verbal interactions that the state intends to regulate. A uniform voice is what the nationalist agenda intends to achieve, and dialects are supposed to be phased out and silenced in the pursuit of societal progress.

Another systematic strategy used to promote Putonghua is the Putonghua Proficiency Test. This test is based on the Ministry of Education's No.16 Decree, "Regulation on the Evaluation of Putonghua Proficiency" (*Putonghua shuiping ceshi guanli guiding*) as well as the "Guidelines for Determination of Level of Putonghua Proficiency" (*Putonghua shuiping ceshi dengji biaozhun,*) issued by the National Language Working Committee under the Ministry of Education in 1997. The resulting test was announced in the "Outlines for Putonghua Proficiency Testing" (*Putonghua ceshi dagang*) in effect since October 1, 2004. The proficiency test has three components, phonetics, lexicon, and grammar, with a maximum possible score of one hundred. Test results are divided into three ranks with two levels in each rank. To achieve First Rank A Level, one must score 97 or above, while the First Rank B Level requires a minimum of 92. TV and radio broadcasters, actors, and Putonghua language teachers must reach First Rank. The Second Rank A level requires at least 87 points, and its B level 80. The third rank A level range is 70 to 79, and B 60 to 69. Other than news reporters and performers, public-facing occupations, such as police officers or schoolteachers, also need to meet a minimum level set by the educational bureau at the provincial or municipal level. Xia, a native Shanghairen policeman in his mid-forties, proudly informed me that he scored a 92, well above the required level of 87. As for schoolteachers in subjects other than Putonghua, a Second Rank B level of 80 is required. Passing the test is only the beginning, since daily language practices in public are closely monitored.

During the other 358 days of the year when it is not Putonghua Promotion Week, Putonghua is reinforced through obligations assigned to various levels of the government and state functionaries. In this way, abstract language policy becomes operational guidelines for public employees' language practices.

From civil servants to schoolteachers and broadcasters, speaking Putonghua is an essential aspect of proper and professional conduct as required by law. In a 2013 interview, the Deputy General Manager of the Shanghai Grand Theatre explained to me how they, being a "Window Organization" (*chuangkou danwei*, a public-facing organization representing the image of the city), are constantly and covertly inspected by the city's Office of the Construction of Ideological Infrastructure Committee (*jingshen wenming jianshe weiyuanhui bangongshi*):

> They would come to our box office, pretending to be customers and asking about performances, to see whether our staff speaks perfect Putonghua. Or sometimes they would just act like tourists asking our security guards for directions. Very sneaky; we always only find out about their visits in the later notice or report they send us. If they spot dialect speaking or untidiness of the venue, they deduct points from our annual ranking as a Model Organization (*wenming danwei*), threatening to take away the plaque.

Though many previously state-owned and funded theatres and art troupes were restructured to take full responsibility for their financial standing in the economic reform era, administratively they still belong to the Shanghai Municipal Propaganda Bureau. Losing the Model Organization plaque would be a serious punishment, a public humiliation that would affect the career trajectory of the organization's leadership. This intricate relation between government and nonprofit organizations indicates that the implementation of the language law is the responsibility of more than just the law enforcement sector. Responsibility is given to various interconnected state and party agencies that painstakingly engage in daily surveillance.

For a project of this scope to reach the individual and affect an ordinary Shanghairen's everyday life, municipal and local agencies maintain strict organizational control. The guiding principle is to treat any effort to promote local dialects as a challenge to the dominance of Putonghua. In early 2013, a team of producers and editors at the Shanghai People's Radio Station submitted a proposal for a citywide Shanghai dialect competition to the Shanghai Spoken and Written Language Working Committee (*shanghaishi yuyan wenzi gongzuo weiyuanhui*) under the Municipal Education Bureau. The proposal was a grassroots effort intended to encourage the Shanghai dialect proficiency among school children. According to one of the station's producers, the committee was interested in the proposal and showed verbal support but required the committee's name to be left off any promotion of the dialect competition. As a municipal governmental agency, it was important not to be seen promoting any kind of Shanghai dialect–related activity. It is also true, though, that without any written governmental approval, no promotional or recruitment material could be distributed in schools, and thus the competition idea was scrapped.

The producer attributed the failed competition to the dilemma faced by school principals and teachers:

> Without a clear order from above, they dared not do a thing. Plus, they are all required to carry out the administrative order to promote Putonghua. How could they participate in the promotion of the Shanghai dialect, when everywhere on campus there are small plaques and posters saying, "Please Speak Putonghua"?

According to the 2001 Language Law, any governmental agency, such as the Municipal Language Committee, is supposed to lead the promotion of Putonghua, and schools are the primary organ for the creation of Putonghua speakers. Messages such as "please speak Putonghua" (see figure 2.1 for the

Figure 2.1   A Window Panel with "Please Speak Putonghua, Please Write Standardized Characters" Painted on a Classroom Door on the Campus of Fudan University in Shanghai. *Source*: Photo by the author.

promotion slogan on a college campus) on small plaques or painted on walls and windows on campuses remind school principals and teachers of their duty, but also promote self-governmentality for everyone to discipline their own linguistic practice.

During my fieldwork in Shanghai in 2013 and 2017, I came across "Please Speak Putonghua" plaques in hospital lobbies, banks, and at public transit customer service counters (see figure 2.2 for the plaque in a clinic). They always face outward to remind clients of the linguistic norm in public places, and their presence also ensures that the staff self monitor their speech.

From my observations, it was only when a client responded in broken Putonghua with a strong Shanghai dialect accent, or completely in the Shanghai dialect, that a bank clerk or receptionist would switch to the Shanghai dialect to accommodate. Usually, those who speak Putonghua poorly are elderly native Shanghairen, who finished school before the

Figure 2.2 A Plastic Plaque Showing "Please Speak Putonghua, Please Write Standardized Characters" Nailed to the Pillar at a Hospital Lobby. *Source:* Photo by the author.

Table 2.1   Language Practices in Public

	Solely Putonghua (%)	Mixed with Predominantly Putonghua (%)	Solely the Shanghai dialect (%)	Mixed with Predominantly the Shanghai dialect (%)	Equally mixed (%)
At government agencies	46.00	26.80	9.60	15.10	2.50
In hospital	35.00	30.50	11.10	19.80	3.70
In retail	28.80	34.20	12.80	21.40	2.90
At leisure venues, such as gym or movie theatre	37.20	30.20	12.40	18.60	1.70
In Public transit such as subway or bus station	32.60	31.80	12.60	21.30	1.70

Communist Party's Putonghua project started in the 1950s or those who live and work in an environment still dominated by the Shanghai dialect. In a telephone survey with a representative sample of 1,008 residents in Shanghai of age 13 and above conducted by the Shanghai Statistical Bureau in 2013 —the same year of my survey research, it was found that 97 percent claimed to speak acceptable or fluent Putonghua, while 81.4 percent for the Shanghai dialect.[24] Though the report does not specify the proportion of natives and non-natives in the sample, it coincides with my survey with native Shanghairen that Putonghua use is increasingly ubiquitous in public places in Shanghai (see table 2.1).

Putonghua dominates four out of the five types of public spaces. Though for "in retail," the practice of mixed Putonghua and the Shanghai dialect is more common than solely communicating in Putonghua, if we add "Solely Putonghua" and "Mixed with Predominantly Putonghua" together, across all five categories, "at governmental agencies," "in hospital," "in retail," "at leisure venues," and "in public transit" claim more than 60 percent, with at governmental agencies reached combined 72.8 percent, and at leisure venues closely follows with 67.4 percent. The practice of solely speaking the Shanghai dialect across all five categories is only around 10 percent. These survey results complement my observations of the Putonghua dominant linguistic scene in public in the early 2010s Shanghai. Even among the older generation who speak Putonghua with difficulty or with a strong Shanghai dialect accent, they unavoidably need to switch to Putonghua to communicate with the younger generation who have limited proficiency in the Shanghai dialect, regardless of native-ness. Among the generation in their thirties or forties, Putonghua has become the default language in public. The rapid shift is a direct result of state-led Putonghua promotional efforts.

The dominance of Putonghua in public spaces explains the scenario described at the beginning of this chapter. The staff's rude response to hearing the Shanghai dialect spoken at a venue reserved for high culture revealed them taking it upon themselves to police linguistic practice. Like many Shanghairen I spoke with, the art center staff deployed their embodied linguistic capital, which dictated the proper uses of both languages. The concert for that night was performed by the United States' National Symphony Orchestra, one of a series of events to celebrate the thirtieth anniversary of the establishment of official diplomatic relations between the United States and the People's Republic of China. Greeting and congratulating messages from thenPresidents Hu Jintao and Barack Obama along with their photos were printed in the playbill. The formalness suggested the only proper language for that event was Putonghua, the national language.

The promotion of Putonghua is not an isolated project; instead, it is integrated into the legal and administrative system under the Chinese Communist Party's leadership. It represents a nationalist vision of a unified, modern, prosperous, and open China. The vision has gained momentum in the last two decades. To influence the behavior of ordinary citizens, the nationalist project of linguistic unification brings together state institutions and all associated organizations. Ultimately, through annual Promotion Weeks, language proficiency tests, and policing and surveillance of language use in public, the state makes explicit the political and socioeconomic significance of Putonghua. This translates Putonghua proficiency into a type of linguistic capital, the conversion of which into economic gain and social status is guaranteed by the state. Public measures are seeping into private life, as adoption of the dominant language ideology increases in native Shanghairen's homes, where they pass it down to their children. Furthermore, the school system has played an active role in imbuing native Shanghairen with the proper linguistic capital, not only through teaching the state-sanctioned standardized national language but also by degrading the Shanghai dialect, and associating Putonghua alone with upward social mobility.

DOMINANT LANGUAGE IDEOLOGY

Through educational obtainment, an individual's possession of linguistic capital is an effective indicator of socioeconomic status, and one of the main tools to achieve it in Shanghai. Nancy Dorian notes that the hierarchy of languages corresponds to social statuses of their speakers, and the correlation goes both ways.[25] If a speaker has power and prestige, it will be projected onto the language they speak, and vice versa. Or, to put it more simply, people are ranked by the language they speak. This ranking explains why many native Shanghairen avoid the Shanghai dialect and adopt the dominant language in the state's Putonghua panopticon. Bourdieu rightfully points out that the decision to speak which language is never a personal choice but in the hands of the state in terms of defining both the linguistic standards and proper occasions for its use.[26] The heavy-handedness of the state's control of language choices also sheds light on the gendered attitudes and practices regarding Putonghua and the Shanghai dialect, in an era with unprecedented economic growth but stagnant progress toward gender equality.

At Home and in School

Language practices in Shanghai homes have been influenced by two other major factors besides state language policies. First, changing family compositions, with increased intermarriage between native Shanghairen and recent internal migrants.[27] However, since language(s) spoken is not part of the demographic data collected by the Shanghai Statistical Bureau annually, it is difficult to sort the city-wide data effectively. For example, determining how many Shanghai dialect speakers are married to non-speakers or to someone who speaks a non-Wu Chinese dialect. The phenomenon of intermarriage certainly suggests an increasing linguistic diversity in the domestic sphere, and thus also Putonghua's increasing status as the common language for everyday communication.

The second factor affecting domestic language practices is a widespread belief in the successful capital conversion of embodied linguistic capital, in the form of Putonghua proficiency, to social, economic, and symbolic capitals in the era of the "China Dream." Because Putonghua has been the medium of instruction in schools since the 1950s, proficiency is associated with a long period of formal schooling, and thus higher educational achievement. In Shanghai in the 1980s, Ramsey observed that some educated, sophisticated Shanghai families had begun to use Putonghua in their homes.[28] From my personal recollection of growing up in Shanghai in the 1980s and 1990s, Putonghua proficiency was by then already an indicator of a child's family background. In the late 1990s, Chen observed that competence in Putonghua in addition to one's local dialect was generally taken as an indicator, albeit not always a reliable one, of one's educational level.[29]

The broader sociohistorical context facilitating the linguistic-to-economic capital conversion involves changes in job allocation during the economic reform era. Instead of *hukou* status or political affiliation, criteria essential in the Maoist era, the job market has turned to a more merit-based system that rewards educational achievement regardless of birthplace. This transition will be discussed in greater detail in chapters 4 and 5. Marius van den Berg observed a strong association between Putonghua proficiency and economic success among young, highly educated professionals in Shanghai in 2005.[30] With such socioeconomic incentives in mind, the proactive accumulation of linguistic capital at home prevails not only in highly educated households but also among those of lower socioeconomic status. Both groups cultivate a home environment geared toward Putonghua proficiency for their children. Even when the Shanghai dialect is used, it is not directed at the children, thus sending the message that the dialect is not theirs.

Table 2.2 shows the responses from 175 survey participants who have daily interactions with children in their households. Only 22.9 percent of surveyed native Shanghairen use "Solely the Shanghai Dialect" to communicate with children, and 12.6 percent use a mixed pattern of Putonghua and the Shanghai dialect with the latter dominates. While "Solely Putonghua" counts 11.4 percent and "Mixed with Predominantly Putonghua" 27.4 percent. Adding up these two sets of corresponding categories, Putonghua with 38.8 percent wins slightly over the Shanghai dialect's 35.5 percent. The languages used to speak with children also follow an age-group pattern with more than half of surveyed respondents aged above 45 use the Shanghai dialect exclusively with children, especially of the group above 65 years old, two-thirds use solely the Shanghai dialect. The age groups below 55 show a Putonghua dominant pattern. For age group 35–44, "Solely Putonghua" and "Mixed with Predominantly Putonghua" add up to 59.1 percent, and the two categories add up to 45.5 percent for the age group of 25–34 years old. Another element in the results is the "Other" category that captures languages other than Putonghua, the Shanghai dialect,

Table 2.2   Language Used at Home with Children by Age

Languages spoken at home with children	19–24 (%)	25–34 (%)	35–44 (%)	45–54 (%)	55–64 (%)	Above 65 (%)	Total (%)
Mix Putonghua, the Shanghai dialect, and English	0.0	1.1	0.0	0.0	0.0	0.0	0.6
Mix Putonghua and the Shanghai dialect of equal amount	25.0	6.8	13.6	0.0	0.0	0.0	9.7
Mixed with Predominantly Putonghua	9.4	34.1	40.9	40.0	14.3	14.3	27.4
Mixed with Predominantly the Shanghai dialect	6.3	17.0	4.5	0.0	28.6	9.5	12.6
Solely Putonghua	15.6	11.4	18.2	0.0	0.0	4.8	11.4
Solely the Shanghai dialect	0.0	15.9	22.7	60.0	57.1	66.7	22.9
Other	43.8	13.6	0.0	0.0	0.0	4.8	15.4
Total	32	88	22	5	7	21	175

or English spoken to children at home. This counts for 15.4 percent of the total and indicates a more diverse domestic linguistic environment which invites further research. It must be noted that the data were collected from a non-probable sampling strategy, and thus the pattern does not represent the overall native Shanghairen population. However, it certainly indicates the domestic linguistic environment for children has been largely taken over by Putonghua. From the interview with Bei, it is apparent that the dominant language ideology explains such pattern. From our interview, I learned that in Bei's family, her husband closely monitored their son's language use. Bei is a native Shanghairen and her husband is originally from Shannxi province in northwestern China. According to Bei, he vehemently objected to speaking the Shanghai dialect at home:

> He thinks the Shanghai dialect is backwards, not compatible with the global city image of Shanghai. Besides, he picks on my mother, who is not highly educated and speaks only the dialect, saying her world is very limited, evidenced by her limited language skill. He doesn't like her speaking the Shanghai dialect to our son. So, when he is around, my mother, though with heavy accent and difficulty, would speak Putonghua to the boy. It is her way to show my husband that she understands his expectation, and his care for the child's future.

The linguistic capital Bei's husband possesses is comprised not only of competence in Putonghua, English, and his native Shannxi dialect but also knowledge of the standing each has in a hierarchy. Immanuel Wallerstein's world-systems theory categorizes countries as core, semi-periphery, or periphery based on their participation in the world economy and global division of labor. Abram de Swaan builds on Wallerstein to describe a world language system as a pyramid-shaped hierarchy. It has English on top, as the sole hyper-central language, and thousands of periphery languages, predominantly used in verbal communications locally, at the bottom. In between are central languages, made up primarily of languages that are the official languages of nation-states of semi-periphery status, but also include super-central languages used for international trade and communication. In de Swaan's mapping, Putonghua is a super-central language, while varieties of non-Mandarin Chinese, particularly those spoken south of the Yangtze River and without a standardized written form, are lower on the pyramid. The Shanghai dialect is thus defined as a peripheral language, despite the sheer number of speakers in comparison to that of the national language of a small country, for example, Icelandic.[31] Bei's husband, like many internal migrants in Shanghai, understands this disparity in linguistic reach and position in the language hierarchy between Putonghua and the Shanghai dialect.

Furthermore, Bei's mother's lower educational level and social status provide proof of the lower status and limited application of the Shanghai dialect.

In turn, proficiency in the Shanghai dialect confirms speakers' low status in society. This again echoes Woolard's findings in her study on the social condition of Catalan and Castilian speakers; the lower socioeconomic status of dialect speakers "furnish[es] convenient evidence that they are not equipped for more authoritative functions."[32] Bei, immersed in the dominant language ideology through her school years in Shanghai, found it difficult to counter her husband's view. Over time, like her mother, she stopped communicating with her son in the Shanghai dialect when her husband was present. Through her husband, the dominant language ideology constructed a predominantly Putonghua environment in the private sphere. Though deprived of the opportunity to learn and practice the Shanghai dialect, Bei's son grew up with the proper, and thus desirable linguistic capital, later to be rewarded in the school system and on the job market.

Nevertheless, Bei's son will still hear plenty of the Shanghai dialect at home, since Bei speaks it with her mother in his hearing. Codeswitching only occurs when the father is present. Other interviewees confirm this kind of codeswitching as a common parenting practice. For example, as a retired native Shanghairen college professor observed to me:

> For example, in the elevator of my building, a parent would say hello to me in the Shanghai dialect. The next second, he would switch to Putonghua to scold the kid: "Stand still!" Automatically, just like that!

This anecdote provides further evidence that native Shanghairen parents constantly make audience-specific language choices. Increasingly, parents choose to communicate with their children exclusively in the national language, a choice that reinforces the power and authority of Putonghua. This not only aligns with the dominant language ideology assigning each language a different status but also facilitates the accumulation of the children's linguistic capital by demonstrating the workings of language ideology.

From my observations in Shanghai, it is clear that generally what distinguishes the middle class is bilingual or trilingual capacity, as opposed to mere Shanghai dialect proficiency. This is because many professionals in Shanghai work for transnational corporations and use English on a daily basis. Those without such language skills are predominantly native Shanghairen senior citizens with less education and a working-class background. This demographic group, by and large, lacks Putonghua proficiency due to leaving school before Putonghua was mandated as the language of instruction, and their lower social status is due largely to the Cultural Revolution (1966–1976), which deprived most of them of the chance for high school and postsecondary education. Nevertheless, many native Shanghairen see the correlation between class status and language skills as proof that dialect proficiency cannot be converted to economic capital.

Qi, a dialect preservation activist, told me about his aunt's firm belief in the correlation between language proficiency and socioeconomic status, and also her resulting linguistic practices:

> Not only when talking to her high-school age daughter, [did she use Putonghua]; even when describing her daughter's classmates and school life, my youngest aunt would switch to Putonghua automatically, even though she was talking to my dad and other siblings in the Shanghai dialect, and regardless of her daughter's presence.

Qi's aunt switched to Putonghua to describe her daughter's world, perceiving it as different from her own, which is populated by lower-class Shanghai dialect speakers. Through conscious codeswitching, she made an explicit distinction between her Putonghua-speaking daughter and her Shanghai-dialect-speaking siblings. Her daughter was, at the time I spoke with Qi, a manager in a Fortune 500 company, earning the highest salary of her generation in the extended family, realizing her mother's aspirations.

From Qi's family's story, we see how linguistic capital, in particular Putonghua proficiency among native Shanghairen, becomes a convenient signifier of social status. To a certain extent, we can understand it as confirmation of the state's propaganda. Putonghua proficiency leads to the realization of the "China Dream" measured by good jobs and high earnings. The "China Dream" turns out to be less an individual aspiration than a promise by the state that political and cultural conformity will be rewarded with economic prosperity and social recognition. Summarizing from earlier studies in various sociohistorical contexts, Grenoble and Whaley argue, "[t]he relinquishing of a native tongue is tied in part to the belief that success in a non-native language is crucial to economic advantage."[33] The shift from a planned to a market economy has opened up venues for individual's upward mobility. In a changing Shanghai, many native Shanghairen made the pragmatic decision to adopt Putonghua.

Qi's story about his aunt also illustrates how the dominant language ideology has influenced native Shanghairen of lower socioeconomic status, many of who now embody and promote that ideology. Bourdieu sees petite bourgeoisie, or the lower-middle-class, as the main contributors to linguistic change, because of the disparity between their socioeconomic aspiration and their limited means to achieve it.[34] The state encodes in their propaganda a promise of upward social mobility and makes explicit that Putonghua is required to fulfill that promise. Qi's aunt belongs to a lower-middle-class or working-class stratum. This is an intermediate position, between bi- or trilingual professionals, and rural-origin migrant workers who speak heavily accented Putonghua and other dialects. Thus, it is not surprising that many of her generation have seemingly contradictory feelings about speaking Putonghua and translating the dominant language ideology into differentiated attitudes and practices. On the one hand, they discriminate against unskilled migrants whose strongly accented Putonghua reveals their rural origins and low educational level. On the other hand, they actively prefer Putonghua and work to create a monolingual Putonghua environment for their native Shanghairen children and eschew the Shanghai dialect at home. Such seeming contradiction in language attitude can be explained by this group's downward social mobility in the last two decades.

The older generation's effort to create a predominantly Putonghua environment at home is assisted by the school system's rigid Putonghua promotion. Many Shanghairen parents told me that after just a few weeks or months of kindergarten, their children had stopped, and even refused, to speak the Shanghai dialect at home. It was despite the fact that most of them were raised in the dialect by their native Shanghairen grandparents. The school system in Shanghai produces linguistic capital by teaching Putonghua, which results in many Shanghairen children being bilingual. Such bilingual capacity is essential for recognition of their differentiated cultural aesthetics and corresponding domains of usage. This is, as Bourdieu stresses, the role schools play in elaborating, legitimating, and imposing an official language.[35] Wu Wei, a computer programmer in his early thirties who developed a free mobile app for typing in the Shanghai dialect, recalled to me how public schools legitimize and establish Putonghua's higher status by deliberately degrading the dialect:

> The idea that speaking the Shanghai dialect is philistine and low-class is deeply rooted. We were taught in elementary school that the Shanghai dialect is rustic, as well as the idea that the Shanghai dialect is of a lower status, not proper for formal settings.

Besides degrading the Shanghai dialect and explicitly disciplining students' linguistic practices, teachers' own language choices in non-pedagogical settings further reproduce the dominant language ideology.

Yan, a native Shanghairen teacher at a private elementary school, provided me with a telling example:

> Usually we teachers consciously use Putonghua at work, because school is a formal setting. But interestingly at meetings with the principal, he would use Putonghua to explain pedagogic materials in a very formal tone. Then, he would switch to the Shanghai dialect when scolding us because of some negative

review. He differentiates, switches back and forth. We as well, if criticizing students' work, we would switch to the dialect.

In Yan's description, the principal did not consistently use Putonghua even in a relatively formal setting. Rather, he switched to the Shanghai dialect to swear, a function believed to be improper for Putonghua. Even though the official language connotes power and authority, it is viewed as unsuitable for certain ways of speaking, regardless of social context. In Yan's telling, swearing in the Shanghai dialect not only reflects Putonghua's formality but hits the spot in another way: Putonghua's relatively plain vocabulary cannot communicate or carry the same force that certain Shanghai dialect words can. This differentiated connotation and use of Putonghua and the Shanghai dialect echoes what earlier studies found in European contexts. For example, both Alexandra Jaffe studying Corsica[36] and Kathryn Woolard on Barcelona[37] conclude that codeswitching is viewed as an inherited component of a value-laden bilingual system. In other words, the symbolic meaning of both languages needs to be understood by both the speaker and the listener for the switch to be effective and meaningful, even though proficiency in both languages is not necessary.

The fact that Yan and her colleagues are aware of the principal's codeswitch makes it apparent that the differentiated functions of the two languages are widely understood. Furthermore, since teachers' critique of students' work follows the same pattern, it is clear that the differentiated social functions of Putonghua and the Shanghai dialect are part of the linguistic capital reproduced in schools. Students learn Putonghua's pronunciation, vocabulary, and grammar in class, but also hear their teachers consciously codeswitch in certain contexts. Outside of class hours, an important part of the linguistic environment in which students learn how, where, and when to use each language. Here, codeswitching does not indicate that the Shanghai dialect has a coarser vocabulary, but instead that social functions and cultural values have been assigned to its use. This further reinforces that the dialect is rude and suited only for devalued activities, such as swearing and scolding.

Through years of immersion in the dominant language ideology, most young native Shanghairen have adopted the image of the Shanghai dialect as backward and informal. As a Shanghai dialect preservation activist pointed out to me, "those self-perceived to be modern and classy refuse to speak the Shanghai dialect." This view is further exemplified by a story told to me by Ouyang, a native Shanghairen. The story is about Ouyang's cousin, who was born in the early 1980s, speaks Putonghua fluently and works as a director at Shanghai TV Station:

It was at the family gathering to celebrate his 30th birthday at a fancy restaurant. His parents, and senior members of the extended family were all present. But he said later that he couldn't give the thank-you speech in the Shanghai dialect. According to him, it's like a physiological [psychological as well] compulsion, that he could not make himself. To him, it is a formal speech, so he could not switch to the local tongue. He apologized to us for his language choice at the end of the speech.

Through this language choice, Ouyang's cousin demonstrated the linguistic capital he embodied. The differentiated aesthetics and status assigned to Putonghua versus the Shanghai dialect prevented him from using the latter even among family members in his speech. Usually, using the dialect in a private, intimate setting, such as among family members or in a close-knit community, signifies trust and solidarity, but Ouyang's cousin was unable to use the dialect, despite his acknowledgment of that intimacy. His apology notwithstanding, the dominant language ideology he adopted dictates the exclusive usage of Putonghua for formal settings.

The decline of the Shanghai dialect competence moves linearly across generations. For example, the cohort born in the 1990s are still able to speak some Shanghai dialect but need to switch to Putonghua from time to time due to their limited vocabulary in the dialect. Those born in the 2000s in general have a passive understanding of the Shanghai dialect but prefer not to speak it. The most profound decline can be seen in the group born in the 2010s, who have little to no knowledge of the dialect and are highly unlikely to acquire any in the school system. The generational difference indicates native Shanghairen parents and grandparents work in accordance with official school policies to create a Putonghua-speaking environment for native Shanghairen children and clearly communicate the message that the Shanghai dialect has few uses, which accelerates the dialect's decline.

Gendered Language Attitudes and Practices

In this language milieu, native Shanghairen's responses to the dominant language ideology break down along gender lines, with women more likely to comply with state policies and guidelines. Robin Lakoff, in her groundbreaking piece about language and women's place, argues that the marginality and powerlessness of women are reflected in the ways they are expected to speak. Women are damned if they do, and damned if they do not, because they are expected to speak in ways that only reinforce and reproduce the inequality and discrimination that they face in society at large.[38] Working within the premise of the complex social construction of gender, the observations made in this study do not suggest a clear-cut, simple correlation between gender and language attitudes and practices among native Shanghairen. Rather, multiple social processes are in action, among which the aspiration for upward social mobility plays an important role.

Peter Trudgill argues from his study in Norwich that middle-class women are more likely to follow the standard-language norms to acquire prestige, while working-class men tend to use vernaculars to show defiance and toughness, hence, proof of masculinity.[39] In another study about gender-based language choices conducted in the 1970s in Europe, Susan Gal explains how German-Hungarian bilingual women in rural villages strategize their language choices and marriage patterns. The German language those young women switch to represents money and prestige associated with newly available factory work in towns. Situated in the transition of the larger society they live in, those young women's language choice is associated with their aspirational lifestyles and the desirable social identity as wives of workers instead of peasants.[40] Though not directly participating in the labor market, those women are able to acquire a higher social status through their (prospective) husbands in a surrogated manner. The prestige or symbolic capital they obtain though appearing to be through converting their linguistic capital, in truth involves their romantic partners' economic, cultural, and social capitals as well. Building from earlier studies suggesting gendered variation and its association with women's position in larger social contexts which provide limited venues for women's advancement socioeconomically, Penelope Eckert argues it is not prestige but power, raw and direct, determines gender-based linguistic variation.[41] In Eckert's study in the Detroit area, women in working-class neighborhoods who are not college educated or hold professional jobs rely heavily on the accumulation of symbolic capital through using the standard language, to articulate and assert their worth and authority.[42] Synthesizing these early works with Bourdieu's framework on the convertibility of symbolic and linguistic capital, I maintain these studies complement each other in revealing the ultimate incentive for the performative aspect of utterances.

Ultimately, the hope appears to be when more women receive higher education, enter the professional labor market, achieve higher socioeconomic status, and obtain power in their own rights, the gender-based language variance will diminish. However, as my study shows, the anticipated transition is more likely wishful thinking than an attainable prospect in urban China. In the case of choosing to use Putonghua over the Shanghai dialect, highly educated and professional native Shanghairen women are quick to shift to the officially sanctioned language, in the hope of bettering their social position and to avoid possible negative consequences academically and professionally. This reality is situated in the inverted association between economic developments and gender equality in China.

Despite the remarkable achievements of the economic reform era, and the grand vision of the "China Dream" in the last decade, women's position in the country remains stagnant, if not worse than before. In 2020, the Global

Gender Gap Index ranked China 106th among 153 countries in economic participation and opportunity, educational attainment, health and survival, and political empowerment. China fell three spots from 2018, when it was 103rd out of 149 countries,[43] while in 2006 China was 63rd out of 115 countries.[44] The latter was the year after the All-China Women's Federation, under the direct leadership of the Chinese Communist Party, issued a statement calling highly educated single women over the age of 27 *shengnv* (leftover women) and urged them to get married and start a family. A drop of forty-three positions in fourteen years cannot be attributed simply to the increase in countries measured. Rather, it reflects the overall trend in the country of increasing gender inequality.

Against this backdrop, Bourdieu's insight on the petite bourgeoisie's tendency for linguistic hypercorrection in order to reinforce linguistic and social hierarchies is useful for understanding gendered language attitudes in Shanghai. Though of varied social class backgrounds, the shared lower social positioning as women in contemporary China results in female native Shanghairen more likely to adopt Putonghua and the dominant language ideology. Minglang Zhou's quantitative study of native Shanghairen college students' language attitudes shortly before the promulgation of the 2001 Language Law indicates women favoring Putonghua in terms of social status and group solidarity, while men favor the Shanghai dialect.[45] The study refutes the general understanding that associates authority and status with a national and official language, and conversely associates insider membership and solidarity with a regional or minority language. More than ten years later, my qualitative observations and survey results in Shanghai provide a more nuanced illustration of gendered language attitudes.

The Shanghai dialect preservation movement is disproportionally made up of men, which is already telling, and they are well aware of how language practices break down along gender lines. Wu Wei, the software engineer, told me:

> [Native Shanghairen] men are more likely to speak the Shanghai dialect, but strangely [native Shanghairen] women are not . . . if you initiate a conversation in the Shanghai dialect, they [women] would respond in Putonghua . . . it is true that through school education we learned the Shanghai dialect is of a lower status, so they [women] refuse to speak it. Men are more protective in terms of their own culture, territorial kind of . . . and women are easily influenced by outside forces.

Wu Wei's reading of gendered linguistic practices weaves together Dorian's argument that a speaker has the status of the language they speak and Lakoff's argument about linguistic discrepancy reflecting social discrepancy in the positions of men and women.[46] In a society where women's social position is generally lower, using the higher status language, in this case, Putonghua, is intended to improve social position, in the hope that they will gain authority and their opinion will be taken more seriously.

Wu Wei, like other Shanghai dialect preservation activists, used the Shanghai dialect in our interviews, while all other native Shanghairen, besides senior citizens with limited Putonghua proficiency, used Putonghua, evidently regarding interviews with a scholar from a U.S. university as a formal setting. The "outside influences" Wu Wei referred to above include formal institutions and their delegates, such as schoolteachers. In line with his observation, I did find that female interviewees readily used Putonghua in interviews, and some also shared experiences that aligned with Wu Wei's observation, such as Yu, who attended college in Shanghai about the same time as Wu Wei.

A Shanghai native in her mid-thirties at the time of the interview, Yu holds an MBA degree and works as marketing strategy manager for a German company's headquarters in Shanghai. She told me in Putonghua that upon entering college, she realized her tendency to speak the Shanghai dialect negatively impacted her presentation skills in the eyes of her professors. It motivated her to practice Putonghua as much as she could, both on campus and at home with her parents. Her behavior exemplifies Grenoble and Whaley's argument about the belief in economic achievement though the adoption of a non-native language.[47] In Yu's case, she made a pragmatic decision to speak Putonghua in order to improve her academic standing, which later delivered her professional success.

Wu Wei and Yu's language attitudes and practices are not outlier cases, as shown by my survey about language choices in school among native Shanghairen (see table 2.3). Native Shanghairen women consistently use Putonghua more than the Shanghai dialect to communicate with teachers, in comparison to men. Across all four school levels, "Solely Putonghua" and "Mixed with Predominantly Putonghua" dominate the language practices at about 60 percent for all three school levels below college. And there is a big jump in Putonghua use in college settings, which can be partly explained by the diversity among college faculty and the student body, but also higher education settings are more likely perceived as formal settings in comparison to other school levels. Thus, Putonghua is a more proper choice under state language policies and the rhetoric of Putonghua promotion. "Solely Putonghua" and "Mixed with Predominantly Putonghua" at the college setting together counts 93 percent for females and 86 percent for males.

The school setting is more significant when we juxtapose language practices in school with those at home. In table 2.4, both men and women speak the Shanghai dialect more at home with parents and other senior family

Table 2.3   Language Used in Schools with Teachers by Gender

Elementary School	Female (%)	Male (%)	Grand Total (%)
Mixed with Equal Amount	4.20	1.10	3.00
Mixed with Predominantly Putonghua	21.10	18.10	19.90
Mixed with Predominantly the Shanghai dialect	6.30	12.80	8.90
Solely Putonghua	46.50	34.00	41.50
Solely the Shanghai dialect	21.80	34.00	26.70
Middle School	**Female (%)**	**Male (%)**	**Grand Total (%)**
Mixed with Equal Amount	5.70	0.00	3.40
Mixed with Predominantly Putonghua	27.00	22.80	25.30
Mixed with Predominantly the Shanghai dialect	8.50	12.00	9.90
Solely Putonghua	36.90	32.60	35.20
Solely the Shanghai dialect	22.00	32.60	26.20
High school	**Female (%)**	**Male (%)**	**Grand Total (%)**
Mixed with Equal Amount	5.10	1.10	3.50
Mixed with Predominantly Putonghua	25.40	28.10	26.40
Mixed with Predominantly the Shanghai dialect	9.40	10.10	9.70
Solely Putonghua	42.80	33.70	39.20
Solely the Shanghai dialect	17.40	27.00	21.10%
College	**Female (%)**	**Male (%)**	**Grand Total (%)**
Mixed with Equal Amount	1.80	3.10	2.20
Mixed with Predominantly Putonghua	23.70	29.70	25.80
Mixed with Predominantly the Shanghai dialect	1.80	3.10	2.20
Solely Putonghua	69.30	56.30	64.60
Solely the Shanghai dialect	3.50	7.80	5.10

Table 2.4   Language Spoken at Home with Seniors by Gender

During School Years, Language Spoken at Home with Parents and Senior Family Members	Female (%)	Male (%)	Grand Total (%)
Mixed with equal amount	4.10	1.10	3.00
Mixed with Predominantly Putonghua	11.00	9.80	10.50
Mixed with Predominantly the Shanghai dialect	24.80	10.90	19.40
Solely Putonghua	4.10	4.30	4.20
Solely the Shanghai dialect	55.90	73.90	62.90

members than in school during their school years, and especially men: "Solely the Shanghai dialect" is 73.9 percent for men, and for women 55.9 percent. Combining "Solely the Shanghai dialect" and "Mixed with Predominantly the Shanghai dialect" includes 80.7 percent women and 84.8 percent men. Furthermore, this juxtaposition demonstrates an important discrepancy in language practices: women are more likely to abide by state language policy and the authority of schoolteachers.

Minglang Zhou explains the gendered language attitudes he observed in 2001 by suggesting that, in a still-patriarchal Chinese society, women are more conscious of social status. Language practices and attitudes are one of the few venues in which they can cultivate and accumulate prestige and social status, and thus they favor Putonghua over the Shanghai dialect.[48] In the ten years since Zhou's study, Chinese society has changed a great deal, while women's position has not progressed apace and has actually regressed. Similar gendered language preference among young females was also observed in Guangdong, where Putonghua promotion over years has led to a gradual increased use of Putonghua in recent years.[49] My survey data from 2013 indicate that despite all the efforts by women to obtain higher education and participate in the professional world, the real change has not come yet, thus they opt for the prestigous standard variety of the Chinese language.

The language pattern stays consistent at workplaces, as table 2.5 shows the languages used with supervisors and colleagues. Two trends are apparent; first, at workplaces Putonghua has a slight majority, 57.9 percent with supervisors and 52.5 percent with colleagues when we add together the "Mixed with Predominantly Putonghua" and "Solely Putonghua" categories. Second, there is a gender-based pattern, with more men using either solely Putonghua or solely the Shanghai dialect, while women demonstrate a more mixed pattern especially in the "Mixed with Predominantly Putonghua" category. With supervisors, 31.7 percent of native Shanghairen women reportedly mix Putonghua with the Shanghai dialect, while the percentage for native Shanghairen men is 18.2 percent. With colleagues, the female and the male percentages are 40.5 percent and 26.6 percent, respectively. In terms of using a single language instead of a mixed pattern, for both Putonghua and the Shanghai dialect, men reported higher percentages. With supervisors, 36.4 percent of men use solely Putonghua, and 20.8 percent solely the Shanghai dialect, while the corresponding female percentages are 28.3 percent and 13.3 percent, respectively. The difference is averaged about 8 percent. This gender-based difference is more salient in communication with colleagues. 24.1 percent of men while 13.2 percent of women solely use Putonghua, while 20.3 percent of men and 10.7 percent of women use solely the Shanghai dialect.

This gendered pattern has been developed against the background of the societal language transition. Literature abounds suggesting women are more

Table 2.5　Language Spoken at Workplace by Gender

With Supervisors	*Female (%)*	*Male (%)*	*Total (%)*
Mixed with Equal Amount	2.5	1.3	2.0
Mixed with Predominantly English	5.8	5.2	5.6
Mixed with Predominantly Putonghua	31.7	18.2	26.4
Mixed with Predominantly the Shanghai dialect	14.2	16.9	15.2
Overall Mixed	**54.2**	**41.6**	**49.2**
Solely English, or Other Foreign Language	4.2	1.3	3.0
Solely Putonghua	28.3	36.4	31.5
Solely the Shanghai Dialect	13.3	20.8	16.2
Overall Single Language	**45.8**	**58.4**	**50.8**
With colleagues	**Female (%)**	**Male (%)**	**Total (%)**
Mixed with Equal Amount	3.3	1.3	2.5
Mixed with Predominantly English	0.8	2.5	1.5
Mixed with Predominantly Putonghua	40.5	26.6	35.0
Mixed with Predominantly the Shanghai dialect	28.9	22.8	26.5
Overall Mixed	**73.6**	**53.2**	**65.5**
Solely English, or Other Foreign Language	2.5	2.5	2.5
Solely Putonghua	13.2	24.1	17.5
Solely the Shanghai Dialect	10.7	20.3	14.5
Overall Single Language	**26.4**	**46.8**	**34.5**

likely to be early adopters of the standard language to better their social positions, but here the pattern in Shanghai, with men being both more conservative by using solely the Shanghai dialect and being more progressive by using solely Putonghua more at work. This finding coincides what Qing Zhang argues about the language practices among Beijing yuppies. Among them, more women speak what Zhang terms cosmopolitan Mandarin, which is non-Beijing local variants of Mandarin mixed with Taiwan, Hong Kong, and Singaporean Mandarin and some English.[50] Because the difference between the Shanghai dialect and Putonghua is much greater than that between the Beijing variant of Mandarin and Putonghua, what the mixed pattern communicates in my study is more complicated than a cosmopolitan, transnational Chinese linguistic market as argued by Zhang.[51] If we add up all four types of mixed pattern: "Mixed with Equal Amount," "Mixed with Predominantly English," "Mixed with Predominantly Putonghua," and "Mixed with Predominantly the Shanghai dialect," the contrast between females and males is even starker. With supervisors, 54.2 percent of women use a mixed pattern, versus 41.6 percent among men. With colleagues, 73.6 percent of women use a mixed pattern, while 53.2 percent for men. Instead of adopting a Shanghainese equivalence of cosmopolitan Mandarin deprived of local Beijing elements, the mixed pattern used by native Shanghairen suggests a Shanghairen identity which is anchored on a cosmopolitan city, which I will elaborate in chapter 4.

The examples above have shown how language ideology dictates individual language choices, and in the process, Putonghua has encroached on the linguistic space once occupied by the Shanghai dialect. However, there is resistance to this trend, as shown by the pragmatic side of Shanghai dialect proficiency in informal settings and the Shanghai dialect preservation activism.

ALTERNATIVE LANGUAGE IDEOLOGY

The transfer of status and power between languages and their speakers in contemporary Shanghai is complicated by residual forces that still grant prestige to the Shanghai dialect. This alternative language ideology, which associates the Shanghai dialect with insider membership, can be immediately converted to social, symbolic, and economic capitals in random social encounters. From my observations, this alternative ideology still thrives in the city. One reason is the presence of the older generation of native Shanghairen, who do not speak Putonghua well, and the migrant-run small businesses catering to them. Working as barbers, street venders, seamstresses, or locksmiths, these migrants are outside the state's employment system, where Putonghua proficiency is highly valued. These workers' quick adoption of the Shanghai dialect leads directly to better customer service, more business, and hence economic capital. And they also deploy the symbolic power of speaking the Shanghai dialect for distinction, as my encounter with a migrant seamstress in 2013 shows.

The seamstress in her late thirties or early forties had a sewing machine set up under a shabby tent outside of an apartment building in a lower-middle-class neighborhood in the Hongkou district in northeastern Shanghai. I approached her, speaking Putonghua, about hemming jeans. My understanding then was that most service-sector workers were non-natives, and thus Putonghua speakers. She treated me rudely, which at first, I assumed was because at 5 yuan (less than one U.S. dollar), the work was barely worth the effort. However, while I was waiting for her to get it done, she let a woman speaking the Shanghai dialect cut in line. The seamstress engaged in friendly small talk in the Shanghai dialect with an evident accent with that woman and quickly finished her equally small sewing job. Other than a slight age difference, nothing would justify this differentiated treatment besides language. The other customer made no effort to switch from the Shanghai dialect to Putonghua when talking to the seamstress. It was almost comical how the seamstress's attitude toward me changed immediately when I switched to the Shanghai dialect. During that encounter, the seamstress demonstrated her Shanghai dialect proficiency to serve a customer and cultivate an insider rapport. At the same time, she used her Shanghai dialect proficiency to establish power and authority over me, whom she initially presumed to be a more recent migrant to Shanghai than her. In a way, she passed along the linguistic discrimination she might have experienced when she first came to Shanghai. This encounter shows that among migrant workers, such as this seamstress, the Shanghai dialect is an important component of their linguistic capital. It can be converted not only to economic capital through business opportunities but also social and symbolic capital to distinguish themselves from more recent working-class migrants. The latter have yet to start the linguistic assimilation, as a means for climbing the socioeconomic ladder.

Better-educated native Shanghairen actively cultivate Putonghua proficiency, while at the same time recent migrants pragmatically try to assimilate by learning the Shanghai dialect. This is the complex linguistic sphere of Shanghai, in which two language ideologies compete for dominance. This is the background of Shanghai dialect preservation activists' strategy to revive the dialect. Dorian summarizes the fate of languages with the principal that "languages are seldom admired to death but are frequently despised to death."[52] The activists try to dissociate the Shanghai dialect from working-class quotidian life and imbue it with higher cultural values, which might be a way to save it from such a fate.

The impact of the dominant language ideology is hard to shake off, especially when some native Shanghairen writers and artists believe in the lower status and lack of aesthetic value of the dialect and integrate such ideology into their work. Marianne Mithun, in her study of the decline of Native American languages, argues that when the strength of native cultures, encoded in the linguistic tradition, is lost or no longer understood, those languages become vulnerable to the same decline and domination by the larger society's language.[53] Jin Yucheng, a famous novelist whose bestseller, *Fan Hua* (*Flowers*), won various national awards, spoke bluntly about the Shanghai dialect's vulgarity:

> It has nothing to do with social class, but essentially [with] the language itself. It is not the issue of topics either, such as domestic conflict, or trivial things, the indecency of the dialect is embedded in each and every sentence. You can find lots of vulgarity and coarseness in ordinary Shanghairen's dialect-speaking.

A bilingual native Shanghairen, Jin was an editor for *Shanghai Literature* for decades before he wrote his award-winning novel. It incorporates the Shanghai dialect to depict urban life in the second half of the twentieth century. To him, the Shanghai dialect, the former *lingua franca* of the city, is essentially a vernacular for daily life, with curse words and vulgar sayings, and thus incompatible with high culture. Considering that the diglossia system is thousands of years old, it is only natural that the written language, which was the basis for Putonghua, is associated with high culture in the form of poetry, theatre, or court documents, while vernaculars are associated with the quotidian. However, linguistically, there is no innate quality of languages that makes them elegant or not. Jin's opinion echoes Dorian's analysis of the ideological contrast between official languages and dialects. An official language is usually regarded as "a rich, rationally organized and rationally organizing instrument; and dialects by contrast, are considered impoverished, crude and most likely inadequate."[54] By using the Shanghai dialect to vividly depict urban life among middle- and working-class native Shanghairen, Jin provides an authentic voice of Shanghai, while also deprives the dialect of higher cultural value.

In an authoritarian state, and especially in a globalizing city representing the state's economic achievement, public protests or dissemination of materials promoting the dialect through state-controlled mass media are highly unlikely. A 2012 study, examining the conflict between Cantonese and Putonghua in Guangzhou, makes plain the uneven power relations between state-backed Putonghua hegemony and those advocating for a place-specific cultural identity.[55] Taking a lesson from the failed protests in Guangzhou, which attempted to reach policymakers through social media and other limited channels, the Shanghai dialect preservation activists have avoided direct confrontation with the state. They have developed narratives to heighten the aesthetics of Shanghai dialect. Emphasizing the cultural value of the Shanghai dialect has become the primary weapon of the preservation movement to counter the state's language ideology. As Dorian argues about language retention, for a small group to fight against the dominant language, a great deal of social and psychological self-confidence in the worth of the language is needed.[56] In this case, classical literature and traditional theatre provide rich sources for the re-establishment and recognition of the cultural values of the dialect.

To alter the Shanghai dialect's association with lower educational levels and working-class urban life, preservation activists learned from the cultural aesthetic claims made by Cantonese preservation activists in Guangdong by pointing to the use of Wu languages in China's traditional high culture. Qian Chen, vice president of the Shanghai Huajixi Troupe, explained to me that ancient Chinese pronunciations are well preserved in the Shanghai dialect, but non-existent in Putonghua:

I have done my research about long vowel sound words (*zhisheng zi*) in poetry of the Tang Dynasty (AD 618–907), for example, Wang Zhihuan's poem *Deng Guanque Lou*(Ascending Guanque Tower) The "*bai ri*" in the first line, "*bai ri yi shan jin* (sun sets by the mountain ridge)," and "*ru*" in the second line, "*huang he ru hai liu* (Yellow River flows into the ocean)," are supposed to be prolonged. Try to read it in the dialect . . . the up and down rhythms are superior! The Shanghai dialect has long-sounding words, but Putonghua does not. Or our national treasure, the Peking opera, in the script of *Si Jinshi* (Four Scholars) there is a line "*bai shang le Xinyang zhou* (going up to the Xinyang county)." In it, "*xin*" has a *jianyin* (sharp sound). Where could you find *jianyin* in Putonghua? Nowhere! The differentiation between *jianyin* (sharp sounds) and its opposite, *tuanyin* (round sounds) in Peking operas is identical to those in the Shanghai dialect.

Qian recited the poetry and sang the opera line in both Putonghua and the Shanghai dialect for me to demonstrate the difference in rhythm and flow, presenting the Shanghai dialect versions as more aesthetically pleasing as well as more authentic. His performance communicated a sense of pride in the cultural value of the Shanghai dialect. Qian made a historical argument for Shanghai dialect's aesthetic value, rooted in what he called the "national treasure" of China. In his comparison, Putonghua, based on Beijing pronunciation, is rootless and artificial, though nevertheless promoted by the state as the default language of the Chinese nation and an inseparable part of the history of the Chinese people. In his telling, Putonghua's incompatibility with ancient poems and traditional theatre demonstrates that the state leans agenda political and not based on historical fact.

Zhu Zhenmiao, then a Ph.D. student in Chinese Language, making an argument similar to Qian's, recited to me a few lines from *Shi Jing* (*The Book of Odes*) in Cantonese over our 2013 interview. *The Book of Odes* is another classical text—a collection of 305 works dating from the eleventh to seventh century BC. To him, the dominant language ideology, which associates classical literature exclusively with Putonghua, is historically and linguistically incorrect. Classical literary works are not only recited in dialects but were also most likely composed in dialects of the ancient Wu or Cantonese language families. Therefore, dialects are historically and linguistically closer to the great works of Chinese literature than the newly invented official language. Historian Gina Tam points out that some phonetic features of Medieval Chinese (AD 25–907) are preserved in southern dialects, such as variations of Wu or Cantonese but are no longer present in the Beijing dialect of the twentieth century, which was the basis for Putonghua's pronunciation.[57]

Shanghai dialect preservation activists claim that dialects not only provide an authentic means to recite the classical literature of China but also possess their own aesthetic value. Grenoble and Whaley argue that a subtle but pervasive predictor of the continued use of a language is the prestige attached to it; for example, through the association with a rich literary tradition.[58] By building this association between the Shanghai dialect and classical Chinese literature, preservation activists are cultivating the aesthetic values of regional dialects. However, the venue to publicize such arguments barely exists, and there is little interest in classical literature among native Shanghairen generally.

CONCLUSION

The 2001 Language Law and the various language polices that followed it coincide with economic reforms that reached Shanghai in the 1990s. These two forces are largely to blame for in the recent endangerment of the Shanghai dialect. Before the 1990s, Shanghai was primarily monolingual. The dialect's primacy was due to both the lack of enforcement of earlier language policies and the planned economy allowing limited social and geographical mobility. Since then, through the state's efforts, the dominance of the official language has limited and even eliminated the Shanghai dialect in certain social spheres. The state promotes a dominant language ideology of Putonghua as clear, modern, and advanced, in contrast to vernaculars such as the Shanghai dialect, which are backward, inadequate, and incompatible with the country's progress. Through Bourdieu's notion of linguistic capital, we have seen how the school system actively indoctrinates students, with the goal of creating a monolingual environment. Over time, native Shanghairen came to believe that Putonghua is the language through which they and their children can prosper and realize the "China Dream." Besides the opinions and stories collected through in-depth interviews about language use in Shanghai, my survey data show women are more likely to adopt the dominant language ideology and speak Putonghua in various settings than men. That is at least in part because, in a patriarchal society, the use of Putonghua can help them achieve social status and upward mobility.

The market for converting linguistic capital into social and economic capitals that the state has created instills and reproduces the dominance of Putonghua. Meanwhile the Shanghai dialect is devalued on the formal market and faces a grim future. The decline of the dialect in public and in private is the background of my investigation of the Shanghai dialect preservation movement. This social movement mobilizes narratives of cultural heritage, particularly the Shanghai dialect's roots in the ancient Wu language family, to fight against the dominant language ideology. Grassroots activists struggle to keep the dialect alive on Shanghai's streets and in native Shanghairen homes. One used an ancient Chinese idiom to express their powerlessness, *tangbi dangche* (a mantis raises its foreleg, trying to stop an approaching wagon). Elderly Shanghairen who retain the dialect, and the businesses catering to them, appear to be the last holdouts. This might sustain the Shanghai dialect for another decade or two at most, if current trends of use continue.

The Shanghai dialect's uniqueness is rooted in its urban nature. Urban redevelopment and expansion over the last twenty years have displaced millions of native Shanghairen to the periphery, where new residential communities located in formerly rural areas. The dispersion and relocation have completely transformed the geographical base of Shanghai's linguistic sphere. What happens when the speakers of an endangered language move away from each other?

NOTES

1. Blommaert, Jan, and Jef Verschueren. 1992. "The Role of Language in European Nationalist Ideologies." *Pragmatics* 2 (3): 355–75.

2. Bourdieu, Pierre. 1991. *Language and Symbolic Power*. Cambridge, MA: Harvard University Press. P.114.

3. Bourdieu. *Language and Symbolic Power*.

4. Woolard, Kathryn A. 1985. "Language Variation and Cultural Hegemony: Toward an Integration of Sociolinguistic and Social Theory." *American Ethnologist* 12 (4): 738–48.

5. Grenoble, Lenore A., and Lindsay J. Whaley. 1998. "Preface." In *Endangered Languages: Language Loss and Community Response*, edited by Lenore A. Grenoble and Lindsay J. Whaley, vii–xvi. Cambridge: Cambridge University Press. P.xv.

6. In the context of this study, I look at dialects of Han Chinese. Minority languages used by ethnic minorities, such as Uighurs or Tibetans, are beyond the scope of this study.

7. Ramsey, S. Robert. 1989. *The Languages of China*. Princeton, NJ: Princeton University Press. P.4.

8. Haugen, Einar. 1972. *The Ecology of Language*. Stanford, CA: Stanford University Press. P.251.

9. Bourdieu. *Language and Symbolic Power,* P.45.

10. Chen, Ping. 1999. *Modern Chinese: History and Sociolinguistics*. Cambridge & New York: Cambridge University Press. P.121.

11. Ramsey. *The Languages of China*, P.14–5.

12. Woolard, Kathryn A. 1998. "Introduction: Language Ideology as a Field of Inquiry." In *Language Ideologies: Practice and Theory*, edited by Bambi B. Schieffelin, Kathryn A. Woolard, and Paul V. Kroskrity, 3–47. Oxford Studies in Anthropological Linguistics. Oxford & New York: Oxford University Press. P.16.

13. Bourdieu. *Language and Symbolic Power*, P.47.

14. Ramsey. *The Languages of China*, P.9.

15. 1955 cited in Chen. *Modern Chinese: History,* P.58.

16. Constitution of the People's Republic of China. Adopted on December 4, 1982. http://english.people.com.cn/constitution/constitution.html; in Chinese: http://www.gov.cn/gongbao/content/2004/content_62714.htm.

17. Law of the People's Republic of China on the Standard Spoken and Written Chinese Language. (Adopted at the Eighteenth Meeting of Standing Committee of the Ninth National People's Congress on October 31, 2000, and promulgated by Order No. 37 of the President of the People's Republic of China on October 31, 2000). http://www.lawinfochina.com/display.aspx?lib=law&id=6233&CGid=. Read the full text of the law in Appendix I.

18. Bourdieu. *Language and Symbolic Power,* P.46.

19. See a full list of the Putonghua Promotion Week slogans since 1998 in the Appendix II.

20. In his report delivered on October 18, 2017, at the nineteenth National Congress of the Communist Party of China, Xi stated the greatest dream for the Chinese nation in contemporary history is to achieve the great renaissance of the Chinese nation. The ramifications include a strong and rich country, revitalization of the nation, and happiness of the people.

21. The nationalist connotation of the dream rhetoric makes the translation into China Dream, instead of Chinese Dream more proper, because the latter might be misunderstood as an ethnicity instead of what is clearly bond by and intended to be associated with state sovereignty.

22. Irvine, Judith T., and Susan Gal. 2010. "Language Ideology and Linguistic Differentiation." In *Regimes of Language: Ideologies, Polities, and Identities,* edited by Paul V. Kroskrity, 35–84. Santa Fe: School of American Research Press. P.65.

23. See, for example, Fincher, Leta Hong. *Leftover Women: The Resurgence of Gender Inequality in China.* London & New York: Zed Books.

   Li, Yinhe. 1997. *Rising Power of the Women [zhongguo vvxing de jueqi].* Beijing: Chinese Social Science Press.

   Li, Yinhe. 1998. *Sexuality and Love of Chinese Women [zhongguo nvxing de ganqing yu xing].* Beijing: China Today Press.

24. 2013 Report of Shanghai Residents' Language Proficiency Survey. (*2013 nian Shanghai shimin yuyan yingyong nengli diaocha baogao*) Shanghai Statistical Bureau. February 7, 2014. http://tjj.sh.gov.cn/tjfx/20140207/0014-266714.html

25. Dorian, Nancy. 1998. "Western Language Ideologies and Small-Language Prospects." In *Endangered Languages: Language Loss and Community Response,* edited by Lenore A. Grenoble and Lindsay J. Whaley, 3–21. Cambridge, MA: Cambridge University Press. P.3–4.

26. Bourdieu. *Language and Symbolic Power,* P.47.

27. To give a snapshot, according to the Shanghai Civil Affairs Bureau, where marriage licenses are issued, of the 147,820 couples married in 2013, 55,373 are of unions were between a native Shanghainese and an internal migrant, more than 37 percent.

28. Ramsey. *The Languages of China,* P.30.

29. Chen. *Modern Chinese: History,* P.30.

30. Berg, Marinus van den. 2016. "Modernization and the Restructuring of the Shanghai Speech Community." *Journal of Asian Pacific Communication* 26 (1): 112–42. P.131.

31. Swaan, Abram De. 2001. *Words of the World: The Global Language System.* Cambridge: Polity Press.P.1–16.

32. Woolard. "Language Variation and Cultural Hegemony," 738–48. P.744.

33. Grenoble, Lenore A., and Lindsay J. Whaley. 1998. "Toward a Typology of Language Endangerment." In *Endangered Languages: Language Loss and Community Response*, 22–54. Cambridge, MA: Cambridge University Press. P.37.

34. Bourdieu. *Language and Symbolic Power,* P.62.

35. Bourdieu. *Language and Symbolic Power*, P.32.

36. Jaffe, Alexandra. 1999. *Ideologies in Action: Language Politics on Corsica. Ideologies in Action.* Berlin & Boston: De Gruyter Mouton. P.28.

37. Woolard, Kathryn A. n.d. "Codeswitching and Comedy in Catalonia." *IPrA Papers in Pragmatics* 1 (1): 106–22. P.117.

38. Lakoff, Robin. 1990. *Talking Power.* New York: Basic Books.

39. Trudgill, Peter. 1972. "Sex, Covert Prestige and Linguistic Change in the Urban British English of Norwich." *Language in Society* 1 (2): 179–95. P.182–3.

40. Gal, Susan. 1978. "Peasant Men Can't Get Wives: Language Change and Sex Roles in a Bilingual Community." *Language in Society* 7: 1–16.

41. Eckert, Penelope. 1989. "The Whole Woman: Sex and Gender Differences in Variation." *Language Variation & Change* 1 (3): 245–67.P.250.

42. Eckert. "The Whole Woman," 245–67. P.256

43. See the full ranking report and index at the Global Gender Gap Index 2020 Rankings. http://reports.weforum.org/global-gender-gap-report-2020/the-global-gender-gap-index-2020-rankings/.

44. See the full report http://www3.weforum.org/docs/WEF_GenderGap_Report_2006.pdf.

45. Zhou, Minglang. 2001. "The Spread of Putonghua and Language Attitude Changes in Shanghai and Guangzhou, China." *Journal of Asian Pacific Communication* 11 (2): 231–53.

46. Lakoff, Robin. 1973. "Language and Woman's Place." *Language in Society* 2 (1): 45–80.

47. Grenoble, and Whaley. 1998. "Toward a Typology of Language Endangerment," 22–54. P.37.

48. Zhou. "The Spread of Putonghua and Language Attitude," 231–53. P.245.

49. Wang, Limei, and Hans J. Ladegaard. 2008. "Language Attitudes and Gender in China: Perceptions and Reported Use of Putonghua and Cantonese in the Southern Province of Guangdong." *Language Awareness* 17 (1): 57–77.

50. Zhang, Qing. 2007. "Cosmopolitanism and Linguistic Capital in China: Language, Gender and the Transition to a Globalized Market Economy in Beijing." In *Words, Worlds, and Material Girls: Language, Gender, Globalization*, edited by Bonnie McElhinny, 403–22. Berlin: Mouton de Gruyter. P.410.

51. Zhang. "Cosmopolitanism and Linguistic Capital in China," 403–22. P.408.

52. Dorian. "Western Language Ideologies and Small-Language Prospects," 3–21. P.3.

53. Mithun, Marianne. 1998. "The Significance of Diversity in Language Endangerment and Preservation." In *Endangered Languages: Loss and Community Response*, edited by Lenore A. Grenoble and Lindsay Whaley, 163–91. Cambridge: Cambridge University Press. P.182.

54. Dorian. "Western Language Ideologies and Small-Language Prospects," P.8.

55. Qian, Junxi, Liyun Qian, and Hong Zhu. 2012. "Representing the Imagined City: Place and the Politics of Difference during Guangzhou's 2010 Language Conflict." *Geoforum* 43 (5): 905–15. P.908.

56. Dorian. "Western Language Ideologies and Small-Language Prospects," P.20.

57. Tam, Gina Anne. 2020. *Dialect and Nationalism in China, 1860–1960*. Cambridge: Cambridge University Press.

58. Grenoble, and Whaley. "Preface," vii–xvi. P.ix.

Chapter 3

Geographical Displacement
and Language Loss

Two main factors have contributed to the endangerment of the Shanghai dialect: the language ideology of the Chinese state that discriminates against regional dialects and the tangible rewards of upward mobility associated with speaking Putonghua. However, these factors have not entirely dismantled the dialect's speech community. The potential language loss has been accelerated by geographical displacement at the center of Shanghai. Large-scale urban redevelopments, which began in the 1990s, have displaced millions from overcrowded inner-city neighborhoods. Traditional *shikumen* alleyway housing that once comprised 85 percent of urban Shanghai's residential neighborhoods has been replaced by glass-façade office towers, high-rise condominium buildings, and elevated expressways. With the disappearance of vernacular landscape, close-knit communities and vibrant linguistic environments once inhabited *shikumen* neighborhoods have also disappeared.

Since the early 1990s, the state-controlled housing allocation system that had formerly redistributed heavily subsidized rental housing according to criteria, such as household registration status, career seniority, or Chinese Communist Party affiliation, was replaced by a market economy for real estate. The displacement and relocation shifted the sociospatial stratification of the city, by sorting residents solely according to their socioeconomic status. As a result, linguistically homogeneous but socioeconomically diverse neighborhoods have turned into linguistically mixed but socioeconomically homogeneous ones.

Two speech communities used to be distinguishable in Shanghai: non-natives who communicate in Putonghua and their own regional dialects and natives who predominantly communicate in the Shanghai dialect. The geographical displacement and relocation of Shanghai dialect speakers in the last three decades have disrupted the "regular and frequent interactions" which are essential for the maintenance and survival of a speech community.[1] These involuntary relocations have further altered the linguistic landscape, though the impact might be obscured by the fact that native Shanghairen are already adopting the dominant language ideology and living under the state's surveillance measures.

Furthermore, the sweeping physical changes wiped out the unique character of Shanghai as embodied in the urban built environment. Drawing on Bourdieu, the city's unique character is a type of symbolic capital, recognized as ambiance and authenticity rooted in the city's semi-colonial history. Sharon Zukin argues that a city's distinctive character nurtures a constant dialogue and negotiation between old and new, and in the process, produces and reproduces its authenticity.[2] The state has built a global city, transforming Shanghai's distinct character in the process. Thus, any of the dialogue Zukin suggests has been replaced in the large-scale demolition and construction. The removal of distinctive residential neighborhoods in the urban center made way for a distanced and cold global modernity, raising Shanghai's status in comparison with global cities of the West but sacrificing its former symbolic capital.

The distinctive character (or aggregated symbolic capital) of Shanghai draws heavily from the historical image of an East-meets-West metropolis. As documented in newspaper articles, novels, photos, and movies, people from all over the world and every walk of life consumed, mingled, and strived for a better life in early twentieth-century Shanghai. Dialogue and negotiation with outside influences were vivacious then, as evidenced in architectural features, fashion, cuisine, ideological trends, and even the development of the Shanghai dialect. It was during that period that Shanghai's unique character took shape.[3] Before the founding of the People's Republic in 1949, Shanghai was viewed at home and abroad as a beacon of modernity and cosmopolitan verve.[4] Under Mao, dialogues and interactions with the outside world were shut down, so the city's rich and vibrant character was frozen in time, preserved and rearticulated as tradition in the collective memories of its inhabitants.

Starting in the early 1990s, policymakers aimed to revitalize Shanghai as a global city. The first step was to "adopt a 'global-city-look' by constructing state-of-art infrastructure and flagship architectural projects" such as bridges, airports, and skyscrapers.[5] Many native Shanghairen complain about the changes wrought by thirty years of massive urban redevelopments in industrial, commercial, and residential spaces. In their eyes, the Oriental TV Tower, the Shanghai World Financial Center, and the China Pavilion at Shanghai Expo 2010 are symbolic of a "world-class city," which has little to do with their sense of home and belonging. In Zukin's words, they are images for the nation and the world to consume.[6] The more those urban spectacles are staged for the world, the less they are relevant to Shanghairen's sense of belonging: "As China's image of growth, Shanghai is pure window display."[7] The symbolic and emotional cost of the new built environment was steep: besides what urban scholars call domicide among the displaced,[8] the cultural and symbolic capitals that the city once possessed are all but gone and replaced. The disappearance of *shikumen* housing neighborhoods also removed the material basis for communities rooted in the Shanghai dialect. Spatially and linguistically, native Shanghairen feel alienated and lost in re-globalizing Shanghai.

INVOLUNTARY MOBILITY

Large-scale redevelopments in Shanghai hollowed out the urban center and led to the fraying of the social fabric. These projects ranged from rebuilding or renewing dilapidated and overcrowded residential areas to upgrading urban infrastructure, such as elevated expressways, bridges, and subways. In this process of dramatic urban landscape change, more than 1.1 million households were displaced from the urban core between 1995 and 2017.[9] Accompanying this massive displacement, urban core districts were merged and previously rural areas outside of Shanghai proper were rezoned to house the displaced.

In this remaking process, three urban districts disappeared from the map, nine rural counties were transformed into urban districts, and the entire tract of rural land east of Huangpu River emerged as the Pudong New District (see figure 3.1). In figure 3.1, the year underneath the district name indicates the date of its urban designation. Besides urban expansion, urban districts that had historically belonged to different domestic or colonial powers in the early twentieth century, and were perceived to possess diverse cultural, economic, and symbolic capitals, were merged (see figure 3.2). For example, Nanshi, which was historically under imperial Chinese jurisdiction, was merged with the previously British and American co-ruled International Settlement and later upper corner Huangpu district in 1991. In 2011, the jewel of the former French Concession, the upper corner Luwan district, was merged north to form the new Huangpu district. Though both are former concessions, their pre-1949 boundaries were tangible in daily life in many ways, for example, different standard voltages for power outlets. More recently, in 2015, another upper corner district, Jing'an district of the former International Settlement, merged north with the lower corner Zhabei district, which had been Chinese-ruled before 1949 and was predominantly working-class and inhabited by the urban poor. The administrative and judicial boundaries between upper and lower corner areas were penetrated and broken down in the process, and the

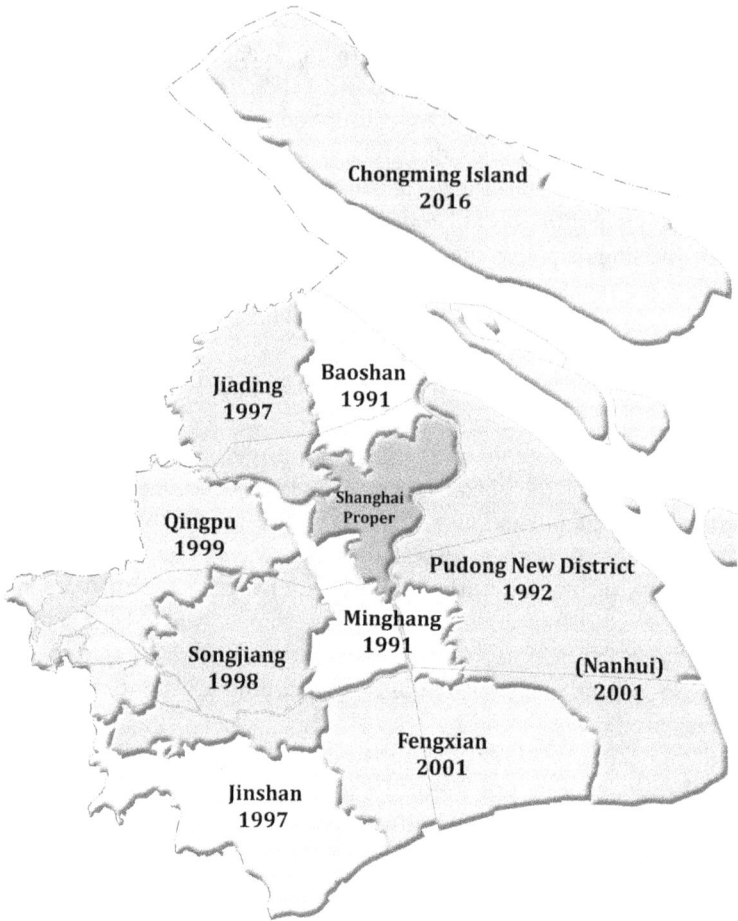

Figure 3.1   Municipal Map of Shanghai. Modified by Author Based on the 2017 July Shanghai Municipal Map. *Source*: Created by the Shanghai Institute of Surveying and Mapping.

cultural and symbolic capitals associated with each district became muddled. The previous sociospatial hierarchy of districts, inherited from the semi-colonial era, required reassessment, and native Shanghairen had to mentally remap their own neighborhoods with different district names and new upper/lower corner alignments.

The demographic justification for the consolidation was the three urban core districts' sharp population decline, which in turn was caused by that highly sought-after land being redeveloped for commercial use in the 1990s. Comparing the 2010 and 1990 censuses, the urban core districts that lost the most residents in the demolition and resettlement process were:

Figure 3.2   District Map of Shanghai Proper. Modified by Author Based on the 2017 July Shanghai Downtown District Map. *Source*: Created by the Shanghai Institute of Surveying and Mapping.

Huangpu, even after swallowing Nanshi district, had the sharpest decrease at 72.4 percent. It is followed by Jing'an district at 49.3 percent and Luwan district at 47.7 percent. Compensation, in the form of either cash or ready housing from developers, relocated inhabitants to the periphery, to either former lower corner districts or even previously rural areas that had been rezoned. One of these, the Minghang district, saw an astonishing fifteen-fold population boom in two decades. The other new urban districts saw sharp population increases during the same twenty-year span. Impressive numbers include Songjiang's increase of 209 percent and Baoshan's 189 percent. The Pudong New District, which did not exist in 1990 but had 1.65 million residents in 2000, surged to 5.5 million in 2010, combined with the previously rural Nanhui district (see table 3.1).

It makes intuitive sense to merge urban core districts that had significantly smaller post-demolition populations, in terms of administrative management. But for the hundreds of thousands displaced, they not only lost residences in a familiar neighborhood with social interactions embedded in the physical space but also the nominal administrative district category within which they can cognitively position themselves in the city. All these on top of losing the symbolic capital associated with living in historically important districts. Doreen Massey argues that the continuity of places is in names. Citing Walter Benjamin, Massey stresses that street names preserve unembodied memories

Table 3.1   Population Change in Shanghai 1990–2018

Shanghai (Urban) Districts	*1990* Census Unit: 10k	*2000* Census, Unit: 10k	*2010* Census Unit: 10k	*Population Increase in Percentage (1990–2010) (%)*	*2018* Statistical Yearbook Unit: 10K	*Population Increase in Percentage (1990–2018) (%)*
Municipal Shanghai	1334.19	1640.77	2301.92	72.53	2423.8	81.67
Huangpu	73.32	66.18	42.97	−72.44	65.38	
Nanshi	82.6	43.5				−67.87
Luwan	47.58	35.59	24.87	−47.73		
Jing'an	48.66	35.8	24.67	−49.30	106.28	−11.40
Zhabei	71.29	70.83	83.04	16.48		
Xuhui	77.66	86.77	108.52	39.74	108.44	39.63
Changning	58.54	60.49	69.06	17.97	69.4	18.55
Putuo	79.62	84.27	128.88	61.87	128.19	61.00
Hongkou	87.97	80.36	85.23	−3.11	79.7	−9.40
Yangpu	112.44	107.95	131.3	16.77	131.27	16.75
Minghang	15.9	65.4	243.12	1429.06	254.35	1499.69
Baoshan	65.9	80.95	190.56	189.17	204.23	209.90
Jiading	53.7	48.64	147.2	174.12	158.89	195.88
Jinshan	55.4	53.01	73.25	32.22	80.5	45.30
Songjiang	51.2	49.55	158.34	209.26	176.22	244.18
Qingpu	46.2	45.89	108.19	134.18	121.9	163.85
Fengxian	52.7	50.42	108.41	105.71	115.2	118.60
Pudong New District	N/A	165.14	504.73	615.79	550.02	679.07
Nanhui	70.6	69.03				
Chongming Island	73.6	65.36	70.34	−4.43	68.81	−6.51%

of people, making the past present against an increasingly rapid succession of changes, thus making these places relatable.[10] In the merging and re-naming of Shanghai urban districts, even that linkage was broken.

In urban redevelopment, the upper/lower corner distinction is reproduced in a spiral pattern. That is, economic capital in the form of property value and symbolic capital in the form of prestige and privilege feed into each other's rise. Land in upper corner Puxi, such as Jing'an, Luwan, and Huangpu districts (with their symbolic capital inherited from the semi-colonial era), garners higher bids from real estate developers, with the government charging higher leasing fees. As a result, social services, including hospitals, public schools, and sanitation, are of higher quality than those of previously lower corner districts, such as Hongkou and Yangpu. As noted by Orum et al. in the Xin Hua neighborhood of the upper corner, the community center provides local residents "a well-stocked library, as well as a building with individual rooms set aside for regular activities such as language lessons, singing and even the use of high-end computers."[11] Those neighborhood-based amenities reactivate and reinforce the privilege of living in the urban core.

Adding insult to injury, much of the land in Puxi once occupied by overcrowded residential housing was redeveloped into office towers and shopping centers, further limiting the housing stock in the upper corner. The prices for apartments in those neighborhoods are pushed ever higher. As a result, the sociospatial stratification represented by an individual's housing location is made starker. Upon displacement, former residents in the urban core were usually offered two options, monetary compensation or move-in ready apartment units, as stipulated by the 1991 Shanghai Urban Housing Demolition Management Plan. However, neither of these options spared them the loss of the proximity to the urban core. Their new housing conditions in large part depended on their own socioeconomic status. The monetary compensation provided by developers fell short of the market price for apartments in the same neighborhood. Moreover, those new apartments offered by developers were sure to be on the periphery of the city, depriving the former residents of their right to the central city. The sociospatial stratification and involuntary downward mobility brought about and intensified by urban redevelopments have left those affected urban core residents dispossessed and bitter.

Guorong and his parents were displaced in 1997 from two rooms in a Western villa in Jing'an district shared by more than ten households. They lived along Nanjing West Road, at the center of the inner ring within two miles of the People's Square, which has high land values and well-developed social services. Their new apartment, meanwhile, is outside of the middle ring in the Meilong area, in the previously rural Minhang district. After more than fifteen years, he was still full of anger and frustration when retelling the account of his relocation:

On that piece of land, the Four Seasons condominium building was built. In 2004 or 2005 when it entered the housing market, the per square meter price was more than RMB 60,000 [approx. US $900/ft^2], now [2013] that has probably more than doubled. At the time of our displacement, the government didn't mention a word of moving back, and the compensation? They gave us an apartment in Meilong and RMB 7,500 in cash. The market price for the apartment we live now, the one the government gave us, is about RMB 2.7 million, but the worth of our old room in our old neighborhood? More than RMB 6 million!

By comparing the market value of the new apartment with the current value of an apartment in his old neighborhood, Guorong expressed a strong sense of injustice. This loss, one that he and his family did not foresee at the time of their relocation, became the root of his bitter feeling of deprivation. In his view, the government and the developer tricked them in the displacement and relocation process. These complaints notwithstanding, the apartment shared by Guorong and his parents is more spacious than their previous two rooms. But beyond the monetary disparity he described between the two apartments, there is a disparity in relation to the symbolic capital of urban-core living. This loss or gain is not calculated in an apartment's square meters of concrete and steel, but in the volume of intangible symbolic capital embedded in the built, social, and cultural environment of each housing location. Though their former dwelling was very crowded, Guorong's family once enjoyed the geographic advantage and pride of association with the city's upper corner.

This initial redevelopment and concomitant relocation of former upper corner residents in the late 1990s had a ripple effect: housing prices close to the edge of the inner ring spiked, as displaced persons opting for monetary compensation from developers tried to buy properties. In turn, when a new round of redevelopment projects took place in the 2000s, the displaced were forced to move to the middle ring or to Pudong where housing units were still affordable. The combined effects of shrinking urban core housing stock and ever-rising housing prices meant that those displaced in the 2010s had to relocate to the outer ring.

All my native Shanghairen interviewees recounted stories about their own or close family members' displacement over the last ten to twenty years, always from the urban core to middle or outer ring areas. Yu, a marketing manager working for a German Fortune 500 company grew up in Huangpu district, a neighborhood within walking distance of the Bund. But now she lives with her husband and two young sons in an apartment beyond the northern edge of the inner ring in Zhabei district. Similarly, Hai, a social sciences professor at a top Shanghai university in his sixties, grew up in *shikumen* housing in upper corner Luwan district in the former French Concession, but now lives in the Jiangwan neighborhood located outside of the middle ring.

On the land where the professor's family house once stood, an artificial lake, part of the upscale shopping and residential Xintiandi neighborhood, can now be found.

A more recent example comes from Du, whose family's *shikumen* house was located in Peide Alley, one of the few remaining *shikumen* housing neighborhoods in Jing'an district. Du's family lived there along with his aunt's and his uncle's families, and also his grandmother. Their relocation contract was signed in the first weeks of 2015. The family successfully negotiated with the developer and the government for four relocation apartments, located in Zhoupu Township in the center of the Greater Pudong Area, beyond the outer ring, though close to subway lines. In exchange for the ownership of four new, more spacious apartments, they said farewell to the urban core.

These experiences of involuntary relocation reinforce a collective social attachment to Shanghai's urban center, which is the only space many native Shanghairen recognize as truly Shanghai. Setha Low and Irwin Altman point out that this attachment to place includes emotional embeddedness, feelings of esteem and belonging, and is especially important to the cultural self-identification and integrity of individuals and social groups; furthermore, this bonding is most salient during times of relocation and societal upheaval.[12] The dispossession of urban central living and its associated symbolic capital is most acutely felt by the displaced, to the degree of threating their self-identification as Shanghairen.

The involuntary sociospatial mobility has created a new linguistic landscape in Shanghai. It is summed up in a popular saying that "English is spoken in the inner ring, Putonghua in the middle ring, and the Shanghai dialect in the outer ring." However, my data about relocation destinations suggest a more complex situation is present. When I spoke with dialect preservation activist Qi in the winter of 2013, he suggested that this saying was no longer accurate and was in fact outdated:

> This saying has been around for almost ten years. The reality now is actually more nuanced, if not reversed. The closer to the urban center, the higher the cost of living. It is true that in [the former] Jing'an or [the former] Luwan district, there are many foreigners, but it is not even close to the degree that the common language in the inner ring is English, even though you can hear more English spoken there than ten years ago.

Despite the increasing presence of affluent foreign expatriates, the commercial and residential spaces within the inner ring remain predominantly Chinese. What has changed is that those central spaces that were once populated by ordinary working-class native Shanghairen are now mainly occupied by the wealthy, who came to Shanghai from different regions of China. Qi further elaborated:

It is again not necessarily true that the suburbs or outer ring and beyond are predominantly populated by displaced native Shanghairen. In Qingpu or Songjiang counties [districts],[13] the cost of living is lower than in the inner city, so it would be easier for them [working-class non-natives] to settle down. What I find accurate is that most [native] Shanghairen now live between middle ring and outer ring.

Though displaced from the most desirable upper corner neighborhoods and relocated to the rim of the inner or middle ring, native Shanghairen still retain relative privilege compared to millions of migrant workers. The majority of non-natives possess neither the access to the heavily subsidized public housing granted through urban *hukou* and state-owned work units before the housing reform nor the financial capacity to purchase housing on the market.[14] The visible presence of affluent foreign expats conceals the reality of better-off non-natives' residency in the urban center and the hardship of the truly disadvantaged migrant workers. It also veils the dispossession and relative deprivation of native Shanghairen. Nevertheless, what relocation stories and the easily debunked popular saying do capture is the close association between urban residency, language, and social class.

CLASS RESTRUCTURING

The massive displacement and relocation of native Shanghairen away from the most desirable upper corner neighborhoods constitute a story of discriminatory urban political economy. But unlike market-initiated and profit-driven gentrification cases in Western contexts, the case of Shanghai illustrates the most recent power shifts on the national scale and suggests the rising of new elites with a political tint.

Since the 1990s, the urban landscape in Shanghai saw the birth of new elites, at the expense of old elites whom the Communist Party had fostered and put into place in the Maoist era. As we saw in chapter 1, the creation of the upper and lower corner distinction in early twentieth-century Shanghai was a manifestation of social hierarchy in the semi-colonial past—when better quality housing was built for, and occupied by, colonizers or affluent Chinese merchants and political elites in the Republic era (1911–1949). From Guorong's family's housing situation over the course of three generations, it is apparent that residency in Shanghai is a story of power beyond the local context. Furthermore, it illustrates shifts in the Communist Party's favoritism. The multiple rounds of relocation and shifts in sociospatial mobility Guorong's family experienced is just one example of hundreds of thousands of families' experiences, and it will serve as the paradigmatic example of shifting social stratification.

Guorong's previous neighbors in his family's former residence, a four-floor single-family house in Zhang Garden,[15] illustrate the important role housing played in the recognition of elite status in Shanghai before the 1990s (see figure 3.3 for photo of a house similar to Guorong's family house in Zhang Garden). The elites of the Republic era were replaced by Communist-era party favorites, a group that included Guorong's grandparents. But later, in the 1990s, those enjoyed privilege in the Maoist era were displaced to make way for the upgrade of urban infrastructure. Guorong described the families sharing that house this way:

My paternal grandfather came to Shanghai with the Liberation Army in 1949 and was assigned housing in the house that once belonged to a senior official of Kuomintang of the Republic [of China] (1911–1949). The four-story house was shared by sixteen households, and the three bathrooms and one big kitchen on the first floor were shared by all.

Guorong gave a vivid description of the privileged in the Maoist era in the house he grew up in. When the old elites of the Kuomintang in the Republic were driven out to Taiwan in 1949, the single-family occupancy house was divided and awarded to the People's Liberation Army officers, Communist Party members employed in the new municipal government, renowned intellectuals and artists useful for the party's propaganda, technocrats, revolutionary workers, and even some old elites who renounced their affiliation with the capitalist West or Kuomintang. Guorong continued:

On the first floor were retired municipal government officials, and a professor from Fudan University. There were six households on the second floor, and from room 201 to 206 were the families of a senior electrician, a single woman recently returned from the U.S., a cameraman working at Shanghai TV Station; both heads of household in room 204 and room 205 worked in the municipal government. The people living in room 206 didn't talk much to neighbors. On the third floor there were four big rooms, occupied by four families. Room 301 was by a guy with connections to the district government. A retiree from the municipal government in room 302 raised many pigeons. I remember visiting him often to see the birds when I was little. The famous movie director Shen Xilin and his wife lived in room 303. The woman who lived in room 304 is said to have connection with Kuomintang, and married a "red" worker to get out of political trouble. Our family occupied the entire fourth floor, two huge rooms. My uncle and aunt lived in the smaller one, and my parents and I lived in the bigger one with grandparents.

A low standard of living was nearly universal in the "redistributive economy" of the Maoist era. Earnings and resources were collected by the state and redistributed to individuals according to their positions in the politically defined and ranked bureaucratic system.[16] Though living in an extremely crowded dwelling, Guorong's family and his neighbors enjoyed the geographic advantage and the sense of being in the center of everything in metropolitan Shanghai. In a previously single-family house, tenants would have shared a bathroom with their neighbors, regardless of whether one worked as a party official in the municipal government, or a famous movie director worked for a state-owned movie production work unit, or a proletarian "red" worker.

Figure 3.3   Photo of Zhang Garden in 2017. *Source*: Photo by the author.

The structural and behavioral dimensions of this pre-reform status hierarchy, as identified by Yanjie Bian, are exemplified by different households sharing that one supposedly single family house.[17] First of all, housing confiscated by the Party shortly after the founding of the People's Republic was granted to people already living in the city, but especially to those who "liberated" the city, such as Guorong's paternal grandfather. Second, those employed by the state directly (such as municipal government officials) or indirectly through state-owned work units (such as the movie director or the senior electrician) were granted top-tier housing. Since income was universally low in the pre-reform era, the party installed a social hierarchy and presented their favorites with state-owned, heavily subsidized rental housing, access to which was contingent on political position, work unit authority, seniority, education, and skills.[18] Since all the residents were tenants of state-owned property, and the rents they paid were "so low and so minimally differentiated by income that they play only a minor role in sorting people across neighborhoods by income," as Whyte and Parish observe.[19]

Besides urban *hukou* status and contingent categories associated with education and profession, an individual's political characterization as "revolutionary" or "anti-revolutionary" was also important. The true revolutionary "red" (proletarian) and anti-revolutionary "black" (bourgeoisie) classes were defined by a mixture of family class origin, individual political attitude, and performances in numerous party-led campaigns.[20] In terms of family class origin, the urban poor and property-less peasants belonged to the "red" class, while the landed gentry, merchants or industrialists to the "black" class. The disadvantage of being categorized as a member of the "black" class could be mitigated through an individual's demonstrated loyalty to the Communist Party's leadership and ideology. For example, the woman living in Room 304 used her marriage arrangement with a revolutionary "red" worker to demonstrate her political attitude, and thus was allowed to remain in her highly desirable housing.

Despite having to share a previously single-family house, the living standards for Guorong and all of his neighbors were still higher than the hundreds of thousands who lived in old *shikumen* housing, which did not have indoor plumbing. Nevertheless, the powerful sense of loss felt by the displaced stems not only from the loss of a home or apartment but from their loss of symbolic capital and privilege, represented by the pride of proximity to the urban center their occupation of state-allocated housing units provides.

Guorong described how he and his neighbors needed to boil water in the large shared kitchen on the first floor and haul it up to their own floor if they wished to take a bath. When he noticed me jotting down that fact, he quickly added, "[r]eally, it was not that bad. It was already much better than the situation in *shikumen* housing." A similar qualification was added to his room, which was 33 square meters he shared with both of his parents from age 3 to 16, and before that, his paternal grandparents as well. That is to say, a space approximately 350 square feet once served as living room, dining room, and bedroom for two couples and the younger couple's child. Guorong's comment that it was "not that crowded" was in comparison to living arrangements endured by the majority of those living in *shikumen* housing. According to data collected by the municipal government, in early 1990s, there were more than 120,000 households in Shanghai with per capita living space under four square meters (approximately 43 ft^2), and more than 30,000 households with less than 2.5 square meters (approximately 27 ft^2).[21] But this relative privilege disappeared when Guorong's family was relocated to Minhang district outside of the inner ring. The harsh reality of life after relocation is the fact that one can hardly afford to move back. As an IT manager with an RMB 150,000 annual income living with his pensioner parents, Guorong does not dare to dream of buying an apartment in his old neighborhood priced in the millions.

On visits to their old neighborhoods, nothing is recognizable apart from maybe the street names for displaced native Shanghairen. This disconnection with the urban built environment or, more precisely, this disorientation in the new urban landscape has socioeconomic roots. Where their old neighborhood once stood are now office towers hosting Fortune 500 company headquarters or upscale commercial complexes beyond their reach. These new offices are not where many of them could hope to find work, and the luxury boutiques are not where many could afford to shop. The space where native Shanghairen used to live, work, and shop—*shikumen* neighborhoods full of alleyway gossip in the Shanghai dialect has transformed into a bland space deprived of vernaculars in both the architectural and linguistic senses.

Truth be told, among those sterile glass-façade office towers and shopping centers, a handful of *shikumen* houses or garden villas have been preserved. But the preservation of historic buildings is mostly driven by economic and political interests rather than by concerns for protecting cultural heritage. Never for the return of the displaced, what has been preserved is a superficial shell for spectacle.[22] *Shikumen* housing preserved at Xintiandi is a Shanghai-flavored display of global consumer culture, with fashion, cuisine, and clubbing taking the place of neighbors mingling in alleyways or buying produce from street vendors and household items from mom-and-pop stores. The redevelopment erased the everyday lived experiences in the original neighborhoods, including the crowding, noise, and dinginess, leaving only their façade intact as spectacle. Xintiandi was not preserved out of nostalgia for the past, but only to create a new site for a modern consumerist lifestyle.[23] Thus, it has nothing to do with the *shikumen*-living lifestyle. The renewed façades and the surrounding pedestrian zone form an Old Shanghai theme park, and inside is a museum gift shop for those curious about the cosmopolitan Shanghai of the 1930s.

For a working-class and middle-class Shanghairen, the architectural shell of their former lived experience increases the sense of loss. The emotional distance they feel from upscale global consumer culture is not closed by familiar-looking architecture; on the contrary, that gulf widens. Behind the *shikumen* façade of those historic neighborhoods, the vibe is alien: a stage-set for a play performed by and for other people. The life associated with *shikumen* housing, be it quarreling over shared kitchen space, children roaming the alleyways after school, or a sense of belonging to one big extended family, is forever gone, razed and bulldozed and rebuilt as something foreign.

David Harvey, in his critique on urban political economy, ponders which segment of the population benefits from the commodification of local culture; who reaps monopoly rent from a place's symbolic capital?[24] Clearly, the answer is not the displaced former residents. The symbolic capital objectified in vernacular *shikumen* housing and its associated ways of living is the charm, distinctive ambiance, and authenticity of those central urban neighborhoods. However, the long-term contributions native Shanghairen made to this reservoir of symbolic capital over decades do not grant them access to these Disneyfied *shikumen* neighborhoods.

Though Shanghai's total municipal area is eight times that of the urban center, historically Shanghairen is the identification reserved for people living in that highly dense core of 86 square kilometers (approx. 21,250 acres, as "Shanghai proper" in figure 3.1). For them, leaving there would mean being thrown out into backward, remote rural areas. Thus, when they were relocated to Meilong in what was previously Minhang Township, or to Zhoupu Township in previously rural Nanhui, native Shanghairen left behind the very urban space that molded their identity.

In essence, the growth machine indiscriminately forced native Shanghairen to pave the road—quite literally, as the homes of Guorong and his neighbors were demolished to make way for the construction of the Nanjing West Road Station on the No.2 subway line. They had to leave so that a new global city could emerge in the economic reform era. As Low and Altman point out, "the place may be a medium or milieu which embeds and is a repository of a variety of life experiences, is central to those experiences, and is inseparable from them."[25] The displacement broke the physical bond native Shanghairen have to the urban core landscape. At the same time, the relocation strengthened their emotional attachment and desire to reclaim the place which had provided them with self-esteem, self-worth, and pride. In order to assert symbolic claims to their old neighborhoods and urban Shanghai lifestyle, and to reaffirm their Shanghairen identity, the Shanghai dialect, an intangible but concrete signifier, came into focus. However, what the natives discover is that the practice of the dialect is also slipping away.

DISPERSAL OF THE SPEECH COMMUNITY

The dislocation and disintegration of *shikumen* communities violently disrupted the territorial condition of the Shanghai dialect. The dialect itself is
an urban hybrid: its birth and development are attributed to the waves of
migrants who came to Shanghai over the last century and half. As such, the
spatial component is vitally important for the dialect's speech community.
Qian Nairong, the renowned Shanghai dialect expert, emphasizes urban
Shanghai as the geographical boundary in discussing the dialect's history
and changes.[26] In the pre-reform era, this urban speech community excluded
the entire Pudong region, as well as the majority of areas outside of Shanghai
proper, which were categorized as rural.

The relocation of more than one million households from the urban center to areas mostly outside of the inner ring, and to Pudong, uprooted the
Shanghai dialect speech community from the territory that defined it spatially. During the first wave of urban renewal and redevelopment in the early
1990s, move-in ready housing was provided to the displaced in the periphery,
which enabled a small speech community to survive. Even today, the dialect
is still spoken in certain "relocation buildings (*dongqian fang*)." As Lu, a
retired editor from *Xinmin Evening News*, explained:

> I have many friends who used to live in the city center, in Jing'an district,
> all native Shanghairen. They were all displaced and relocated to Hanghua or
> Minghang [in the late 1990s].[27] Those were bleak and desolate areas, very
> remote when they moved. Now it is more connected with the urban center
> through the subway line, and there are lots and lots of non-natives [living there].
> The funny thing is as soon as you climb up the stairs of old relocation buildings,
> you hear the Shanghai dialect [in hallways].

Lu expressed amazement at discovering those island speech communities, so
removed from the urban center. It clearly shows the importance of geographical proximity for language vitality. For the Shanghai dialect to be sustained
outside one's homes, not only speakers but also a neighborly space for speaking it are needed. These are the two prerequisites for the dialect to survive as
a language in active, social use, as opposed to surviving as tape recordings
played in a folk culture museum.

In addition to the survival of these pockets of Shanghai dialect speech
communities, Lu also vividly illustrates the segregated housing situation in
those recently developed outer areas. Those displaced from the center formed
small dialect speech communities in their new buildings and homes, though
surrounded by new housing developments inhabited mostly by lower-middle-
class non-natives due to those peripheral areas' relatively low housing and

rental prices. Lu's description of the linguistic space in those neighborhoods sounds similar to depictions of a Chinatown in the North American context: an island of a "foreign" language, marginalized from mainstream society, but nevertheless persevered. What is different is the fact that these Shanghai dialect speakers do not live in a foreign land but rather still live in their home city of Shanghai.

To investigate the linguistic scene in a relocation neighborhood, I traveled to Sanlin Township, outside of the middle ring in Pudong, in the winter of 2013. At that time, it looked quite desolate and bleak. Getting out of the Pusan Road Station of the No.11 subway line, I saw broad but empty sidewalks, new, gated apartment complexes, vacant lots, and no shops at all (see figure 3.4). Ling Jie, the principal of a private kindergarten there, told me that the neighborhood was much better than seven years before when she had opened the kindergarten. The kindergarten made its name by teaching the Shanghai dialect. Ling explained her kindergarten's popularity:

There are many relocation buildings here in Sanlin to house those displaced by the Shanghai Expo 2010. For those parents relocated from Puxi, they had a strong sense of loss, away from the atmosphere and culture of urban Shanghai, so teaching their kids the Shanghai dialect is such a big draw.

Figure 3.4   Outside of Pusan Road Subway Station in 2013. *Source*: Photo by the author.

The parents' responses to their children learning the Shanghai dialect, as described by Ling, suggest a positive future instead of endangerment for the dialect. What is less helpful, however, is the current linguistic landscape in Sanlin. Since those already living in Sanlin do not speak the urban version of the dialect, the common language they share with those relocated from Puxi is Putonghua. Besides, recent migrants who do not speak the Shanghai dialect also live in Sanlin. The prevalence and dominance of Putonghua is the linguistic context of the kindergarten's Shanghai dialect initiative. If the dialect were still the *lingua franca*, as was the case in Shanghai before the 1990s, teaching it would not be a subject in the kindergarten curriculum. And if Shanghai's transformation had not necessitated relocating Shanghairen to previously rural Pudong, the use of the dialect would not have to serve as their only connection to urban-core living and a much-needed reaffirmation of their Shanghairen identity—all the other markers of that identity would still be in place.

To relocated parents, their removal from inner ring Puxi neighborhoods has two dimensions, geographic and linguistic. Though the urbanization process rezoned Sanlin Township as part of urban Shanghai, this categorical change did not shorten the distance. The old homes they cannot afford to return to lie across the Huangpu River. At the very least, these families hope to continue speaking the Shanghai dialect at home with their children, to maintain their connection to the city and assert their Shanghairen identity. Studies have shown school-age children to native Shanghairen parents and grandparents in Shanghai quickly lost dialect competence after entering the public-school system, where Putonghua is the medium of instruction.[28] In light of how linguistic capital is heavily endowed in the school system, dialect lessons, and the use of it as medium of instruction offered at Ling Jie's Modern Baby Kindergarten in this remote Pudong neighborhood not only contribute to the preservation of the Shanghai dialect but also bring the warmth of home to those displaced households. Geographically, they are displaced; but linguistically, they still hold onto Shanghai's urban culture through dialect speaking.

Across the Huangpu River in Puxi, the rapidly diminishing space for dialect speaking is due to natives' voluntary adoption of Putonghua and the increasing presence of Putonghua-speaking non-natives. The logic of the real estate market, coupled with a deep-rooted desire to live in the upper corner among native Shanghairen, worked to dismantle islands of the speech community in relocation neighborhoods. Living in the periphery means an inconvenient daily commute, poor infrastructure, and limited social services. The one positive is families can live in larger and newer units. The initial relocation was involuntary, but over time, those with more financial resources purchased housing closer to the urban center and sold or rented out their apartments in relocation buildings often to non-natives.

Guorong, who has lived in Meilong with his parents since their relocation in 1997, explained the transition to me:

Buildings in our neighborhood are mostly relocation buildings initially inhabited by old neighbors from the urban center. At the beginning, you heard the dialect spoken everywhere, but now it is totally different. If you walk around my neighborhood in the morning, all you hear is quarrels over dogs, whose dog bit whose, Putonghua with Shanxi accent, with Northeastern accent, but absolutely no Shanghai dialect. I don't hear many people in my neighborhood speaking the dialect anymore.

It appears that many of Guorong's relocated neighbors moved away, but he and his family stayed. Over the years, his neighborhood has changed from a community of relocated native Shanghairen to a mixed community of both natives and non-natives from all across the country (mostly non-natives, according to Guorong). The workings of the real estate market created a residential community that was socioeconomically more homogeneous, but linguistically more heterogeneous.

This is in stark contrast to pre-1990s Shanghai, when housing was controlled and redistributed by the municipal government and state-owned work units. More often than not, employees of various ranks, seniority or professions lived in the same building, owned by a single work unit, which hired only those with a Shanghai *hukou*. As Whyte and Parish point out, the pattern of residential neighborhoods during that period was not completely homogeneous, but differences that were visible tended to be less related to social class.[29] From Guorong's example, a proletarian worker lived next door to a famous movie director and to municipal government officials. All of them shared one bathroom.

Relocations over the last two decades not only moved millions of Shanghairen away from the metropolitan core to more diverse neighborhoods but also changed their relation to public space in the neighborhood they live in. The overcrowded living conditions in *shikumen* housing meant intermingling in public spaces, such as alleyways and shared kitchens, spatial conditions that built a close-knit community of Shanghai dialect speakers. This condition disappeared in the relocation and the associated adoption of apartment living. To illustrate the change, Yan, an elementary school teacher in her late thirties, compared her childhood experience with her son's:

When I was young [1980s], I played with neighbors in the alleyway all the time. Now my son is nine years old. What does he do after school? Watching TV alone at home. It's very difficult for him to make friends in the neighborhood because most of his classmates don't live close by, or they need to stay at home to do homework.

Yan made this comparison to explain why her son did not speak the Shanghai dialect with his classmates and friends. To her, this is not merely the result of the language ideology taught to him at school, or the Putonghua he hears on television, but also the linguistic environment and social circles. Sacrificed in the housing upgrades along relocation are opportunities to interact with neighbors and children's opportunities to play with classmates after school: opportunities, presumably, to practice the Shanghai dialect. As Yan elaborated:

> Compared to our times, they don't play with each other much. I remember when I was in elementary school, we didn't even have landline telephones, and you didn't need it. You just went out into the alley and shouted out: "let's meet up after dinner and play!" Kids would then show up and play all sorts of alleyway games.

During childhood, Yan lived with her parents and grandparents in an old *shikumen* housing complex in working-class Hongkou district, close to the industrial end of the Bund. Now she lives with her husband, mother, and son in a nice three-bedroom condo in the Jiangwan area of Yangpu district, beyond the middle ring. She does not seem to regret moving away from *shikumen* housing, in contrast to those research participants who grew up in Western-looking villas or upscale *lilong* housing in the former foreign settlements. To her, the cash compensation from relocation enabled her and her family to purchase nicer housing in an upscale (albeit more remote) neighborhood. What she lamented was the loss of community and tangible social circles close to home. Instead of the everyday mingling in shared courtyards and alleyways of her old neighborhood, now interactions with neighbors are mostly limited to "Hello" and "Bye" when riding the elevator together. Both the circle of classmates living close by and the afterschool alleyway games she once enjoyed are not available to her son, who has his own room in their apartment.

The reconstruction of Shanghai dialect speech communities is not as easy as building residential high-rises. Since, for a language to survive, people in that speech community must practice the language with each other on a regular basis. Geographical proximity is vital for such interactions. Although Gumperz's relational definition of a speech community emphasizes the presence of non-speakers to identify the boundary,[30] living in close proximity with non-speakers of Shanghai dialect inevitably leads bilingual Shanghairen to use Putonghua. Furthermore, modern apartment lifestyles, conducted largely behind locked doors, limit the opportunity for interaction between neighbors.

The linguistic landscape inside of the inner ring, though not dominated by English, is not very accommodating to the Shanghai dialect. Putonghua dominates the linguistic space in those new upscale condominiums. Using *hukou* status as the indicator for native-ness, He and Wu reveal that 35 percent of the residents in Zhongyuan Liangwancheng, an upscale new housing development near Suzhou Creek within the inner ring are non-natives.[31]One typical example of language policing in such residence comes from Zoe, a native Shanghairen in her mid-thirties and a senior marketing director at an international educational organization, whose husband is a financial officer at a big tech company. They live in one of those upscale high-rise condos. Zoe explained the reasons behind the changed linguistic environment in urban central Shanghai as twofold: the geographical dislocation and dispersal of native Shanghairen as well as the influx of non-natives who speak Putonghua, to whom the Shanghai dialect is as unintelligible as a foreign language. She went on:

> There is nowhere in Shanghai now that can claim to have solely native Shanghairen residents. Say you initiate a conversation with a stranger in your building in the Shanghai dialect. It is more than likely that s/he [being a non-native] would reply in Putonghua and even give you a dirty look suggesting the rudeness of using [an informal] language that they don't understand.

The way she was treated by equally affluent neighbors when initiating a conversation in the Shanghai dialect explains why she now regards Putonghua as a default language choice:

> Encountering situations like that a few times and you [being a native] would stop using the Shanghai dialect with strangers. There is no solution, no future for the dialect. There is no space for it.

Zoe sees a dim future for the dialect since the public space for its practice evaporated in the process of relocation and internal migration. In that environment, she found the most practical choice was to speak Putonghua. Many of her fellow native Shanghairen make the same choice, since the residential neighborhoods they live in are also mixed.

Between the dispersal of the Shanghai dialect speech community and the impossibility of reconstructing such a community in the various residential neighborhoods across the city, the outlook is grim for the dialect. In the global city-building process, what is lost in the minds of millions of native Shanghairen is the city's symbolic capital imbued in the vernaculars, meaning both the architectural features in *shikumen* housing neighborhoods and the language that inhabited such urban spaces. In the last three decades, nationwide urbanization has made Chinese urban centers uniform. When the visual cue for distinction is nowhere to be found, the bewildered can only rely on audible traces. But even the latter is fading.

LOSS OF URBAN CHARACTER

A city loses its character when features such as vernacular architecture and neighborhood layout are destroyed in favor of a uniform architectural scene and lifestyle. The result is a city no different from any other city. In the economic reform era, this is exactly what has happened to many, if not all, Chinese cities through the public-private partnership leading the urbanization and redevelopment process. This singular trajectory of urban changes grew from the idea to "catch up with the West," initiated by the central government and facilitated by real estate developers. The erasure of local characteristics was carried out in the name of progress and modernization.

The visible proof of Shanghai becoming a node in the network of global cities is its new uniform look, which signifies consumerism and accommodation for capitalist globalization. After decades of neglect and disinvestment in the Maoist era, this global-city look initially made natives proud and non-natives feel welcomed and included. At the same time, vernacular built environments, such as *shikumen* housing, alienated non-natives who were not familiar with the lifestyle associated with it. According to the Shanghai Statistical Bureau, roughly 80 million square meters of residential neighborhoods were demolished or taken through eminent domain between 1995 and 2013.[32] With the city changed beyond recognition, the earlier excitement among natives was replaced by bewilderment and disorientation. Proshansky et al. explain that individual place identity involves memories, feelings, attitudes, preferences, and values associated with everyday physical environment.[33] The overhaul of familiar residential neighborhoods and the new uniform urban landscape made native Shanghairen realize that there is no longer a distinctive place they can identify as Shanghai. There is no way to differentiate the city from other Chinese cities and to anchor their place identity.

The nationwide urbanization and building frenzy in the economic reform era brought to China uniform-looking modern infrastructure, similar to redeveloped Shanghai, though on a smaller scale. Decentralization of power provided great freedom for local governments to implement entrepreneurial development policies.[34] Inspired by the success of urban renewal projects that increased property values and attracted investment in top-tier cities like Beijing and Shanghai, municipalities across the country have begun replicating the process. Redevelopment of urban centers and suburbanization to house the displaced urban population have occurred in economically vibrant cities such as Guangzhou in the Southeast, the northern industrial cities Shenyang[35] and Dalian, and big cities in the Yangtze River Delta region close to Shanghai, such as Hangzhou and Suzhou.[36]

Government officials in partnership with real estate developers care little about the consequences for locals' place identity. The city's new image on the national or even global stage can positively affect the politicians' career trajectory and benefit the city's coffers, negating possible setbacks from the locals' complaints. City officials regard the symbolic capital carried by global-oriented urban landscapes as leverage in inter-city competition.[37] Winning this competition means attracting tourists and capital investments, and catering to the emerging middle class.[38]

Urban redevelopments in China involve two steps: a massive upgrade of urban infrastructure to adopt a uniform global-city look, followed by a few preservation-themed projects with a vernacular flavor, to seek a competitive edge in tourist attraction despite the destruction of the local culture and social fabric brought about in the initial upgrade. In the search for a competitive edge through the urban built environment, a few major second-tier cities, such as Nanjing,[39] the provincial capital of Jiangsu province, Kunming, the provincial capital of Yunnan province,[40] and Chengdu, a major political, economic, and cultural center of Sichuan province in Western China,[41] have experienced preservation-based redevelopment and gentrification since the 2000s. Some others, instead of drawing inspiration from vernacular architectural features, opted to copy proven, global models of redevelopment.

Seeing the success of Xintiandi, the profit-driven, preservation-anchoring redevelopment project in Shanghai, mayors of other Chinese cities sent invitations to the architect responsible for the project, asking the team to clone Xintiandi in their cities. The Xihu (West Lake) Xintiandi has already been completed in Hangzhou, a two-hour train ride south of Shanghai. Chongqing, inland in Sichuan province opened its (Xin)Tiandi in early 2019.[42] Just like Xintiandi in Shanghai, these projects do not bring historical relevance to their cities; instead, they bring global consumer culture to China's new rich. Even when a few vernacular architectural elements are incorporated into redevelopment, the essence of the urban space is permanently altered. Borrowing an old Chinese saying, it is using an old bottle to sell new wine (*jiu ping zhuang xin jiu*). This practice can only fool dilettantes, while appealing only to those who value the outlook of global modernity more than vernacular flavor.

The irony of nationwide urban redevelopments is that when cities try to imitate each other, the strategy can fail to boost local standing, since "the advantage of being the first to do it has been lost" as Molotch et al. argue in their comparative study of two Californian cities.[43] Furthermore, these copycat measures have brought uniformity and McDonaldization[44] to the urban landscape across the country, at the expense of distinctiveness. It may appear counterintuitive that inter-city competitions generate less innovation. In this way, glass-façade office towers are really no different from renovated historic landmark buildings. Both represent the sweeping forces of state-led economic reform and entrepreneurism practiced by local governments.

Over the course of just twenty years, Chinese urbanites found themselves surrounded by identical-looking office towers and residential high-rises. They treat them less as spectacles than surrogates for a Western lifestyle and modernity, which had been denied them for decades. The rise of other Chinese cities means Shanghai is no longer the only modern metropolis in China, a title and recognition native Shanghairen held dear for decades now slipping away more quickly than they can comprehend. It is against this back-drop that native Shanghairen came to realize the loss of Shanghai's distinct character and found anew the importance of the Shanghai dialect as an endur-ing symbol of their city's uniqueness.

Having already witnessed Shanghai's urban center altered beyond recogni-tion, native Shanghairen are even more surprised to see how widespread that alien, modern look is across the country. For example, Peng, a product man-ager in a French company, traveled around the country regularly for product launches and roadshows. Besides Shanghai, Beijing, and Guangzhou, the three top-tier cities, he has been to many second- and third-tier cities with populations of more than one million. He was disappointed by a general lack of distinct character in urban China:

> Because of work, I have been to many Chinese cities, big or small, more than thirty a year. Even though some of them claimed to be tourist cities, none of them, no Chinese city has its own character.

Peng emphasized those cities were recognized as "tourist cities" (*lueyou chengshi*), which is a recognition awarded by the Chinese National Tourism Administration based on the evaluation of a city's distinct tourism resources and the development of the tourist industry. By invoking that category, Peng stressed that if those cities, recognized as such, failed to demonstrate local character, then other cities without the title would appear to possess even less unique character or distinctiveness.

What exactly is the distinct character of a city? Other than historic land-marks or spectacles, how could we tell one city apart from another? Peng suggested that the vanishing vernacular landscape was the answer:

> To me, a city's characteristics are the Forbidden City in Beijing, the Drum Tower in Xi'an, or some folk arts in the Northwest. But the distinguishing features between Chinese cities? Really, any city in Mainland China, northeast to Shenyang, or south to Guangzhou, every downtown looks the same, no difference!

To him, landmarked historical sites are certainly distinctions, but the urban built environment is much more than a few tourist sites. Moreover, not every city in vast China is blessed with being a capital of past dynasties.[45] He elaborated on the sameness of those urban China downtowns in this way:

> In Chinese cities, all neighborhoods look the same. All buildings look the same, all shopping malls look the same, even all railway stations! Airports? After the [Shanghai] Pudong International Airport was built, the design and blueprints were sold to many cities. All look the same, even the interior design and materials!

His examples, such as identical shopping malls or transit hubs, are the kind of non-places Auge identifies that "cannot be defined as relational, or historical, or concerned with identity."[46] The non-places constructed during China's economic boom over the last three decades do not have locally rooted anthropological meanings, and certainly do not integrate residents' earlier experiences with the locale. As Relph writes, what they represent is placelessness.[47] Those characterless urban centers are places without distinguishing features. Anonymous, placeless urban built environments are more accommodating to the global economy, which is hostile to unstandardized, unruly, locale-specific vernacular architecture, and urban planning.

The creation of non-places is consistent with the ideology of neoliberal urbanism, as a way to generate monopoly rent for developers and to accommodate capitalist globalization. Over our lunch interview at a restaurant on the Bund with the view of the Pudong waterfront CBD (see figure 3.5), Wendy, a female native Shanghairen and a senior marketing manager at an American company, pointed out how China embraced global city-building by eliminating local character:

> Look, do you see [the Pudong waterfront skyline has] any difference from the Victoria Harbor in Hong Kong? The decision makers at the municipal and the central government level don't think Shanghai needs any distinctive character. China now doesn't appreciate diversity.

The creation of identical urban landscapes follows capitalist globalization's logic of rationality, functionality, and revenue maximization. To replicate proven models for generating revenue is a guaranteed road to success, which extends to urban spatial configurations. Therefore, there is no space for less-profitable configurations generated locally, with vernacular features for non-profit-generating purposes, such as a sense of belonging, collective memories, or local solidarity. These prototypical built environments in globalizing cities are celebrated by policy makers as modern and cosmopolitan. But they are rootless and placeless in the eyes of locals who are often excluded culturally if not financially.

Figure 3.5   View from the restaurant M on the Bund, Located on the Seventh Floor of the Nissin Shipping Building at No. 5 The Bund. *Source*: Photo by the author.

Considering the identical-looking urban landscapes, what is left to identify a particular place, to differentiate one urban center from another? Ge, a well-traveled retired radio station editor and Shanghai dialect preservation activist, vividly described the importance of language, for him, in distinguishing a city:

> It is highly homogenized, anywhere you go in China. Last year I went to Qaramay City. The city is a rich oil town and looks identical to Shanghai! I felt I had never left Shanghai after getting off the plane there. A joke I always tell is that if I parachute out of a plane blindfolded, I can't tell where I am after landing. How did I realize that I was no longer in Shanghai? There are Uyghur there speaking their language.[48] Language is the only tool to tell the difference.

An ethnic minority's language is the only indicator Ge could find to tell one city apart from another. The example he gave, Qaramay City, is located in the northern desert area of the Uyghur Autonomous Region, close to the border of Kazakhstan, and more than 2,600 miles away from Shanghai, which sits on the Pacific coast. Being Han Chinese, Ge did not find the cultural and ethnic characteristics he had anticipated in that city which historically has a large Uyghur population.[49] That is to say, even remote cities in ethnic minority autonomous regions are not spared from the ubiquitous placeless look of the new urban China.

Beyond the urban built environment, the vision of the "China Dream" has further strengthened the uniformity of the linguistic sphere in China. While ethnic minorities are still guaranteed some freedom to speak their own language—though this has diminished in recent years, Putonghua is the mandate official language for the Han Chinese majority. For them, regional dialects, like the Shanghai dialect, serve as an ever more important signifier for their city and their own identity. To Peng, to preserve the local dialect is the last hope to combat the total loss of urban character:

> The only thing left is dialect, to tell where you are from and who you are! If the linguistic difference is also wiped out, then there is no distinguishing feature of the people, or of the city.

It is the urban landscape, and the people living in it, that imbue a city with soul. The modernization and developmental policies of the economic reform era and the sweeping power of capitalist globalization have transformed the landscape of urban China and Chinese citizens. As Peng stressed, if deprived of a linguistic difference, one could hardly tell the origin and identity of any individual. This might sound alarmist, since, after all, individual identity is multifaceted and fluid. When native Shanghairen like Peng express their anxiety about the future of the Shanghai dialect and the associated Shanghairen identity, they express a sense of powerlessness in the face of the state, which has demonstrated its might in totally transforming urban China over the last three decades.

CONCLUSION

"An ocean receiving hundreds of streams" (*hai na bai chuan*) has been the motto of Shanghai for more than a century. It portrays Shanghai as a place that absorbs various global and domestic trends, including architectural styles, fashions, cuisines, languages, and lifestyles, and appropriates them as her own. It is this kind of hospitality, this kind of embrace of diversity and autonomy, and this kind of witty reappropriation that characterized Shanghai before 1949. It sits in sharp contrast to the uniform urban life in the Maoist era, which was characterized by blue and grey outfits, limited goods sold through a ration system, and universal conformity to a singular Communist ideology. In the reform era, China's door to the West was reopened, but the inflows have been highly controlled in the economic sphere and censored in the cultural sphere. The central government's developmental policies modeled urban China after a single version of global modernity in the hope of catching up with, if not surpassing the West. On the ground, this has meant providing a welcoming environment for capital investments and the flow of labor forces.

The soul or distinctive character of Shanghai is more than an attitude toward outside influences, as captured in the motto but an integration process worked out by millions of Shanghairen. Since the opening of the Treaty Port in 1843, the changes that occurred in Shanghai were never wholesale replacement of the old with the new, as seen recently in Pudong and many parts of Puxi, but a battle and a negotiated incorporation process that strived to maintain vernacular roots while embracing outside trends. Once the most Westernized city in Mainland China, Shanghai is at a crossroad. It is in a transitional phase and must strike a balance between the Western culture it was once familiar with, and the rising and dominant Chinese national culture and identity represented by Putonghua. So far, Shanghai does not seem to be ready to completely give up its own identity.

If *shikumen* housing characterizes Shanghai's hybridity in the most visible and tangible way, then the Shanghai dialect is its intangible counterpart, rooted in the city's history, and an essential though now more and more ambiguous part of Shanghairen identity. The hostility toward the all-encompassing and uniform global-city look is born organically from natives' lack of agency in the reproduction of urban space. The top-down policies in the redevelopment of Puxi and urbanization of Pudong clearly denied this very agency, at least on the highly censored and controlled official platforms and physical space.

The image of Shanghai that is presented to the world now is a non-place of consumption or transaction for national and global elites. To reinstall the city's authenticity would not mean to close the door and lock the city back up but to interpret, appropriate, and integrate outside flows to produce something unique of its own. This is the process that led to the creation of hybrid *shikumen* housing nearly a century ago and to the creation of the hybrid Shanghai dialect, which has continually updated itself by inventing new vocabulary to capture the zeitgeist—until 2001, when Putonghua started to dominate the city's linguistic landscape.

In this regard, the preservation of the hybrid Shanghai dialect is the key to rescuing the city's dying authenticity. Over the last two decades, the state's language policies were accompanied by city-wide urban redevelopment. Under the logic of urban political economy and the real estate market, the Shanghai dialect speech community was dispersed to various neighborhoods with mixed-origin residents. Out of practicality, as well as under the influence of the dominant language ideology, most bilingual native Shanghairen now choose to speak Putonghua. Nevertheless, this does not mean that they are willing to see the extinction of the dialect or accede to a monolingual future. Since the majority of natives are bilingual in the dialect and Putonghua, the language conflict between the natives and non-natives is not an issue of daily communication but rather conflicts about what makes an authentic Shanghairen identity, and hence who has the right to the city.

NOTES

1. Gumperz, John J. 1972. "The Speech Community." In *Language and Social Context: Selected Readings*, edited by Pier Paolo Giglioli, 219–31. Harmondsworth: Penguin.

2. Zukin, Sharon. 2010. *Naked City: The Death and Life of Authentic Urban Places*. Oxford & New York: Oxford University Press. P.xi.

3. See for example

Lee, Leo Ou-fan. 1999. *Shanghai Modern: The Flowering of a New Urban Culture in China, 1930–1945*. Cambridge, MA: Harvard University Press.

Lu, Hanchao. 1999. *Beyond the Neon Lights: Everyday Shanghai in the Early Twentieth Century*. Berkeley, CA: University of California Press.

Gamble, Jos. 2003. *Shanghai in Transition: Changing Perspectives and Social Contours of a Chinese Metropolis*. London & New York: RoutledgeCurzon.

Yeh, Wen-hsin. 2007. *Shanghai Splendor: Economic Sentiments and the Making of Modern China, 1843–1949*. Berkeley, CA: University of California Press.

Bergère, Marie-Claire. 2009. *Shanghai: China's Gateway to Modernity*. Stanford, CA: Stanford University Press.

Wasserstrom, Jeffrey N. 2009. *Global Shanghai, 1850–2010*. London & New York: Routledge.

4. Rudolph, Jennifer, and Hanchao Lu. 2008. "Mirrored Reflections: Place Identity Formation in Taipei and Shanghai." In *Urban China in Transition*, edited by John Logan, 161–81. Malden, MA: John Wiley & Sons.P.164.

5. Ren, Xuefei. 2011. *Building Globalization: Transnational Architecture Production in Urban China*. Chicago & London: University of Chicago Press. P.13.

6. Zukin, Sharon. 1995. *The Cultures of Cities*. Cambridge, MA: Blackwell. P.8.

7. Greenspan, Anna. 2014. *Shanghai Future: Modernity Remade*. New York: Oxford University Press. P.53.

8. Shao, Qin. 2013. *Shanghai Gone: Domicide and Defiance in a Chinese Megacity*. Lanham: Rowman & Littlefield Publishers.

Zhang, Yunpeng. 2018. "Domicide, Social Suffering and Symbolic Violence in Contemporary Shanghai, China." *Urban Geography* 39 (2): 190–213.

9. Shanghai Statistical Bureau. 2012. *Shanghai Statistical Yearbook 2011*. Beijing: China Statistics Press. http://tjj.sh.gov.cn/tjnj/nje11.htm?d1=2011tjnje/E0205.htm.

———. 2018. *Shanghai Statistical Yearbook 2017*. Beijing: China Statistics Press. http://tjj.sh.gov.cn/tjnj/20190117/0014-1001529.html.

10. Massey, Doreen. 1995. "Places and Their Pasts." *History Workshop Journal* 39: 182–92. P.187.

11. Orum, Anthony M., Sidney Bata, Li Shumei, Tang Jiewei, Sang Yang, and Nguyen Thanh Trung. 2009. "Public Man and Public Space in Shanghai Today." *City & Community* 8 (4): 369–89. P.384.

12. Low, Setha M., and Irwin Altman. 1992. "Place Attachment." In *Place Attachment*, edited by Irwin Altman and Setha M. Low, 1–12. Human Behavior and Environment. Boston, MA: Springer US. P.4–6.

13. This is yet another example of how native Shanghairen are slow to adopt the re-classification of rural counties as urban districts, even after more than ten years. See figure 3.1 for the locations of the mentioned districts.

14. Logan, John R., Yiping Fang, and Zhanxin Zhang. 2009. "Access to Housing in Urban China." *International Journal of Urban and Regional Research* 33 (4): 914–35.

15. Zhang Garden was initially built as a spacious park west of the International Settlement where elites came for leisure. Later, as an upscale residential neighborhood, it occupied the area north to West Beijing Road, south to Weihai Road, east to Shimen No.1 Road, and west to Shanxi South Road. See Pan, Lynn. 1982. *In Search of Old Shanghai*. Hong Kong: Joint Pub. P. 68–70. And Nien, Cheng. 2010. *Life and Death in Shanghai*. Reissue Edition. New York: Grove Press.

16. Bian, Yanjie, and John R. Logan. 1996. "Market Transition and the Persistence of Power: The Changing Stratification System in Urban China." *American Sociological Review* 61 (5): 739–58.

17. Bian, Yanjie. 2002. "Chinese Social Stratification and Social Mobility." *Annual Review of Sociology* 28: 91–116.

18. Logan, Fang, and Zhang. "Access to Housing in Urban China," 914–35.

19. Whyte, Martin King, and William L. Parish. 1984. *Urban Life in Contemporary China*. Chicago & London: The University of Chicago Press. P.84.

20. Bian. "Chinese Social Stratification and Social Mobility," 91–116.

21. Shanghai Municipal Government Press Release, August 8, 2003. The State Council Information Office of the People's Republic of China. http://www.scio .gov.cn/xwfbh/gssxwfbh/xwfbh/shanghai/Document/320761/320761.htm. Retrieved August 14, 2020.

22. Ren. *Building Globalization*.

23. Shen, Jie, and Fulong Wu. 2012. "Restless Urban Landscapes in China: A Case Study of Three Projects in Shanghai." *Journal of Urban Affairs* 34 (3): 255–77. P.264.

24. Harvey, David. 2001. "From Managerialism to Entrepreneurialism: The Transformation in Urban Governance in Late Capitalism." In *Spaces of Capital: Towards a Critical Geography*, 345–68. New York: Routledge.

25. Low, and Altman. "Place Attachment," 1–12. P.10.

26. Qian Nairong. 2007. *Shanghai Dialect (shanghai fangyan)*. Shanghai: Wenhui Publishing. P.12.

27. Hanghua area sits between the middle and the outer ring, and Minghang district is mostly outside of the outer ring.

28. See for example

Jiang, Bingbing. 2006. "Bilingualism and Linguistic Harmony: Research on Shanghainese Students' Language Usage (*shuangyu yu yuyan hexie: laizi shanghai-shi xuesheng yuyan shiyong qingkuang de diaocha*)." *Rhetoric Learning (Xiuci Xuexi)* 6: 64–6.

Jiao, Chengming. 2009. "Report on Shanghai Native Students Linguistic Behavior (Shanghai *tuzhu xuesheng yuyan yingwei baogao*)." *Applied Linguistics (yuyan wenzi yingyong)*, no. 1: 27–37.

Sun, Xiaoxian, Bingbing Jiang, Yijia Wang, and Lihua Qiao. n.d. "A Survey of Shanghai Students' Use of Putonghua and Shanghai Dialect (*Shanghaishi xuesheng putonghua he shanghaihua shiyong qingkuang diaocha*)." *Yangtze River Academic (Changjiang Xueshu)* 3: 1–10.

29. Whyte, and Parish. *Urban Life in Contemporary China,* P.84.

30. Gumperz. "The Speech Community," 219–31. Harmondsworth: Penguin.

31. He, Shenjing, and Fulong Wu. 2007. "Neighborhood Changes and Residential Differention in Shanghai." In *China's Emerging Cities: The Making of New Urbanism*, edited by Fulong Wu, 185–209. New York: Routledge.P.193–97.

32. Chart 18.4 Demolition and Eminent Domain of Properties, 1995–2013. Shanghai Statistical Yearbook 2014 [in Chinese]. Retrieved February 17, 2016, from http://www.stats-sh.gov.cn/tjnj/nj14.htm?d1=2014tjnj/C1804.htm.

33. Proshansky, Harold M., Abbe K. Fabian, and Robert Kaminoff. 1983. "Place-Identity: Physical World Socialization of the Self." *Journal of Environmental Psychology* 3 (1): 57–83.

34. Ren. *Building Globalization,* P.138.

35. Zhou, Yixing, and Yanchun Meng. 1997. "Shenyang's Suburbanization: Suburbanization Comparison between China and The Western Countries (*shenyang de jiaoquhua jianlun zhongxifang jiaoquhua de bijiao*)." *Acta Geographica Sinica (Dili Xuebao)* 4: 3–13.

36. Xie, Shouhong, and Yuemin Ning. 2003. "Urbanization and Suburbanization: The Dual Engines to Spatial Change of Chinese Metropolis under Transitional Era: A Case Study of Guangzhou." *City Planning Review (Chengshi Guihua)* 27 (11): 24–38.

Zhang, Wenxin, and Liang Zhu. 2003. "The Situation and Countermeasures of Population Suburbanization in Big Cities of China." *Journal of Beijing Normal University (Natural Science)* 39 (3): 417–21.

37. Yeoh, Brenda S. A. 2004. "Cosmopolitanism and Its Exclusions in Singapore" *Urban Studies* 41 (12): 2431–45.

38. Robinson, Richard, and David S.G. Goodman. 1996. "The New Rich in Asia: Economic Development, Social Status and Political Consciousness." In *The New Rich in Asia: Mobile Phones, McDonald's and Middle-Class Revolution*, edited by Richard Robinson and David S.G. Goodman, 1–18. London & New York: Routledge.

39. Song, Weixuan, and Qiyan Wu. 2010. "Gentrification and Residential Differentiation in Nanjing, China." *Chinese Geographical Science* 20 (6): 568–76.

40. Zhang, Li. 2006. "Contesting Spatial Modernity in Late-Socialist China." *Current Anthropology* 47 (3): 461–84.

41. Huang, Xing, and Yongchun Yang. 2010. "The Characteristics and Forming Mechanisms of Gentrification in Cities of Western China: The Case Study in Chengdu City (*Zhongguo Xibu Chengshi Shenshihua Xianxiang jiqi xingchen jizhi yi Chengdushi weili*)." *Progress in Geography (Dili Kexue Jinzhan)* 29 (12): 1532–40.

42. "City Centre Master-Planned Communities-Property Developments-Property Developments-Shui On Land." Accessed September 12, 2020. https://www.shuionland.com/en-us/property/Community/detail/cc.

43. Molotch, Harvey, William Freudenburg, and Krista E. Paulsen. 2000. "History Repeats Itself, But How? City Character, Urban Tradition, and the Accomplishment of Place." *American Sociological Review*, 791–823. P.818.

44. Ritzer, George. 1999. *Enchanting a Disenchanted World: Revolutionizing the Means of Consumption*. Thousand Oaks, CA: SAGE Publications.

45. Beijing has been the capital city of in China since BC 770. Xi'an is the current provincial capital of Shannxi. Historically it was the starting point of the Silk Road, and hosted the capital of thirteen kingdoms and empires since BC 202.

46. Augé, Marc. 1995. *Non-Places: Introduction to an Anthropology of Supermodernity*. London; New York: Verso. P.78

47. Relph, Edward. 1976. *Place and Placelessness*. London: Pion.

48. A Turkic language with an Arabic-based alphabet spoken in the Xinjiang Uyghur Autonomous Region.

49. The interview took place in the fall of 2013, before the re-education camps started to operate in Xinjiang province.

Chapter 4

Social Integration and New Shanghairen as Euphemism

Over the last thirty years, reforms of the household registration (*hukou*) system have brought in millions of non-natives to Shanghai through a selective process. With reforms in place, these internal migrants can work, live, and enjoy public services in Shanghai in nearly the same way as native Shanghairen. The educational attainment and entrepreneurship-based selection system has given birth to a selective pattern of social integration between natives and non-natives, with Shanghai dialect proficiency wedged awkwardly as the ultimate differentiator.

At the time of my follow-up research in summer 2017, 14.55 million of the 24.18 million residents in Shanghai had Shanghai *hukou*.[1] That means at least 39.8 percent of long-term residents in Shanghai are non-natives. As I will show later in this chapter, a sizeable number of college graduates who attended universities in Shanghai were granted Shanghai *hukou* upon graduation, and as such, the actual number of non-natives will be higher than this percentage. With a Shanghai *hukou* status, non-natives are no longer strictly Waidiren (Outlanders), which is a derogatory term in contrast to Shanghairen. By examining the patterns of social integration at work, in social circles, and family life, I argue that whereas previously regional difference was the key determinant of who would be recognized as Shanghairen, socioeconomic status and lifestyle are now most important. And the officially sanctioned category New Shanghairen is treated as a euphemism by native Shanghairen to indicate that non-natives can never be accepted as genuine members of the community. In the evaluation process, Shanghai dialect proficiency plays a pivotal role, even though the younger generations of native Shanghairen are no longer fluent.

The loosening of the *hukou* system, and especially the reforms at the end of 1990s and early 2000s, allowed greater geographical mobility for Chinese citizens, who were then allowed to move to, and settle in more economically developed regions. This measure was applauded by some social scientists and seen as symbolic of the tearing down of the legal and institutional framework maintaining what was called a dual society[2] or "apartheid."[3] Conversely, other scholars like Solinger predict the persistence of subtle social and cultural barriers.[4] Wu and Treiman claim that the *hukou* system would continue to shape individuals' socioeconomic status and life chances.[5] Almost thirty years after the beginning of the reforms, my study in Shanghai shows that the effects are more nuanced than predicted in earlier literature. On the one hand, migrants now have better overall chances for structural acceptance and integration as institutional barriers represented by *hukou* status have receded; on the other hand, social and cultural boundaries are effectively maintained through language and lifestyle. Instead of a dual society characterized by those with an urban *hukou* and those without, the current social stratification in Shanghai is based on a combination of *hukou*, including the newly invented, second-tier Shanghai Resident Permit and socioeconomic status. More specifically, a selection mechanism has been put in place to integrate certain highly educated and wealthy non-natives into the job market and social circles, while less-educated rural migrants are excluded.

Before reforms of the *hukou* system in the 1990s, three pillars of self-identification firmly established a Shanghairen identity legally, geographically, and linguistically: Shanghai *hukou*, urban residency, and fluency in the Shanghai dialect. Previously these three were inseparable and worked simultaneously; for example, if one was born in Shanghai to Shanghai-*hukou*-holder parents, *hukou* status was granted automatically. The individual's *hukou* would be registered in a household registration booklet associated with a single urban Shanghai address. These two pillars would have implied the third: fluency in the dialect. Collectively, these affirmed a Shanghairen identity.

Over the last three decades, state developmental policies aiming to remake Shanghai into a global city have disrupted the legal (*hukou*) and material (urban housing) basis for determining a local identity and have diminished the privilege this identity once carried. Such privilege once meant that, through their *hukou* status, Shanghairen had convenient access to public services within their central urban neighborhoods. However, as I detailed in the previous chapter, urban redevelopment and economic reforms not only displaced millions of natives from the zone of privilege in the urban center but also extended Shanghai *hukou* status and its associated benefits to recent migrants. National studies conducted shortly after reforms, in the early 2000s, show that the *hukou* system still performed a crucial role for population control and facilitated the uneven distribution of talents and resources between economically vibrant coastal regions and inland areas, intensifying spatial inequality.[6] In the case of Shanghai, from the short-lived blue-stamp *hukou*, to the recently implemented Shanghai Resident Permit, differentiated legal statuses for supposedly equal Chinese citizens is a highly effective way to mobilize a selective labor force and direct investment capital into the most aggressively developing urban areas. The municipal government incentivizes labor and capital movement through granting access to top-quality social services and a modern urban lifestyle, on top of a business friendly environment.

With the commercialization of urban housing and the expansion of *hukou* issuance to non-natives, proficiency in the Shanghai dialect plays an increasing role in defining and signifying Shanghairen identity. The significance is outside the realm of legal or socioeconomic status but derives from knowledge accumulated by living in an East-meets-West metropolis distilled in the vernacular. Borrowing from Bourdieu, we can understand Shanghai dialect proficiency as a linguistic capital nurtured by decades of institutional privilege.[7] In the early twentieth century, the experience of living in a cosmopolitan metropolis transformed the early generation of internal migrants settling in Shanghai. They provided their children with unique cultural and social capitals, which were interdependent with the economic capital connected to both urban residence and cultural consumption. Over the course of many years in the city, they gradually adopted the Shanghai dialect in their everyday communication outside of homes and introduced new vocabulary into it. After 1949, those Shanghai residents enjoyed decades of economic and social privileges granted by the Communist Party's *hukou* system and the planned economy that favored urban areas. Fluency in the Shanghai dialect is regarded as a badge for insider membership and structural privilege. Over just two generations, this exclusive experience influenced ways of thinking, speaking, and behaving. Competence in the Shanghai dialect still serves as an effective barometer for identifying non-natives and judging their characters and worth in everyday interactions. Minority languages serve the boundary-maintenance function in relation to rights and representation, as Stephen May argues in another context.[8] Holding onto this exclusive last pillar of Shanghairen identity, older generation Shanghairen mitigate the material, linguistic, and symbolic loss they have experienced in the reform era. Dialect proficiency also buttresses their claim to the city as genuine Shanghairen, as opposed to the New Shanghairen. The latter is a label invented and promoted by the municipal government to welcome highly educated and entrepreneurial internal migrants.

Using Bryan Turner's differentiation of two dimensions of modern citizenship, namely social membership and the right to an allocation of resources,[9] I investigate the selective acceptance and social integration of highly educated and better-off non-natives in Shanghai in three areas—workplace, social circle, and family. For rural, less-educated migrant workers, social exclusion persists. Rural migrant workers, as a group, were not even mentioned when my native Shanghairen interviewees discussed non-natives' social integration. As for the allocation of resources, the transition from the state- to market-dominated redistribution of public resources promotes the social inclusion of non-natives, especially those with high cultural and economic capital, into comfortable urban living in Shanghai. Thus, urban citizenship in Shanghai is enjoyed fully by those of high socioeconomic status with a Shanghai *hukou*, regardless of origin. In reaction to the loss of exclusive rights and entitlement to urban resources, native Shanghairen use dialect proficiency to challenge non-natives' claim to Shanghairen identity. Furthermore, some better-off native Shanghairen also engage in performative acts of policing fellow natives if they do not take pride in being dialect-speaking, genuine Shanghairen. Through these language attitudes and practices, bilingual native Shanghairen can deploy Putonghua and the Shanghai dialect to effectively maintain the boundary of Shanghairen identity and dismiss the municipal government's newly invented category.

SELECTIVE INTEGRATION IN THE WORKPLACE

Studies on rural migrant workers in urban China in the economic reform era have revealed their precarious life as second-class citizens in their own country, working in cities thousands of miles away from their home villages and without a local *hukou*. These non-natives, employed in low-status jobs, are just as essential for Shanghai's development into a global city as newer highly skilled migrants. At the lower end of the job market in the early 2010s, employers used the flexibility granted by *hukou* reforms to take advantage of rural migrant workers' geographical mobility without assisting them to obtain local legal status.

Sociological studies in the 1990s and early 2000s show large-scale layoffs in urban China due to structural changes in state-owned enterprises through consolidation, mergers, assets restructuring, and closedowns.[10] As a result, hundreds of thousands of native Shanghairen were pushed into early retirement and low-status jobs in the service sector. Drawing data from Shanghai's Statistic Yearbooks, Davis finds that from 1990 to 1995, more than 600,000 industrial jobs disappeared—510,000 of which were in production.[11] At that time, China's major urban centers like Shanghai focused on attracting the super-rich and recruiting highly educated labor for expanding the tertiary sector.[12] Starting in the early 2000s, when those laid-off native Shanghairen workers who moved to service jobs began to retire, and Shanghai was experiencing massive urban redevelopments, it was more and more common to see rural migrant workers in trades, restaurant services, manufacturing, and construction.[13]

Ten years after those earlier studies, occupational segregation continues, with less-educated rural migrants clustered in low-end jobs. Data from 2013 is represented in table 4.1, drawn from a report published by the Shanghai Statistical Bureau titled "Non-Shanghai Hukou holders count more than half of Shanghai's labor force."[14] The areas listed, manufacturing, construction, hospitality and restaurants, and repair and other services, all have more non-native than native workers. Although non-natives accounted for roughly the same percentage of Shanghai's labor force as natives in 2013 with 51.2 percent, their proportions in the four listed sectors are consistently higher.

My observations in stores, restaurants, barbershops, and other retail or hospitality settings in 2013 align with those statistics. In those settings, the language I overheard was predominantly Putonghua with different regional accents. In addition, when I asked my native Shanghairen interviewees about where they would usually encounter non-natives outside of their own workplace or immediate social circle, they pointed to low-status service jobs in restaurants, supermarkets, or as janitors and couriers. To help me understand the prevalence of rural migrant workers occupying those jobs, Jianyuan, a retired native Shanghairen, described to me his grocery shopping routine:

> That's why during the Spring Festival [week-long Chinese New Year holiday], we have nowhere to buy fresh groceries in the wet market [fresh food market with individual venders]! They [rural migrants] all go back home. This is the [only] time that I use my fridge. Usually I buy fresh veggies and meat daily from the wet market across the street.

The inconvenience he described shows how the typical wet market labor force is comprised entirely of non-native rural migrant workers. Their annual departure for their hometowns during the Chinese New Year holiday brings the whole market to a halt.

Table 4.1   Non-natives Participation in the Labor Force

	Manufacturing	*Construction*	*Hospitality and Restaurant*	*Repair and other services*	*Total*
Total Labor Force	2,524,700	912,594*	296,100	64,700	6,500,400
Non-natives	1,486,700	608,700	172,922*	37,785*	3,328,600
Non-native's percentage (%)	58.90	66.70	58.40	58.40	51.20

Another industry that continues to be dominated by rural migrant workers is construction. As indicated in table 4.1, 66.7 percent of workers in that sector are non-natives. In our 2013 interview, Zhenhai, who worked as a project manager at the Shanghai Construction Group, described to me how workers' home regions correspond to the occupational hierarchy in construction:

> Those senior architects or technicians are mostly [native] Shanghairen; many of our internal project meetings are conducted in the Shanghai dialect. Since now we do more management than actual construction, we don't directly hire laborers, but outsource the job to contractors. They are all non-natives, some from Sichuan province, and some from Hunan province. Below them, the laborers are from everywhere!

In the construction industry, according to Zhenhai, native status remains directly related to seniority and expertise, unlike in other sectors that allow non-native college graduates to climb quickly. Little has changed since the early 1990s, when Kam Wing Chan observed that it was the state-owned construction enterprises that hired rural migrants as temporary or contract workers to perform the strenuous labor shunned by urbanites.[15]

The parts of *hukou* reforms most relevant to rural migrant workers are legal residence and access to manual labor jobs in urban areas. The reforms allow millions of rural migrant workers to meet the demand created by two conditions. On the one hand, the urban government allows rural migrants to set up small businesses, such as shoe-repair shops, barbershops, tailor shops, grocery stores, and restaurants,[16] for which there are unmet needs in urban centers.[17] On the other hand, this growing market sector demands more unskilled labor than what the native population is willing or able to supply.[18] Those migrant workers are also now entitled to public services, such as healthcare and education for their children, which are available after establishing residency in Shanghai through a Shanghai Resident Permit, as detailed in chapter 1.

Regardless of the mobility and opportunities on the job market provided to non-natives, the *hukou* system remains intact as a major divide between the rural and the urban populations, as Chan and Buckingham observed in the mid-2000s.[19] Loosening restrictions to facilitate the flow of capital and labor does not shake the dual citizenship structure, although it does open up space for a selective few non-natives to acquire Shanghai *hukou*. Rural migrant laborers, in other words, are still far from being integrated into urban Chinese societies as exemplified in 2010s Shanghai. Instead of granting all non-natives Shanghai *hukou*, and providing public services accordingly and non-discriminatively, a new legal category was invented to differentiate the highly sought-after migrants, with more education and greater wealth, from less educated but equally needed migrant laborers. The latter meets the demand for low-paying service sector jobs, but with little prospect of obtaining a Shanghai *hukou*, which would legally integrate them into the native Shanghairen community. One native Shanghairen interviewee put it candidly to me: "Rural migrant workers? They are not even considered when we think about the New Shanghairen label!" The lowly educated, rural-origin nonnatives, evidently, to the most can enjoy the access to urban resources, but are forever deprived of the social membership, despite being equal Chinese citizens, according to Bryan Turner's argument on the two dimensions of modern citizenship.

In order to build Shanghai into a global city, with a strong tertiary sector of the economy and research and development facilities for both domestic and international corporations, the municipal government promises Shanghai *hukou* to attract college-educated non-natives, while largely ignores the millions of manual laborers who quite literally built the globalizing city. Against this backdrop of the local government's talent-seeking mentality, the retreat of the state's role in job allocation based on an individual's *hukou* status and the decentralization of state power in *hukou* reforms, one group of non-natives in Shanghai enjoy a much better chance for social acceptance and upward social mobility. This group includes those who have obtained Shanghai *hukou* through educational credentials or financial investment. Xuefei Ren suggests it being a new and more complex social stratification than the clear-cut polarization of natives versus non-natives,[20] with the former holding stable good jobs with full access to public services, while the latter working manual jobs with various institutional barriers and contingencies.

Institutional changes to the *hukou* system and changes in hiring processes granted both state-owned and private companies' autonomy to move toward more merit-based recruitment, which gave rise to China's new business elite. According to Margaret Pearson, these elites can be roughly categorized into two groups. One is the contingent of private entrepreneurs and the other is comprised of "foreign-sector managers"—Chinese nationals who manage the foreign-backed businesses that have been allowed to operate in China since the late 1970s. Within this group, there are also professionals and technocratic managers in both foreign and domestic firms. Members of the business elite group tend to be young and well-educated—in their twenties and thirties at the time of Pearson's research in the late 1990s.[21] These new business elites enjoy higher incomes and a standard of living in Shanghai not necessarily accessible to native Shanghairen.

I surveyed and interviewed native Shanghairen who work in organizations owned by either the state or foreign corporations, as well as by domestic entrepreneurs, and asked them about their non-native bosses and coworkers. Reportedly, the hiring process in many industries has moved away from a

Table 4.2   Language Spoken at Workplace with Colleagues by Age

Language Spoken with Colleagues	19–24 (%)	25–34 (%)	35–44 (%)	45–54 (%)	55–64 (%)	Total (%)
Mixed with Equal Amount	0.0	4.3	0.0	0.0	0.0	2.8
Mixed with Predominantly English	0.0	1.7	4.2	0.0	0.0	1.7
Mixed with Predominantly Putonghua	50.0	37.1	37.5	20.0	14.3	37.8
Mixed with Predominantly the Shanghai Dialect	10.7	28.4	37.5	20.0	28.6	26.7
Solely English, or Other Foreign Language	0.0	4.3	0.0	0.0	0.0	2.8
Solely Putonghua	39.3	18.1	8.3	0.0	0.0	18.9
Solely the Shanghai Dialect	0.0	6.0	12.5	60.0	57.1	9.4
Grand Total	28	116	24	5	7	180

hukou-based system. That is to say, non-native status no longer serves as a barrier for employment in Shanghai. It results in mixed-origin workplaces and diverse linguistic space at work. Table 4.2 shows the languages used by 180 native Shanghairen survey respondents who were in the labor force during the 2013 research by age group. Two patterns are apparent. First, Putonghua either used exclusively or predominantly accounts for a combined 56.7 percent, much more than the combined result for the Shanghai dialect at 36.1 percent. The second pattern is the younger the age group, the more Putonghua is used at work, while the older the age group, the more the Shanghai dialect is used. For the age group 19–24 years, Putonghua usage either exclusively or predominantly accounts for 89.3 percent in total, while 14.3 percent for the age group 55–64. When using solely the Shanghai dialect counts 0 percent and 6 percent for age groups 19–24 and 25–34, it is close to two-thirds for 45–54 and 55–64 age groups. The sample size has its limitations, skewing toward the younger groups, which are predominantly college-educated in my non-representative sample. The survey results show mostly language choices in office settings, which supplement and correspond to my interview data.

Kerry, a native Shanghairen who holds an Australian passport and has a bachelor's degree from the University of New South Wales in Sydney, had worked at HSBC's headquarters in Shanghai for ten years at the time of our 2013 interview. She told me about their new recruits, who are mostly non-natives:

> They mostly have graduate degrees from domestic top universities such as Tsinghua University or Peking University. In big companies like ours, they are entitled to the same benefits as native Shanghairen. They occupy relatively high-up positions.

Evidently, non-natives with educational credentials from top domestic universities fare well in the eyes of foreign banks. Hometown or origin matters little compared to educational credentials and skillset. This hiring strategy is a way to control operational cost: the tendency for foreign corporations to replace higher salaried employees transferred from overseas, with relatively lower paid domestic ones.

This wide-spread practice has ramifications not only in home-region based social circles, but also in the languages spoken in the workplace. I interviewed Jane in 2017. Originally from southwestern China, she had completed her undergraduate education in Shanghai and earned her master's degree in London. She described the personnel at a British advertising agency, where she held a c-suite position, thusly:

> When I started working in 1999, all members of the management were Taiwanese, Hongkongers, or Shanghairen who have lived abroad for many years. That's how the company could "hold" up a so-called "international level." Thus, the language for daily communication [in the office] was either Putonghua, or "English: there was no other way" in the overall "environment," in the "working environment, unless administration" personnel, "finance" personnel, all those employees who held positions [in function departments] that could be quickly "localized," are Shanghairen. They would never reach the "executive level." The overall [labor market] "hierarchy," the overall employment at the "professional level" has totally changed. Except some [state-owned] traditional mass media, such as TV stations of radio stations, they might still have a large proportion of native Shanghairen employees, but it won't be long, since the overall [labor market] structure has been changing.

Compatible with the multilingual workplace Jane described, she constantly codeswitched between Putonghua and English. The latter is marked with quotation marks in the interview excerpt. It is safe to speculate that this was the style of communication at her work. It exemplifies how speaking the Shanghai dialect indicates the local identity in an unfavorable light at an international workplace. Since, despite Jane's colleagues' presumptive Putonghua and English proficiency, office emails are uniformly in English, as is the case in a majority of foreign companies in Shanghai. Thus, the Shanghai dialect's boundary-maintenance function, previously a marker of the speaker's local and at the same time cosmopolitan character, now only signifies provinciality, limited international experience, and, as Jane told me, most likely limited chances for professional advancement. From my interviewees' personal experience, those holding top management-level jobs are often not-natives, or to be more precise, hardly any are native Shanghairen with little experience overseas. In such a workplace hierarchy, native Shanghairen possess little if any advantage, and the language they speak is regarded as a sign of lower status.

From HSBC's headquarters to an international advertising agency's Shanghai branch, highly educated native Shanghairen no longer enjoy guaranteed job placement, as they did in the planned economy. Instead, they need to compete for positions both domestically, and even internationally. The following two examples will show that even in state-owned organizations that are traditionally dominated by native Shanghairen, merit rather than Shanghai *hukou* is now the determining factor for advancement.

Despite what Jane suspected, previously exclusive state-controlled sectors, such as mass media, no longer favor native Shanghairen. A native Shanghairen journalist who worked for *Xinmin Evening News*,[22] and preferred to remain anonymous, described her non-native colleagues:

> They [non-natives] are very good at earning high scores at university entrance exams [which determine one's major such as the highly sought-after Journalism], which means most [new recruits] since 2000 are not [native] Shanghairen. Instinctively they want to integrate into the Shanghai society, so they work really hard. They work overtime a lot and seek quick promotions. . . . Now *all* the mid-level managerial positions at our newspaper are held by non-natives.

We see a clear career trajectory for those non-natives trying to make it in the newspaper industry in Shanghai from her telling. Beginning in high schools, non-natives originating from less developed inland regions aim to earn a diploma from a top domestic university based on standardized test scores. After obtaining that degree, they compete with natives to earn a highly sought-after position as a journalist in the *Xinmin Evening News*, a newspaper that, by the time of my interview had enjoyed the largest readership in the city for decades. To natives, this position is a good and comfortable career destination; however, according to my interviewee, it is a mere start for non-natives. For a better and more secure future in Shanghai, they continued to push themselves further to acquire managerial and editorial positions.

The journalist's slight critique of her non-native coworkers' careerism aside, both recruitment and internal promotion appear to be merit-based, or at least they seem to be dissociated from one's status as a native. Although there is no way for me to measure whether non-natives are more qualified than their native Shanghairen counterparts in the newspaper's hiring and internal promotion process, she seemed embittered and expressed a sense of relative deprivation of privilege, which was once associated with a Shanghai *hukou*.

Another sector that has experienced this shift in hiring practices is the once rigidly *hukou*-based top-tier public schools. Dong, a sophomore at Fudan, a nationally top-ranked university in Shanghai at the time of our 2013 interview, and a graduate from the prestigious high school affiliated with the university, reflected on his experience with his high school science teachers:

> None of my high school teachers are [native] Shanghairen. Not to mention Shanghai dialect, they don't even speak proper Putonghua! Some of them have such a heavy accent; for example, my math teacher is from Henan Province and holds a master's degree from Fudan University. It took my classmates and me a good month to distinguish "*suo yi shuo*" [therefore] and "*shuo yi shuo*" [let's say] in his lectures.

When I expressed my surprise about the inadequacy of his former teacher's Putonghua fluency, since there is a mandatory language test for a teaching certificate, Dong stressed that in terms of academic credentials, his math teacher was of the top rank, so language skills was probably overlooked in the hiring process. This example shows the emphasis on merit: besides the applicant's *hukou* status, even the national standard language requirements can be ignored as well.

The example of the math teacher also shows that a grey area exists in Shanghai's job market. Instead of automatically excluding people without a Shanghai *hukou*, employers have the flexibility to bypass national or municipal regulations in their recruitment of the best and brightest in the country. The existence of this grey area is likely due to the labor shortage at the professional level in public services brought on by the rapid increase of the urban population. Besides education in the example above, the healthcare sector has experienced a similar transition. Le, a nurse who works in the Pediatric Hematology and Oncology Department at the Shanghai Children's Medical Center, explains the high percentage of non-native medical doctors employed there:

> The chance for native Shanghairen medical school graduates to obtain a job in AAA [*san jia*][23] top-rank hospitals such as ours is slim because we want to recruit those with more experience or having studied abroad [regardless of *hukou*]. I can safely say in AAA hospitals in general, non-natives account for 70 percent among medical doctors.

The competitive job market at the children's medical center is another example of how little Shanghai *hukou* status matters. The above cases in mass media, the public school system, and in hospitals demonstrate that in Shanghai today, with the *hukou* barrier in the hiring process eliminated, highly educated and hardworking non-natives appear to enjoy a better chance of integration into the workplace, and thus upward social mobility.

At the same time, my native Shanghairen interviewees are keenly aware of the boundaries between native Shanghairen and highly educated migrants, likely due to the lack of Shanghai dialect proficiency in the latter group. Their descriptions of the diversity of workplaces contain a hint of disappointment and surprise that the state-owned sectors, which are known to practice local protectionism, operate now just like the private sector. I argue it is likely the very fact of being state-owned that requires those organizations to comply their hiring process with the municipal government's recent *hukou* reforms, as well as to compete with the private sector for talents from across the country. Thus, native Shanghairen no longer enjoy job allocation or promotion as it was under the planned economy, which was largely based on *hukou* and seniority, if not membership of the Communist Party.

The private sector in Shanghai, reborn in the economic reform era that began in the early 1980s, has also experienced increased participation by non-natives, as both entrepreneurs and employees. Yingli, a native Shanghairen in her early 30s who worked as a sales aide in a heavy machinery company at the time of our 2013 interview, recounted the higher-up personnel at her workplace:

> The head of our sales department is from Zhejiang Province. The big boss of the company is her uncle twice removed, and her husband, also a non-native, has his own business. They are senior level white collars, if not higher.

In her eyes, her bosses, being non-natives, are doing much better than native Shanghairen like herself. Also better off are her non-native coworkers:

> Our sales representatives need to have an engineering background and willingness to travel. They are earning good money. With their high commission rate, they were all able to purchase housing in Shanghai. They got married in Shanghai, and now have children. Really, they are better off than us. Look at their nice cars!

It is apparent at her workplace that *hukou* is irrelevant to one's employment opportunities or material success. Being a native Shanghairen, Yingli seemed pleased with her office job because, since she had no engineering background, she did not see herself becoming a successful sales representative in the company. The sales aide position she preferred allowed more time with her young daughter.

The shift from hiring practices based on *hukou* or other ascribed status, such as family political background, to a merit-based job market has contributed to Shanghai's prosperity and development into a global city. These upwardly mobile non-natives' educational credentials, career achievements, and incomes appear to grant them membership to a privileged, mixed-origin community in Shanghai. Native Shanghairen, meanwhile, remain wary of these recent migrants and the change they have brought. In native Shanghairen's reflections about their non-native colleagues, the fact of their non-nativeness is clearly marked out, even when complimenting their merits, qualifications, or work ethics. Thus, the native/non-native distinction remains vividly present. Despite the fact that more and more non-native professionals occupy positions at managerial levels and above, their non-nativeness still associates them with the derogatory term, Waidiren. This means changed practices in the workplace have not led to a smooth integration into Shanghai's social life for many highly educated and wealthy non-natives, as I will show next.

SOCIAL CIRCLES

With such a large-scale influx of internal migrants, achieving full-scale social integration into Shanghai's social life in more than twenty years is likely to be wishful thinking, given how diverse the groups of both natives and non-natives are. Indeed, while most of my fifty native Shanghairen interviewees reflected that through school, work, or simply by being neighbors, they have an increasing number of non-native friends, boundaries persist. First, there is a distinction based on education and social class. Even without that, however, proficiency in the Shanghai dialect and its associated cultural capital remain the ultimate barrier for meaningful inclusion.

For the younger generation, those who grew up in the 1990s and especially those who grew up in the early 2000s, the presence of highly educated non-natives was common in schools and workplaces. There is a general trend of friendship between natives and non-natives based on shared lifestyle and experiences. *Hukou* status and Shanghai dialect proficiency appear to matter little. For example, Dong, a native Shanghairen born in 1996 studying at Fudan University at the time of our 2013 interview, described his circle of friends to me:

> As long as we have shared experience and memories, I will make friends with
> them. I have a good friend since high school that is a non-native and doesn't

speak the Shanghai dialect. We play soccer together and are now enrolled in the same university.

Since Dong's non-native friend attended the same top-rank public high school, I can safely predict that the friend's parents belong to the group of state-sponsored non-natives, who are either highly educated or wealthy and have acquired Shanghai *hukou*. Only with Shanghai *hukou* can non-natives send their children to public high schools, because it is beyond the free nine-year mandatory education that local governments need to provide for internal migrants' children, regardless of their *hukou* status. In this case, the friendship between Dong and his non-native friend is likely based on the similar socioeconomic backgrounds of their families, their shared interests in sports, and shared experience during high school.

Another example of friendship developed through education is Jin, who is more than fifteen years Dong's senior. She worked for the Bank of East Asia and was enrolled in an MBA program at the China Europe International Business School[24] at the time of our interview. She regarded those who only make friends with native Shanghairen as narrow-minded:

> I don't mind making friends with non-natives. We are all Chinese, as long as you are a nice person [then we can be friends]. I am enrolled in an MBA program, and many of my classmates are non-natives. They are all brilliant people. I am not that kind of narrow-minded person who only make friends with [native] Shanghairen.

The non-natives in her narrative are certainly highly educated, resourceful, and likely belong to the upper middle class. The similar socioeconomic background and shared graduate school experience, which includes half-a-year studying in Paris and traveling around Europe together, brought Jin and her non-native classmates close. Her inclusive friendship circle is not limited by others' *hukou* status or birthplace but anchored on socioeconomic status, educational credentials, and professional experience.

Dong's and Jin's stories exemplify how friendship between natives and non-natives formed in elite educational settings. Yan, a teacher at a private elementary school in her late thirties at the time of our 2013 interview, remarked to me, "[t]here are more and more non-natives living in Shanghai. About half of my friends now are non-natives." She regarded this transition as an inevitable consequence of demographic changes in the city over the last two decades rather than a preference based on social class or shared exclusive experience. The sheer number of non-natives among Shanghai's population as the reason for integration makes intuitive sense. However, I still characterize this pattern as transitional, because of the observed reactionary self-segregation in non-natives' social circles.

At a time when more and more natives are making friends with non-native classmates, coworkers, or the parents of their children's classmates, Chen, who works at a research institute housed in Shanghai Normal University, shared her observation of her non-native coworkers' formation of their own social circles:

> Those just relocated to Shanghai for work are very eager to make friends through the Internet. As soon as they find someone from the same hometown, they call each other every day and have meals every day! I couldn't imagine such frequency with anyone except for one's boyfriend or husband.

Chen, a lifelong Shanghairen who was in her early thirties at the time of our interview, could not understand this kind of social networking that is developed between non-natives solely based on shared home origins, "How could you call those friends? You just have meals together, without *any* connection or understanding at a deeper level. Maybe it is because they are lonely."

Besides this loneliness factor Chen alluded to, non-natives coming to the city for work do not have a ready platform, such as a college campus, to jumpstart their social life. In an effort to build their own social circle outside of the native Shanghairen community, they seek people from their own hometown to form social circles. On the one hand, Chen's observation affirms earlier research on the new generation of urban migrants that hometown-based bonds remain central to non-natives' social networks;[25] on the other hand, Shanghai is China's global city, and as such attracts highly educated Chinese with experience overseas, a group referred to as *Haigui* (returnee from overseas).[26] Chen elaborates on the nuances within the non-native community from her observations:

> One kind is that they originate from [less developed] inland provinces, having studied abroad, and now come to Shanghai to work. And the other kind is a purely home-region-based network, such as from Anhui [province] or from Hubei [province]. Neither group would hang out with [us] native Shanghairen.

Unlike those teenage children of non-native Shanghairen whom Dong went to high school and formed friendships with, Chen's non-native colleagues, with different life experience from hers, form separate social circles.

In Chen's eyes, the social circle non-natives cultivate is intentionally with other non-natives. Kerry's observation of nuanced boundaries at the HSBC (China)'s headquarters in Shanghai echoed Chen's:

> It is fairly segregated in my office. Outside of the native Shanghairen circle, there is the Waidiren who have never been abroad, and Waidiren who studied

overseas, and the third non-native group is 100% foreigners. They don't hang out across those lines.

Kerry's observation illustrates that in a foreign bank, social circle formation follows a similar segregated pattern as in a research institute housed on a public university campus. Meritocratic hiring processes do not necessarily mean a full integration at the social level in any workplace. Shared life experience is the apparent culprit, but linguistic differences also play a role.

In my follow-up research in 2017 with non-natives, the language spoken at workplaces stands out as a major contributor to highly educated non-natives' sense of alienation. It is reportedly not felt as discrimination but rather as an invisible barrier to forming meaningful relationships. Lin describes her reaction to such experiences resulted in all her friends being fellow non-natives:

> If you want to build personal connection outside of work, to feel close and inti-mate [with native Shanghairen], the Shanghai dialect is the language to use. It instantly feels different if you can speak the Shanghai dialect or get the joke in the Shanghai dialect when encountering a native Shanghairen.

However, she doesn't speak the dialect and can only observe such closeness from the outside. In the next chapter, I will elaborate more on non-natives' reactionary self-preservation in forming their social circles in Shanghai. The triangulation of experiences and observations from both natives and non-natives demonstrates how social segregation is mutually maintained and feeds into exclusion. With the diminishing relevance of *hukou*, shared socio-economic status and educational experience bring more social integration between natives and non-natives. However, home origin and the persistent language barrier continue to maintain and reproduce mutual exclusion, with the latter more readily identified by non-natives, but often overlooked by bilingual or trilingual native Shanghairen.

INTERMARRIAGES

The gradual and selective integration taking place in native Shanghairen's social circles runs parallel to recent changes in marriage patterns. A quick tally of the marriage status of my fifty native Shanghairen interviewees in 2013 shows that in comparison to the generation in their fifties and sixties, the generation in their thirties and forties shows a higher percentage of union between natives and non-natives. At the time of the interviews, of the fifty, five of my interviewees were still in college and below the legal marriage age,[27] and eight are in their thirties or forties but still single. The remaining thirty-seven interviewees were all married. Six are of 55 or older in age. Of those in their thirties and forties, sixteen are married to natives, while fifteen to non-natives. Marriage status was not one of the criteria of my research subject recruitment, and this snapshot supplements the data from the Shanghai Civil Affairs Bureau, where marriage licenses are issued. Of the 147,820 couples married in 2013, 55,373 are of union between a native Shanghairen and a non-native, accounting for more than 37 percent. According to a report in the *Xinmin Evening News* on February 28, 2014, titled "Shanghai has the highest percentage of native and non-native unions across the country with men's average first marriage age at 34," the intermarriage rate in 2013 was 10 percent higher than it was in 2012.[28]

We can interpret this increasing rate of intermarriage between natives and non-natives as a deepening of social integration. Furthermore, unions of this kind might lead to the decline of prejudice against non-natives in the future, even though observations so far are at the individual level and hard to generalize. Yu, in her early thirties when we spoke in 2013, explained to me how her opinion changed after marrying a non-native, a graduate school classmate, from neighboring Zhejiang province:

> Years ago, I would comment on some uncivilized behavior of a native Shanghairen by saying something like, "What the hell, are you a Waidiren?" I wouldn't say it now. It used to be very common that whenever something uncivilized, or bizarre happened, native Shanghairen would attribute it to Waidiren. It's very likely that because my husband is a Waidiren, my opinion has changed. Also, I am more open to people from elsewhere in general.

Yu's self-reflection illustrates how years of college and office life, living and working side by side with non-natives, and later marriage to a non-native, have changed her attitude toward non-natives as a group. However, what I have noticed is when an individual non-native has been accepted and absorbed into native Shanghairen's families and social circles, such integration does not necessarily extend beyond that native Shanghairen family and close friend's network.

Yin, a native Shanghairen who has worked her entire professional life in a state-controlled art institute that once followed a rigid *hukou*-based hiring process, described to me how language always marks out non-natives and makes social interaction less smooth:

> It is very common to see intermarriage, for example a few of my best female friends married non-natives. And they [need to] speak Putonghua at home. Sometimes when we have a dinner party, I need to converse with them in Putonghua, otherwise their husbands can't understand.

On the one hand, her observation exemplifies the increase in native and non-native unions and the gradual social integration of non-natives through marriage; on the other hand, the need to speak Putonghua to accommodate non-natives made Yin uncomfortable and created a social distance between her and her friends. For her, the required linguistic accommodation makes a friendly setting less intimate and reinforces the outsider status of her friend's spouse. As we will see in the next chapter, the linguistic insider-outsider dichotomy makes non-natives feel just as awkward and alienated as native Shanghairen do, if not more so.

Discomfort and prejudice based on linguistic differences are never the full story. In the case of Shanghai and the Shanghai dialect, it is tainted by wealth and social class, as Yin went on to say:

> As far as I know, most intermarried couples live in/moved into the native Shanghairen's place. That's why I always say the intention of non-natives marrying native Shanghairen is suspicious. Those closely involved cannot see as clearly as those outside.

These comments should be understood in the context of the practice of work units providing state-owned housing only to their employees with Shanghai *hukou* in the pre-economic reform era. Units were later sold at a heavily subsidized rate to the sitting tenants in the early years of the reforms. Taking into consideration the skyrocketing housing prices in Shanghai, Yin suspected that many non-natives married native Shanghairen more out of material concerns, such as the availability of free or cheap housing, than out of love. This suspicion judging said non-natives' character readily communicates discrimination.

Such view is more prevalent among the older native Shanghairen who often hold stronger prejudice against non-natives. These opinions are difficult to change, and the process is slow. For example, Hui, who moved to Shanghai after college in Harbin, a provincial capital in northeastern China, obtained her Shanghai *hukou* through employment, and later married a native Shanghairen. She told me about the earlier opposition of the union from her native Shanghairen husband's family:

> Some native Shanghairen families really discriminate against non-natives. [Before we got married] my father-in-law . . . said to [my husband], "It needs to be a native Shanghairen girl! Why the hell do you want a Waidiren?" He didn't say it in front of me, but my careless husband slipped it out years later that his parents initially objected. . . . Even though my father-in-law said so back then, he didn't interfere with our relationship when my husband insisted on marrying me, or made life difficult for me after we got married. In their mind, they

categorically don't accept a Waidiren as their daughter-in-law, but after the fact, they couldn't find much in me to discriminate against, rather, have discovered how capable a person I am.

Hui's experience is not unique among non-natives who try to gain acceptance in the Shanghairen community. Years into her marriage, Hui appears to have gained her in-laws' acceptance, at least in part due to the fact that she is so professionally successful that her employer sought and acquired Shanghai *hukou* for her, on top of her other qualities. Such favorable evaluation, however, is not extended to other Waidiren whom Hui's in-laws do not know personally.

Increasing integration in the professional world and in social circles, as well as increasing intermarriage, are positive steps toward social integration for highly educated non-natives in Shanghai. Once a crucial criterion for defining who is a Shanghairen, Shanghai *hukou* has diminished in significance for boundary keeping. In its place, socioeconomic status plays an ever more important role for rights and entitlement, sanctioned by the municipal government through the granting of *hukou* status and its second-tier cousin, Shanghai Resident Permit to qualified non-natives. Despite the institutional inclusion and accommodation, there remains persistent criterion that native Shanghairen use to judge non-natives or to decide to which degree they are welcomed into the native Shanghairen community: Shanghai dialect proficiency.

An unintended consequence of the integration of non-natives into the native Shanghairen community is the decline of exclusive linguistic space for the Shanghai dialect. However, this does not mean that the Shanghai dialect has lost its significance for Shanghairen identity and its symbolic capital of distinction. As Kathryn Woolard observes in the linguistic accommodation practiced by bilingual Catalonians in Barcelona to Castilian-speaking migrants, the codeswitch means "the denial of access to the full membership in the solidary local group; those who cannot penetrate the language barrier cannot penetrate group boundaries."[29] In a case closer home, Shaohua Zhan concludes from his study of inner Mongolian migrants' social integration in Beijing that the separation of social circles and identity-based exclusion are the two mechanisms used to maintain social boundaries.[30] The element missing in Zhan's study about social exclusion is the one preeminent in the case of Shanghai: language. In northern China, various mutually intelligible Mandarin dialects are spoken, while the Shanghai dialect is unintelligible to non-Wu Chinese speakers. Shanghai dialect proficiency now performs the exclusive function to safeguard the "genuine" Shanghairen identity and maintain the boundary, when legal status, socioeconomic status, or property rights no longer suffice. In the next section, I will explore the officially created and endorsed category of New Shanghairen and its connection to Shanghai dialect proficiency.

WHO IS A (NEW) SHANGHAIREN?

In the same period that Shanghai *hukou* lost its aura of exclusivity, a new category, New Shanghairen, was invented and promoted by the Shanghai Municipal Government.[31] It is used in government documents and state-controlled mass media to differentiate the highly educated, Shanghai *hukou* holding non-natives from their poorer and less-educated counterparts. For Bourdieu, struggles over classification of regional identity, which is based on birthplace or proficiency of the vernacular, is the struggle for power to legitimate grouping and ungrouping.[32] Official categorization notwithstanding, native Shanghairen evaluate non-natives' level of assimilation through their Shanghai dialect proficiency, and then decide whether to grant them insider membership as Shanghairen. Based on data I have collected through in-depth interviews, a near consensus among native Shanghairen is that Shanghai dialect proficiency is an essential part of Shanghairen identity. To become a genuine Shanghairen, on top of Shanghai *hukou* status, residential property ownership, or long-term residency, non-natives must master the dialect.

In this process of re-classification, millions of rural-urban migrant workers are excluded due to their lack of the legal claim to the city represented by a Shanghai *hukou*. Many of them are street venders, barbers, locksmiths, or seamstresses (e.g., the seamstress who speaks fluent Shanghai dialect in chapter 2), who rely heavily on neighborhood business, and thus have economic incentives to learn the Shanghai dialect. Indeed, many of them have obtained working knowledge of it and are able to conduct simple conversations with native Shanghairen customers. However, because of their lack of a Shanghai *hukou* and their low socioeconomic status, they are not included in the New Shanghairen category in either the official rhetoric or in the minds of native Shanghairen. In contrast, highly educated non-natives with Shanghai *hukou* appear to care little about dialect acquisition, evidently from interviews with both natives and non-natives. Such dismissal fuels the negative perceptions native Shanghairen have about non-natives and generates lasting unease and contentions.

Dialect Acquisition

Shanghairen identity now relies to a great extent on a shared linguistic culture. Decades of economic reforms and urban redevelopments have resulted in economic inequality, dispersed residential communities, and varied lifestyles among native Shanghairen themselves. In John Gumperz and Jenny Cook-Gumperz's work about language and identity, they highlight that group members' shared culture does not necessarily rely on residence in proximity or being socioeconomically homogenous.[33] It is also important to remember that those who identify as genuine Shanghairen are themselves second- or third-generation migrants from other parts of the country. Thus, local rootedness is less relevant to the social identity of Shanghairen than language and shared cultural values. A common understanding among sociolinguists is that language displays and communicates social identities through self-representation.[34] Besides using Shanghai dialect proficiency to flaunt their own local identity, my native Shanghairen interviewees also readily judge non-natives' linguistic practices, in relation to their claim to any sort of Shanghairen identity.

Language has historically played an important role in social exclusion and discrimination in Shanghai. Emily Honig notes the prejudice held against Subei people in Shanghai, who were impoverished refugees fleeing war and famine north of the Yangtze River in the early twentieth century.[35] Although low socioeconomic status and poor education were the basis of discrimination, their distinctive accent when speaking the Shanghai dialect singled them out and resulted in overt discrimination and social exclusion. To distinguish them from other internal migrants, a derogatory Shanghai dialect term was born, "*gangbo nin*" (*Jiangbei ren*, people from north of the Yangtze River). The status of a language is closely related to the status of its speakers. As Nancy Dorian argues, if the people who speak a language have little power and low prestige, their language is unlikely to be well thought of, and vice versa.[36] Viewed through this lens, the opinion of Subei people's accented Shanghai dialect roots in the discrimination of their poor origin and lower social status.

Similar to how Subei people in the early twentieth century were marked out, the first-generation migrants in the early decades of the economic reform era, primarily of rural origin, are called in the Shanghai dialect, in a manner seemingly factual but nevertheless derogatory, *xiawo nin* (*xiangxia ren*, country bumpkin). Later, to include the more recent urban migrants of various origins and socioeconomic backgrounds, Shanghairen coined the equally derogatory *nwadi nin* (Waidiren). Both terms denote class as well as regional distinctions, despite the fact that many of the latter group, who have acquired Shanghai *hukou* through academic credentials or wealth, and are of a higher socioeconomic status than many native Shanghairen—as shown earlier in this chapter and will be explored further in the next chapter. The fact that native Shanghairen group are not socioeconomically homogeneous adds another layer to the nuanced and ambivalent relationship between a speaker's social position and their language. The association between the Shanghai dialect and Shanghairen identity is influenced by the alternative language ideology. That is, despite the lower status of the Shanghai dialect when compared to Putonghua nationally, the local dialect is still able to assert symbolic power of prestige and exclusivity, owing to its long history as the *lingua franca* of a cosmopolitan metropolis.

The self-aggrandized native Shanghairen identity has faced challenges before the officially endorsed classification, New Shanghairen. Jennifer Rudolph and Hanchao Lu discovered in late 2000s that a new category, quasi-Shanghainese (*zhun* Shanghairen) was invented and adopted by non-natives who successfully settled down and adapted to urban living in Shanghai to address themselves.[37] However, native Shanghairen in my research usually dismiss such self-identification of non-natives. They stress the importance of behavioral change for non-natives to qualify as Shanghairen, a.k.a. acquisition of the Shanghai dialect, which their own parents or grandparents did voluntarily as migrants to Shanghai in the early twentieth century. By tacitly invoking their family's migration history, they stress the significance of purposeful adherence to local linguistic culture and norms, which they find lacking among recent highly educated migrants.

Native Shanghairen who hold a personal and professional stake in preserving the Shanghai dialect often express a strong association between Shanghairen identity and dialect proficiency. Qian Chen, a famous Huaji Xi performer (Shanghai vernacular theater) in his early fifties and at the time of the interview the vice president of the Shanghai Huaji Xi Troupe, spoke fervently about the voluntary cultural assimilation of earlier migrants, such as his own family, when I asked about the definition of New Shanghairen in relation to the recent waves of internal migrants to Shanghai:

> We are not true Shanghairen either! I was born in Shanghai, but my parents and my paternal grandparents came from the adjacent Zhejiang Province. We have undergone the transition from New Shanghairen to Old Shanghairen. It is the same.

He invoked his family's migration history to stress that Shanghai dialect acquisition is a rite of passage to become a Shanghairen. Therefore, the new generation of migrants who are unwilling to learn and speak the Shanghai dialect cannot qualify. Adding the prefix old or new serves little purpose. However, the linguistic environment in Shanghai now is very different from that of the early twentieth century. When Qian Chen's grandparents and parents migrated to Shanghai, the national language, Guoyu, was rarely spoken, and almost non-existent, even in formal settings or schools. Instead, the Shanghai dialect was the *lingua franca* in the city.

For motivation to learn the dialect, Qian focuses on love for or emotional attachment to the city rather than the pragmatism of earlier migrants, who acquired the dialect to get by or to find work. According to Qian, adopting the Shanghai dialect is both a requirement and a demonstration of Shanghairen identity: "Being a Shanghairen, you should love your city, and love your mother tongue!" In his opinion, to be recognized as Shanghairen, migrants need to shed their hometown affiliations and wholeheartedly embrace the dialect as adopted mother language. Otherwise, one cannot truly belong. To understand Qian's frustration, one must understand that Huaji Xi performances rely on the audience's Shanghai dialect proficiency. Qian bears witness not only to the decline of dialect proficiency but also to his own shrinking audience, the lifeblood of his art.

Echoing Qian Chen, another native Shanghairen dialect preservation activist, Wu Wei completely rejected the official New Shanghairen category: "First and foremost, if that person doesn't know how to speak the Shanghai dialect, s/he is not a Shanghairen, regardless of the 'New' prefix, or *hukou*." His assertion places Shanghai dialect proficiency above *hukou* status, and likely also above the migrants' long-term residency in Shanghai, not to mention socioeconomic status. To him, linguistic competence is the sole determinant of genuine Shanghairen identity.

Ordinary native Shanghairen view the linkage between Shanghairen identity and Shanghai dialect proficiency with more nuance than preservation activists. Zhejun, a native Shanghairen in his mid-thirties and a junior faculty member in STEM at a top university in Shanghai, shared his opinion in our 2013 interview:

> Firstly, whoever can speak the Shanghai dialect is definitely a Shanghairen. I mean whoever can speak accent-free Shanghai dialect: you can identify that person as a genuine Shanghairen. However, it is not necessarily true that those who are unable to speak the dialect are Waidiren. . . . I regard those with Shanghai *hukou*, living in Shanghai for years and with no intention for leaving Shanghai as Shanghairen. . . . But, at the level of acceptance, I only recognize those able to speak the Shanghai dialect. I would regard them as Shanghairen from head to toe. Otherwise, the recognition stops at the surface. In the native Shanghairen circle, if you speak Putonghua, it would still be very difficult, if not impossible, for us to accept you as a Shanghairen.

His ambivalence is representative of other native Shanghairen I interviewed. They do not have a straightforward conceptualization of Shanghairen identity; rather, their opinions vary at the group and individual levels and based on abstract or concrete criteria. For example, Zhejun holds that accent-free

Shanghai dialect competence, which is very difficult for non-natives to acquire, guarantees insider membership recognized by native Shanghairen. But if one were to break down Shanghairen identity into more concrete criteria, such as legal status, length of residency, and the intention and financial capacity to stay, it is only sensible to regard those non-natives as Shanghairen. However, at the end of the day, when Zhejun imagined encountering a non-speaker at a social gathering, the invisible barrier remained acutely present in his mind.

My native Shanghairen interviewees usually view the effort that non-natives put into learning and practicing the Shanghai dialect in a favorable light. Cheng, for example, is the manager of the customer service department of a state-controlled performing arts venue. While his employees are predominantly native Shanghairen, he highlighted the experience of a non-native employee for me:

> A manager in our security department is from Shandong province. He speaks very good Shanghai dialect, and is well integrated into our society. However, his level of fluency is rare.

Cheng acknowledged that his employee's Shanghai dialect proficiency stood in stark contrast to most non-natives. Other interviewees, whether they worked in state-owned or foreign companies, echoed his observation that in general their highly educated non-native colleagues held a somewhat indifferent if not negative attitude toward the Shanghai dialect. I will delve into the reasons for non-natives' language attitude and practices in the next chapter and allow non-natives to defend themselves.

It remains that the crucial factor for local identity is determined by embodied linguistic capital. Regardless of achieved legal and socioeconomic status, a part of Shanghairen identity is forever elusive without the capability to converse in the Shanghai dialect. Only those who truly desire Shanghairen identity can achieve this linguistic capital. As Zhu Zhenmiao, another dialect preservation activist says:

> I regard those enthusiastically learning the Shanghai dialect as Shanghairen, without a doubt, even if they are not fluent, and came to the city only a few years before. Their active learning demonstrates his/her identification with the local culture.

According to his interpretation, non-natives' attitude toward learning the dialect is more important than fluency in speaking it. Their enthusiasm connects these particular non-natives to the whole set of cultural values and ways of thinking shared by native Shanghairen. At the same time, Zhu Zhenmiao rejects both institutional criteria of moral ownership and *hukou*-based legal recognition:

> Conversely, even if you were born in Shanghai and lived here your whole life, without stepping foot outside of the city boundary even once, as long as you think of the Shanghai dialect as backward and useless, and urge your child to speak Putonghua, I don't count you as a Shanghairen.

He excludes anyone, even native-born Shanghairen, who devalue the local linguistic culture. This tribalistic line of thinking echoes where Peng, a native Shanghairen non-activist stood on this issue: "Whoever speaks the Shanghai dialect is [part of the Shanghairen] family." Safe to say, the opposite also holds true in his mind.

To sum up, tensions between dialect proficiency and Shanghairen identity, new or not, remain beyond the formal criteria of legal or socioeconomic status. The spectrum of acceptance and the linkage between Shanghai dialect proficiency and Shanghairen identity indicates that as long as non-natives are willing to learn the dialect, even if they cannot attain accent-free fluency, native Shanghairen acknowledge that effort and respect it. From their own narratives, an Us vs. Them dichotomy is still apparent, in the sense that *they* should speak *our* language if they want to be welcomed in *our* city. This puts more emphasis on hospitality rather than a willingness to share ownership. As Jacques Derrida makes explicit, hospitality requires one to be the "master" of the house, city, country, or nation.[38] Hence, the expectation for linguistic assimilation reestablishes the ownership of the host, and to a certain degree, the owner's control of the people who are being hosted. Native Shanghairen understand themselves as "moral" owners,[39] who have the right to determine the language spoken "at home." At an institutional level, however, a different understanding emerges. Not only does the central state determine the language spoken but also since a selected group of non-natives are granted Shanghai *hukou*, the state grants them legal right to share ownership of the city. Furthermore, the state supports, and continuously encourages non-natives to speak Putonghua instead of the Shanghai dialect. Disjunctions between moral, legal, and institutional forms of integration in the city contribute to the ambiguity surrounding the association between dialect competence and acceptance as Shanghairen. This in turn engenders more conflicts around the languages spoken in Shanghai.

Language Contention in Public

The lack of Shanghai dialect proficiency among non-natives generates discomfort and annoyance among native Shanghairen, and these emotions even spill over to include native Shanghairen who opt to speak Putonghua in public. In this section, I focus on native Shanghairen's experience of informal social encounters with non-natives with little to no knowledge of the Shanghai dialect or fellow natives who can speak it, but choose not to. The reaction toward non-natives' linguistic practice is similar to what Woolard observed in 1980s in Barcelona among Catalans, who viewed migrants who spoke only Castilian as adversaries, and even as agents of the oppressive state.[40] In the telling of native Shanghairen, non-natives backed by state language policies, do not allow the former to speak the Shanghai dialect in public. This infringes on the natives' linguistic right to the city, undermines the conversion of linguistic capital into social and symbolic capital in public, and threatens to wipe the Shanghai dialect from the city's auditory landscape altogether. Over such encounters with non-speakers, native Shanghairen feel pressured to switch to Putonghua, and at the same time, non-natives feel alienated in a linguistic environment which still values the Shanghai dialect. The other kind of linguistic conflict happens between native Shanghairen themselves, when those who are fluent in the dialect opt not to speak it, exemplified by a confrontational scene I observed in a Shanghai subway car.

Since the Shanghai dialect and Putonghua belong to two different linguistic families, my bilingual native Shanghairen interviewees uniformly reported that effort is required to switch between the two or "switch brains" as some put it, which linguists suggest is a type of language ideological construct. Applying such ideology, native Shanghairen claim that it is out of convenience that they prefer to speak the dialect when the intended audience is a fellow native. In such cases, my interviewees reported that non-natives within earshot would interpret this language choice as a form of social exclusion and insist that native Shanghairen communicate in Putonghua. My interviewees in turn regarded the request as an intrusion, since they never intended to include any nearby non-natives in the private conversation to start with.

Using the analogy of a host accommodating guests, Peng, a native Shanghairen graphic designer in his early forties quoted earlier in this chapter, found non-natives' attitudes and practices disrespectful, and to a certain extent suggested that it was an attempt by the guest to take over the host's position:

> Their attitude is "I don't understand [the Shanghai dialect], so no one is allowed to speak it when I am around, even though the communication is between native Shanghairen and I am not part of it."

Indeed, to non-natives, the unintelligibility of the Shanghai dialect is a clear sign they are being excluded from a conversation. But to native Shanghairen, like Peng, such view by non-natives is discriminatory against the Shanghai dialect:

> They think the Shanghai dialect is backwards, not decent, so that they don't *need* to learn it, and they don't *want* to learn it.[41] They will be happy when the Shanghai dialect is eliminated.

Peng's opinion shows the linguistic deprivation and oppression he felt. The language contention here is tricky to arbitrate because both parties feel vulnerable and oppressed. Unlike in other studies of linguistic discrimination and injustice experienced by minority groups, in Peng's telling, the language being discriminated against is supposed to be dominant and prestigious locally but with inferior, minority status nationally. The conflict is the result of two competing language ideologies that index Putonghua and the Shanghai dialect in opposite order. Though we should take with a grain of salt Peng's opinion of non-natives' intention or attitudes toward the death of the Shanghai dialect, his perception and the sense of hurt, degradation, and vulnerability need to be registered.

Most native Shanghairen interviewees, like Peng, spoke about the desire for a mutually respected boundary in their shared linguistic space. However, as the social integration of natives and non-natives intensifies, a linguistically segregated social space becomes ever difficult to create or to maintain. Such unsatisfied desire can easily appear outright xenophobic as Peng suggested offhandedly:

> *Ru Xiang Sui Su* (the equivalent of the Western idiom, "When in Rome, do as the Romans do"). If they don't want to learn, if they reject the Shanghai dialect, then please go home. Shanghai does not welcome you!

The hostile nature of his comment and attitude toward non-natives who refuse to learn the Shanghai dialect is certainly reactionary; that natives like him are experiencing the endangerment of their local dialect and have no political or social means available to slow or revert the top-down measures. Thus, non-speakers as an abstract group unavoidably become the target of retribution. In this case, both natives and non-natives are the aggressors and victims, in the Bourdieusian sense, of symbolic violence that stems from the state's overarching sociolinguistic structure and results in both parties feeling inferior and violated.

My investigation of the linguistic contentions between natives and non-natives reveals that Shanghai dialect incompetence among non-natives generates and escalates conflicts, though due to no fault of their own. According to Gumperz, intergroup conflicts arise when interactions normally seen as routine, in this case speaking the dialect to strangers, are repeatedly met with unforeseen communication problems.[42] These conflicts do not go away with the intensity and frequency of encounters; rather, every new isolated encounter adds to the misunderstanding and frustration. Therefore, growing social integration does not necessarily erase boundaries between natives and non-natives. Instead, mutual misperceptions harden the distinction between natives and non-natives, despite occasional outlier cases.

The evidence discussed above is further compounded by my ethnographic observation in late 2013 and in summer 2017 in public spaces in Shanghai, such as subway stations or retail settings, , where all conversations strangers initiated with me were in Putonghua. As soon as they heard a trace of my Shanghai dialect accent, native Shanghairen I met would immediately switch to the Shanghai dialect, with a slight smile and a knowing look, signaling closeness and trust shared among insiders. However, such shared insider status is impossible if native Shanghairen opt not to speak the dialect. As Zhenmiao stresses above, this would amount to a public repudiation of their Shanghairen identity.

In the afternoon of a warm fall day in 2013, I took the No.10 subway train heading downtown from Wujiaochang—a formerly industrial working-class neighborhood in northeastern Shanghai, newly revitalized as a shopping and residential area—I encountered the following scenario.

In the subway car, two boys were playing with each other close to the subway car door area, while most passengers were looking at their smartphones. The younger one was probably six or seven years old and the older one eight or nine. The younger child's mother looked to be in her late twenties or early thirties, tall and slender, fashionably dressed with long wavy hair and wearing make-up. The older child's mother wore no make-up, with loose-fitting clothes and her hair in a messy bun. The two mothers did not converse with each other but were both paying attention to the boys. It is very likely that the two boys got to know each other through school, and the two mothers became acquainted through their sons.

The boys were nudging each other and giggling. The older one was trying to teach some rules to the younger one, who protested loudly. The younger child's mother immediately grabbed her son by the arm and told him in a firm tone in Putonghua: "Lower your voice." The boy obeyed.

It is an example of the authority Putonghua holds that parents tend to discipline their children in it, as the embodied dominant language ideology dictates. That public teaching moment was not only an occasion for a mother to teach proper manners and civility to her son but also to demonstrate which language is proper in that given circumstance. Furthermore, she clearly associated good behavior in public with a correct language choice.

The fashionable mother whispered to her son, then asked the older boy in Putonghua: "You both are Shanghairen children, why don't you speak the dialect?" The older boy made a face and responded in Putonghua: "I don't like speaking the Shanghai dialect." With at least three pairs of eyes on him (four including mine), he retreated to lean against his mother, whose facial expression conveyed nothing except a little bit of "whatever."

The fashionable mother clearly used that question to show distinction, to communicate both her Shanghairen identity and also good parenting through teaching her son and his friend to respect their own linguistic heritage and thus to take pride in being native Shanghairen. She explicitly emphasized the linkage between Shanghai dialect competence, language choice, and Shanghairen identity. As Mikaela Marlow and Howard Giles argue from their study on Pidgin speaking in Hawai'i, those competent enough to navigate a multilingual setting maintain the highest social and symbolic power and perceive themselves to be legitimately positioned to evaluate and criticize others' language choices, and whether those choices violate linguistic norms associated with a particular identity.[43] In this subway scenario, the fashionable mother was publicly criticizing and policing the older boy.

I cannot be sure about the reason for the silence of the older boy's mother, but from her looking away, it was apparent that she was aware of the suggested exclusive linkage between Shanghai dialect competence and Shanghairen identity. She simply had no desire to confront the criticism. Her "avoidant response" is one of the typical ways to respond to language criticism as identified by Marlow and Giles.[44] Several possibilities could explain her non-response. For one, she may have married a non-native, making Putonghua the primary language at home, with her husband imposing the dominant language ideology on her and their son, similar to Bei's experience in the previous chapter. Or, being of a lower social class background, she believed in the association of speaking Putonghua and upward social mobility. The third possibility was she didn't care much about speaking the Shanghai dialect and had no interest in engaging in a public debate.

The fashionable mother did not stop there, she continued by suggesting that her son sing a nursery rhyme in the Shanghai dialect. The theme of this century-old song was laughing at, if not outright humiliating, non-natives. She started the first line, "*Xiangwo nin* (*xiangxia ren*, country bumpkin) coming to Shanghai," waiting for her son to join in. "Country bumpkin coming to Shanghai," he sang in a very low voice in the Shanghai dialect, eyeing the older boy. The older boy certainly knew the lyrics and understood their humiliating implication, so he protested, in Putonghua: "My mom is Shanghairen too!"

The century-old rhyme responded to the rural-to-urban migration that characterized Shanghai in the first half of the twentieth century. It was a time when quick linguistic assimilation held economic incentives, such as bringing more business to one's street-vending or being able to find a factory job. It was the time when the Shanghai dialect held a higher status than all the other languages in the city, and newcomers all aspired to learn it. At the time, internal migrants comprised more than 80 percent of the city's population.[45] As Emily Honig points out, in the case of impoverished migrants from the adjacent northern Jiangsu province (Subei), social discrimination against them was presented as language criticism of their distinctively accented Shanghai dialect; but at its core was their low socioeconomic status.[46] This derogatory rhyme, still popular today, thus hints at the general public's persistent association of Shanghai dialect proficiency with higher socioeconomic status and urban sophistication.

Although only eight or nine years old, the older boy already exhibited an understanding of such belief; hence, why he made the assertion that his mother was a Shanghairen in an attempt to defend her. His "aggressive response"[47] in confronting the fashionable mother in Putonghua furthermore indicates his conscious choice to use a language of authority to stress his point. What he appeared to try to convey was that his and his mother's Shanghairen identity was unquestionable, and which language to speak was up to them and none of others' business.

The fashionable mother pressed: "Then why you don't speak the dialect?" To which, he raised his voice in reply, "I don't want to!" and then turned to hide his face in his mother's embrace. The older boy's mother did not discipline her son for raising his voice in that instance, unlike what the fashionable mother did earlier. With a faint grin, the fashionable mother took it as a victory for her symbolic power when her young opponent retreated. She then continued the rhyme with her son: "Country bumpkin coming to Shanghai, doesn't know how to speak the Shanghai dialect," here, the son did not know the rest of the lyrics, so she finished for him: "yummy, yummy, stir-fry pickles." The whole time, the older boy's mother looked away without responding.

This wrestling of symbolic power using the children's competence and willingness to speak the Shanghai dialect was the fashionable mother's deployment of her linguistic capital, in the form of an intimidation, or worse, symbolic violence toward her opponent.[48] In response, the older boy's mother agreed to disagree. Most likely she assumed speaking Putonghua well would help her son attain higher socioeconomic status, while speaking the Shanghai dialect would provide little practical incentive other than the pride of being Shanghairen. It is an identity that she and her son took for granted, regardless of their linguistic practice. In contrast, the fashionable mother perceived Shanghai dialect competence as an indicator of urban sophistication, and consequently of Shanghairen identity. If, according to sociolinguists, languages are used to index social groups by displaying behavioral, aesthetic, affective, and moral contrasts between groups,[49] then the fashionable mother speaking the Shanghai dialect in this observation can be understood as a social performance of Shanghairen identity's symbolic power and the alternative language ideology fostered by the historical socioeconomic index of speakers and non-speakers.

Typically, highly educated middle-class natives comfortable and secure in their social position, tend to see themselves as capable of judging who counts as Shanghairen based on language choices. Such pride inevitably leads to the image of genuine Shanghairen, as arrogant, with a sense of superiority communicated by using the dialect even to non-speakers. Yue, a college senior originally from the adjacent Zhejiang province, was visibly agitated when answering my question about Shanghairen identity during our 2017 interview:

> Shanghairen often feel superior to others or self-aggrandize. It is fine if they are indigenous, but they are new as well. It was only because their parents or their grandparents moved to Shanghai, and they grew up in Shanghai. They identify as Shanghairen, and regard us as country bumpkins. But our parents are relatives! They just blatantly show superiority.

Her personal experience with her Shanghairen cousins clearly demonstrates the discriminatory undertone to the claim of Shanghairen identity as the opposite of "country bumpkin." And she rightfully challenges the claim of nativity, suggesting one's birthplace is not sufficient to declare a Shanghairen identity, at least not as a basis for discrimination. As we have seen, even within the native Shanghairen community, symbolic violence is mobilized against those who no longer speak the dialect.

CONCLUSION

Since the early 2000s, economic and household registration reforms have enabled and facilitated the increasing social integration of non-natives in Shanghai. Due to these reforms, we have seen a shift from a dual society largely based on an individual's *hukou* status to one based on a more nuanced criteria for stratification. I have shown that the earlier, overt exclusion and discrimination based on *hukou* status has since declined significantly in the workplace, in social circles, and in families—the three dimensions of social membership. However, the increasing social integration does not necessarily mitigate cultural differences. Rather, it sometimes backlashes by reducing linguistic space for the Shanghai dialect.

The disappearance of legal and social barriers between natives and non-natives has also created confusion about the criteria that define Shanghairen identity. The three pillars of this identity, *hukou*, urban residency, and Shanghai dialect proficiency, have been shaken by both internal and external forces. There is likely to be ever-increasing integration in the future, as new generations find the significance of *hukou* further diminished, and market forces become central to social resource allocation, in terms of obtaining previously *hukou*-based privileges such as education, health care, or housing. In addition, the younger generation, born and raised in Shanghai to non-native, native, or mixed parents, will mostly acquire Putonghua as their mother tongue. In the next chapter, I will show how highly educated non-natives navigate the treacherous terrain of the linguistic and social space in Shanghai and articulate their own identity in China's global city.

NOTES

1. 2018 Shanghai Statistical Yearbook. Table 2.1 Total Households, Population, Density of Registered Population and Life expectancy (1978–2017) http://tjj.sh.gov.cn/tjnj/nj18.htm?d1=2018tjnj/C0201.htm. Retrieved July 16, 2020.

2. Chan, Kam Wing. 1994. *Cities with Invisible Walls: Reinterpreting Urbanization in Post-1949 China.* Hong Kong&New York: Oxford University Press.

3. Alexander, Peter, and Anita Chan. 2004. "Does China Have an Apartheid Pass System?" *Journal of Ethnic and Migration Studies* 30 (4): 609–29.

4. Solinger, Dorothy J. 1995. "The Floating Population in the Cities: Chances for Assimilation?" In *Urban Spaces in Contemporary China: The Potential for Autonomy and Community in Post-Mao China*, edited by Deborah S. Davis, Richard Kraus, Barry Naughton, and Elizabeth Perry, 113–39. Cambridge: Cambridge University Press.

5. Wu, Xiaogang, and Donald J. Treiman. 2004. "The Household Registration System and Social Stratification in China: 1955–1996." *Demography* 41 (2): 363–84.

6. Wang, Fei-Ling. 2004. "Reformed Migration Control and New Targeted People: China's Hukou System in the 2000s." *The China Quarterly* 177 (March): 115–32.

7. Bourdieu, Pierre. 1987. *Distinction: A Social Critique of the Judgement of Taste.* Translated by Richard Nice. Cambridge, MA: Harvard University Press.

8. May, Stephen. 2011. *Language and Minority Rights.* New York: Routledge. P.134–6.

9. Turner, Bryan S. 1993. "Contemporary Problems in the Theory of Citizenship." In *Citizenship and Social Theory*, edited by Bryan S. Turner, 1–18. London & Thousand Oaks: SAGE Publications Ltd. P.2.

10. Lee, Ching Kwan. 2007. *Against the Law: Labor Protests in China's Rustbelt and Sunbelt.* Berkeley, CA: University of California Press.

11. Davis, Deborah S. 1999. "Self-Employment in Shanghai: A Research Note*." *The China Quarterly* 157 (March): 22–43. P.33.

12. Wang. "Reformed Migration Control," 115–32. P.120.

13. Feng, Wang, Xuejin Zuo, and Danching Ruan. 2002. "Rural Migrants in Shanghai: Living under the Shadow of Socialism1:" *International Migration Review* 36 (2): 520–45. P.529.

14. Shanghai Statistical Bureau. June 26, 2014. http://www.stats-sh.gov.cn/fxbg /201406/271085.html

15. Chan. *Cities with Invisible Walls,* P.144.

16. Wu, Xiaogang, and Yu Xie. 2003. "Does the Market Pay Off? Earnings Returns to Education in Urban China." *American Sociological Review* 68 (3): 425–42.

17. Solinger, Dorothy J. 1999. *Contesting Citizenship in Urban China: Peasant Migrants, the State, and the Logic of the Market.* Berkeley, University of California Press. P.14.

18. Wu, and Treiman. "The Household Registration System," 363–84. P.365.

19. Chan, Kam Wing, and Will Buckingham. 2008. "Is China Abolishing the Hukou System?." *The China Quarterly* 195 (September): 582–606. P.582.

20. Ren, Xuefei. 2011. *Building Globalization: Transnational Architecture Production in Urban China.* Chicago & London: University of Chicago Press. P.173.

21. Pearson, Margaret M. 1997. *China's New Business Elite: The Political Consequences of Economic Reform.* Berkeley, CA: University of California Press. P.3–7.

22. Founded in 1929 in Shanghai, it is the oldest daily newspaper still in operation in mainland China.

23. It is the top rank of hospitals in China, according to the ranking system developed by the State Council. For a total registered long-term population of 25 million, there are only 35 AAA hospitals, including specialist ones.

24. CEIBS was ranked No.1 in Asia and No.17 in the world for its full-time MBA program by Bloomberg BusinessWeek in 2014. At the time of the writing, it is ranked No.5 in the world by Financial Times in its Global MBA Ranking 2020. http://ran kings.ft.com/businessschoolrankings/ceibs. Retrieved July 18, 2020.

25. Liu, Ye, Zhigang Li, and Werner Breitung. 2012. "The Social Networks of New-Generation Migrants in China's Urbanized Villages: A Case Study of Guangzhou." *Habitat International* 36 (1): 192–200.

26. Its homophone, *haigui* which means sea turtle is often used to contrast this group of non-natives in Chinese cities with those local talents who have never gone abroad for study or work. The latter group is often referred to in a self-deprecating way as, *tubie*, local turtles.

27. According to the People's Republic of China Marriage Law, the legal marriage age for male is 22, and female 20.

28. Li, Xin. 2014. "Shanghai Has the Highest Percentage of Native and Non-Native Unions across the Country with Men's Average First Marriage Age at 34 (*Shanghai liangdi hunyin bili quanguo zuigao nanxing pingjun hunling 34 Sui*)."

Xinmin News. February 28, 2014. http://shanghai.xinmin.cn/msrx/2014/02/28/2364 5449.html. Retrieved July 18, 2020.

29. Woolard, Kathryn A. 1989. *Double Talk: Bilingualism and the Politics of Ethnicity in Catalonia.* Stanford, CA: Stanford University Press. P.82.

30. Zhan, Shaohua. 2011. "What Determines Migrant Workers' Life Chances in Contemporary China? Hukou, Social Exclusion, and the Market." *Modern China* 37 (3): 243–85. P.260–1.

31. The first official mention of the category New Shanghairen is the December 13th, 2001 Issue of the People's Daily – Oversea version, citing then Municipal Communist Party Secretary of Shanghai, Huang Ju. P.5.

32. Bourdieu, Pierre. 1991. *Language and Symbolic Power.* Cambridge, MA: Harvard University Press. P.221.

33. Gumperz, John J., and Jenny Cook-Gumperz. 1982. "Introduction: Language and the Communication of Social Identity." In *Language and Social Identity*, edited by John J. Gumperz, 1–19. Cambridge & New York: Cambridge University Press. P.5–6.

34. Lippi-Green, Rosina. 1997. *English with an Accent: Language, Ideology and Discrimination in the United States.* London & New York: Routledge. P.5.

Miller, Jennifer M. 2000. "Language Use, Identity, and Social Interaction: Migrant Students in Australia." *Research on Language & Social Interaction* 33 (1): 69–100.

Schiffrin, Deborah. 1996. "Narrative as Self-Portrait: Sociolinguistic Constructions of Identity." *Language in Society* 25 (2): 167–203.

35. Honig, Emily. 1992. *Creating Chinese Ethnicity: Subei People in Shanghai, 1850–1980.* Yale University Press.

36. Dorian, Nancy. 1998. "Western Language Ideologies and Small-Language Prospects." In *Endangered Languages: Language Loss and Community Response*, edited by Lenore A. Grenoble and Lindsay J. Whaley, 3–21. Cambridge: Cambridge University Press. P.3–4.

37. Rudolph, Jennifer, and Hanchao Lu. 2008. "Mirrored Reflections: Place Identity Formation in Taipei and Shanghai." In *Urban China in Transition*, edited by John Logan, 161–81. Malden, MA: John Wiley & Sons. P.172.

38. Derrida, Jacques. 2000. *Of Hospitality.* Translated by Rachel Bowlby. Stanford, CA: Stanford University Press.

39. Zukin, Sharon, Philip Kasinitz, and Xiangming Chen. 2015. "Spaces of Everyday Diversity: The Patchwork Ecosystem of Local Shopping Streets." In *Global Cities, Local Streets: Everyday Diversity from New York to Shanghai*, 1–28. New York: Routledge.

40. Solé, Carlota. 1987. Articulació social i cultural. In Salvador Aguilar et al., *Visió de Catalunya: El canvi i la reconstrucció nacional des de la perspectiva sociològica*. Barcelona: Diputació de Barcelona. Pp.321–30. Cited in Woolard. *Double Talk*, P.49.

41. Italics to show emphasis in the original interview quote.

42. Gumperz, and Cook-Gumperz. "Introduction: Language and the Communication of Social Identity," 1–19. P.2–3.

43. Marlow, Mikaela L., and Howard Giles. 2010. "'We Won't Get Ahead Speaking like That!' Expressing and Managing Language Criticism in Hawai'i." *Journal of Multilingual and Multicultural Development* 31 (3): 237–51. P.240.

44. Marlow, and Giles. 2010. "'We Won't Get Ahead Speaking," 237–51. P.246.

45. Zou Yiren. 1980. *Research on Population Change in Old Shanghai. [Jiu Shanghai renkou bianqian de yanjiu].* Shanghai: Shanghai People's Press. P.112–13.

46. Honig. *Creating Chinese Ethnicity.*

47. Marlow, and Giles. 2010. "'We Won't Get Ahead Speaking," 237–51. P.246.

48. Bourdieu. *Language and Symbolic Power.*

49. Irvine, Judith T., and Susan Gal. 2010. "Language Ideology and Linguistic Differentiation." In *Regimes of Language: Ideologies, Polities, and Identities*, edited by Paul V. Kroskrity, 35–84. Santa Fe: School of American Research Press. P.37.

Chapter 5

Honorary Shanghairen or Forever Waidiren?

In the experience of native Shanghairen, fluency in the Shanghai dialect is the linguistic pillar of Shanghairen identity—the other two pillars being Shanghai *hukou* and urban Shanghai residency. But this fluency is largely missing among recent highly educated migrants. They are recognized as New Shanghairen by the Shanghai Municipal Government. Their legal residency in Shanghai is buttressed by their educational level, personal wealth, and ever more accommodating internal migration policies. The lack of Shanghai dialect proficiency creates few obstacles for these migrants to develop an attachment to the city. However, it does prevent them from being recognized *by others* or self-identify as a Shanghairen; rather, they are forever considered Waidiren (outlanders). In response, these better-off migrants adopt what I call, a flexible resident identity. While living in Shanghai long-term, they keep their *hukou* in their hometown, and some of them also acquired foreign permanent resident permit. Their personal wealth and skillset provide the geographical mobility on a global scale, hence a flexible identity simultaneously attached to multiple places in a strategic way. In the process, the acquisition of the Shanghai dialect for the purpose of social and cultural integration is largely rendered of little significance and dismissed.

The so-called new-generation migrants of recent years differ from the first generation of migrants, who were mostly unskilled and of rural origin coming to Shanghai in the 1980s and early 1990s.[1] This distinction corresponds to *hukou* reforms, the nationwide urbanization process, and urban redevelopments in Shanghai and the migrants' hometowns, as well as the implementation of the 2001 Language Law countrywide. Economic migrants' decision to stay in Shanghai or return to their hometowns is often subject to institutional barriers,[2] employment, and language proficiency.[3] Shanghai Resident Permit, a second-tier category, was invented and implemented in 2002 as part of *hukou* reforms, through which the institutional and legal barriers for highly educated migrants to stay in Shanghai have to a large extent been eliminated. Moreover, the amendments to the resident permit measures issued in 2013 and 2017 expand the public services the permit holders are entitled to in Shanghai, making the permit nearly on par with a Shanghai *hukou*.

Recent research has shown that the new generation of migrants attaches less value to *hukou* since the access to its previously corresponding benefits is granted by other legal statuses.[4] Departing from it, my work shows that these New Shanghairen's attachment to Shanghai mostly results from a set of pull and push factors, including lifecycle events, cultural affinities, as well as growing unfamiliarity with their hometowns over the years. Furthermore, the state-sponsored dominance of Putonghua, which has been gradually—though at times reluctantly—adopted by native Shanghairen, mitigates linguistic discrimination faced by the migrants who do not speak the dialect.

When I returned to Shanghai in 2017 to conduct follow-up research, I found my highly educated migrant interviewees' sense of belonging and entitlement to social resources are largely based on their socioeconomic status, even though mediated by their *hukou* status. It aligns with my findings from interviewing native Shanghairen in 2013 that migrants' linguistic competence or home region does not matter much in terms of social integration. This leads me to emphasize migrants' place attachment to Shanghai not as New Shanghairen but captured in a new, flexible resident identity.

PLACE ATTACHMENT TO SHANGHAI

The increasing amount of research investigating people-place relationships revives Low and Altman's conceptualization of place attachment.[5] In the Chinese context, as elsewhere, despite mobility and globalization, place continues to be a meaningful object of strong attachment, either in its abstract and imagined monolithic form, for example, the name of a city, or in its concrete and lived form, as in the case of a residential neighborhood.[6] Given how diverse metropolitan Shanghai is, my interviewees articulate their varied attachments to Shanghai based on environmental aesthetics, social integration, or lifecycle stages, though all mediated by *hukou*.

A Shanghai *Hukou* Matters

When articulating the self-identification process, *hukou* is the factor mentioned most by my non-native research participants. Whether they migrated to Shanghai in the 2000s, when a *hukou* was still essential, or in the early to mid-2010s, when a Shanghai Resident Permit was sufficient, not a single interviewee in my sample of twenty identifies as a Shanghairen. At most, one suggested awkwardly in a joking way that they are what the municipal officials call New Shanghairen. In the first two decades of economic reform, geographical mobility brought millions of migrants to cities, but *hukou* as an institutional barrier prohibited equal rights, rendering them second-class citizens in their own country.[7] In a different context, Findley and Stockdale argue that the status of being a migrant is paramount for an individual's overall identity—that they are forever in-between.[8] The recent *hukou* reforms in Shanghai have eased the precarious condition for college-educated migrants and laid a foundation for many to build up place attachment.

Jane, for example, belongs to the first generation of college graduates who faced job uncertainty and liberty at the same time, when the Ministry of Education unbundled college education from job assignment in the mid-1990s. Under the planned economy, college graduates used to be assigned a position relevant to their major in their hometown or home province upon graduation. In theory, this mechanism, paired with the nationwide college entrance exam system (*gao kao*) sent the brightest students to the top universities in the country and returned them to their hometowns to contribute to local development. It also controlled population mobility, demand for jobs, and social services in big cities where graduates of top universities would otherwise cluster. Since the late 1990s, developmental policies, in conjunction with *hukou* reforms, have accommodated college graduates' desire to stay in big cities, to blaze their own paths, as long as they can meet the demand of labor markets there.

After this change, graduation season required college seniors to find employers who would facilitate the necessary *hukou* transfer, thus connecting the graduate's *hukou* with the company's physical location. Otherwise, the graduate's *hukou* would revert to their hometown, reestablishing their legal residence and access to public services. Jane believed that the universe aligned to allow her to stay in Shanghai, when she told the story of the summer of 1999 shortly before her college graduation:

> I still remember it vividly: it was two weeks before the deadline, my advisor reminded me of the *hukou* issue, inquiring whether I was able to find a qualified employer [in Shanghai]. I told her no, and was thinking to myself, it would be okay to go back to work in the provincial TV station there. It wouldn't be that bad. But then this company hired me and took care of the *hukou* issue within one week! Even my advisor said it was unheard of, almost impossible. Maybe it is fate. I felt very lucky.

Before the series of reforms to the *hukou* system detailed in chapter 1, *hukou* status determined life chances for college graduates in the city where they attended college, if different from their hometown. The uncertainty of employment compounded with that of legal status results in college-educated non-natives' extreme anxiety and vulnerability. An employment-based, time-delimited opportunity window could be detrimental for non-natives' sense of belonging, and as Gonzalez puts it in a different context: privatizes risk.[9]

Though this institutional barrier has been gradually eliminated through *hukou* reforms, for the cohort that graduated nearly twenty years later in 2017, many of its constraints remain. Despite this second-tier legal status, a Shanghai Resident Permit guarantees legal residence and right to work for non-native college graduates, the sense of both precarity and place attachment is still mediated by *hukou*. Especially for those with limited resources and at early stage of their careers in Shanghai, *hukou* is a legal status as powerful and significant as work visa or permanent residency for international migrants in their destination countries. It plays a paramount role for most non-natives' attachment to Shanghai. As Gong, a college graduate working for a tech start-up in 2017, put it: "Only after I get a Shanghai *hukou* would I feel this is my city, and that I would self-identify as a New Shanghairen."

Liu, in her mid-twenties, landed a curriculum consulting position at a college in Shanghai, after obtaining her master's degree in Education in early 2017. Three months later, during our interview that June, she explained the new changes of the *hukou* system to me:

> Usually at the end of every May or early June, there is a *luohu* (settling *hukou*) policy announced for that year's graduates. If you intend to stay in Shanghai, you need to submit the application by June 15. Before doing so, you need to calculate your points to see whether you meet the threshold.[10] My [Shanghai] *hukou* would have been associated with the employer, in my case, the college that I started working for in March. But the most recent policy requires one's *hukou* to be associated with a residential address, even if it's a rental. There is now a *gonggong* (public) *hukou* account in every *juweihui* (neighborhood committee office) that non-natives can apply to be associated with, you just bring your lease with other documents.

As a recent graduate, Liu would need to be well informed about the new procedure of transferring her *hukou* to Shanghai. What she experienced is less precarious than the weeks before Jane's graduation back in 1999. The measure for processing non-native's *hukou* applicable to her case was passed in 2013. The measures she referred to were updated yet again in December 2017 and in effect since January 1, 2018.

Though a postgraduate degree opens the door for legal status, the constant changes for acquiring it still make new-generation migrants feel their situation in Shanghai precarious. Those who graduated from colleges in Shanghai between 1999 and 2017 told me that various conditions affected their *hukou* transfer to Shanghai. An annual adjustment of criteria leaves many graduates, as Jane said, in fate's hands. The constantly changing measures require non-native graduates to be up to date and act swiftly before new rounds of policy changes are implemented. It intensifies their sense of uncertainty and powerlessness in the lead-up to graduation. Lan's 2003 cohort at another nationally highly ranked university in Shanghai were able to permanently transfer their *hukou* to the municipal collective *hukou* hosted by the Shanghai College Graduates Career Center, an office under the Shanghai Municipal Government (*shanghaishi gaoxiao biyesheng jiuye zhidao zhongxin*) upon graduation. Their undergraduate degrees were enough to ensure legal status for both work and residency in Shanghai. But eleven years later, for Junlin's 2014 cohort, an undergraduate degree is no longer sufficient to qualify for a Shanghai *hukou*. Instead, a master's degree is needed, as Liu attested.

The municipal government of Shanghai has strategically implemented new categories to differentiate non-natives' *hukou*, from the earlier *jiti* (collective) *hukou* to the most recent *gonggong* (public) *hukou* in 2017. Nominally, it is a step away from socialist terminology, such as the "collective" used in "collective farming." Essentially, it is a neoliberal approach, as the local state retreats further from a central planning role. Previously all college graduates' dossiers were managed at a central municipal office. Now Shanghai's decentralized urban governance keeps dossiers and recent non-natives' *hukou* registered with their residential addresses across the whole city, and leaves the management of non-natives' *hukou* to low ranking governmental clerks at neighborhood committees.

In this way, highly educated non-natives enjoy the convenience of having a *hukou* associated with their residential address—the same setup as for natives and have access to public services that a genuine Shanghai *hukou* would guarantee. As soon as the non-native is able to purchase housing in Shanghai, their *hukou* can be transferred from the previous *jiti hukou* or the current *gonggong hukou* to be associated with their property, thus legally they would be the same as a native Shanghairen. Yet *hukou*, though fundamental in urban China for one's legal status, is merely the base on which migrants build their place attachment.

Pull and Push

When involuntary geographical mobility eroded native Shanghairen's place identity bound with particular neighborhoods in the city, voluntary mobility brought highly educated young migrants into the city. With urban space of various scales, they continuously engage with meaning-making and attachment cultivation. Using the pull and push framework to study the new-generation migrants' gradual formation of place attachment to Shanghai, I employ Gustafson's typology to examine the relationships between self, others, and environment.[11]

One important pull for migrants' place attachment to Shanghai is spending formative years in the city. Those who attended colleges in Shanghai and remained in the city afterward grew into adulthood there. This is a crucial period of personal growth, when one develops independent thoughts and preferences, explores possibilities, and has the liberty to decide for oneself about friends, a career path, and even which neighborhood to live in. This experience of self-discovery makes the attachment personal and roots it in a particular place. As Lan, who completed both her undergraduate and master's degrees in Shanghai, explained to me:

> I had actually spent more time in Shanghai than in my home city, Shenyang. I was born in a small town in the Liaoning province where my father worked for a hydropower station in a nearby mountainous area. I was born and raised there until the second grade, when my parents thought it would be better to live in Shenyang, the provincial capital for my education. I left Shenyang at the age of 18 to attend college in Shanghai; . . . Entering college, that is when real life starts and you can decide what to do, including friends' circle, etc. The center of my life has been in Shanghai. When I left for Shenzhen, I didn't think I would live in Shenzhen for the rest of my life. It was just a temporary relocation for career. My plan at that time was to return to Shanghai within five years.

The social integration in Shanghai that Lan has developed since college led to the active cultivation of continuous connections with Shanghai. Even when she was transferred to her employer's Shenzhen headquarters, she vowed to come back to Shanghai, and she did. In contrast to the provincial capital where her parents live and which she still regards as her hometown, the physical and cultural environment in Shanghai attracts her.

It is clearly a self-environment relationship involving the pull from Shanghai and the push from Shenyang, as Lan elaborated:

> What matters is that you live here, how intimate your relationship with the city is. It's not like I started to feel at home after buying the apartment. I felt that way leading up to my undergraduate graduation that I didn't want to leave Shanghai at all. I didn't want to go anywhere else because other places are unfamiliar. I don't really like my hometown. I grew up there. I know the kind of urban culture there, and I don't like it. Where I like the most is here [in Shanghai]. My college classmates are here, especially the few native Shanghairen dorm mates who are now my best friends.

Her assertion exemplifies geographer Yi-fu Tuan's argument that an individual's attachment to a place comes with familiarity and ease, with the sense of security and warmth, as well as the absence of desire for other places.[12] Again, Lan makes a clear distinction between the cosmopolitan Shanghai she is attached to and the provincial hometown she wants to leave behind. The former symbolizes the wealth of her personal experience, in her words, an "intimate relationship," and provides a sense of spatial-temporal continuity for her personal growth and for her meaningful relationship with others and the environment—bridging Gustafson's typology with Lalli's argument on urban-related identity.[13] Such social integration with the city—and with native Shanghairen—is nevertheless mediated by educational level and socioeconomic status.

As Liu et al.'s study on new-generation migrants shows, contrary to the first generation, comprised mostly of rural-to-urban, unskilled migrants who generally relied on hometown-based bonds, the new generation of urban migrants are more likely to form non-kin, non-territorial networks determined by educational attainment and income level.[14] Among the highly educated young migrants in my study, the non-territorial element is present in the social circles of their domestic partners, friends, colleagues, and neighbors, which lean more toward fellow migrants from other parts of the country rather than toward native Shanghairen. An important reason, one often overlooked, in previous studies, is language.

Shared regional languages or dialects signal insider membership and connote trust, especially when used to form communities in migrant cities like Shanghai. A vast diversity of regional dialects are spoken across the country, especially the mutually unintelligible non-Mandarin dialects. It is not surprising that first-generation migrants' support and friendship networks are bonded by language. In Shanghai, such a native place bond among sojourning communities goes back to the late nineteenth century.[15] More than a century later, what is different about the role language plays in forming migrant communities is the national promotion of Putonghua through the school system. In Shanghai and other Chinese cities, Putonghua has been mandatory at all level of schools as the medium of instruction, following the 2001 Language Law. Uniform instruction has produced linguistic homogeneity among highly educated migrants to Shanghai. The shared Putonghua proficiency facilitates non-territorial networks among migrants originating from different corners of the country.

Using relationship with others as the anchor point for place attachment, in addition to friendships formed on college campuses, many of my interviewees mentioned dating and starting one's own family as another point of attachment. Zheng, in his late thirties, has a trajectory similar to Lan's. He originates from northeastern China and completed undergraduate study and secured a Shanghai *hukou* in the early 2000s. He held a managerial-level job, married a fellow non-native from a different province and had a five-year-old daughter at the time of our interview in 2017. He stressed the importance of marriage and starting his own family as reasons to feel attached to Shanghai:

> The first few years after graduating from college, or even after my parents joined me in Shanghai, I didn't necessarily feel attached to the city. But it all changed after getting married. Now I feel my family is here, I work here, and I live here. The whole city is my turf. It's like animals are territorial. Humans are like that too.

Invoking the rhetoric of territoriality, besides the significance of family, Zheng also asserts his right to the city based on his job and residency. Not to mention the *hukou* status that buttresses his claim legally. Interestingly, similar rhetoric of territoriality was used by Wu Wei, the native Shanghairen software engineer who was active in the Shanghai dialect preservation movement during my 2013 field research. Wu's assertion is more linguistic and cultural than legal or financial. While Zheng sees no incentive to learn the Shanghai dialect, and has no intention to, Wu communicated his frustration about recent migrants' unwillingness to learn it. In Wu's mind, when in Rome, do as the Romans do. However, the national language policy would disagree, not to mention, as shown in chapter 2, that more and more young native Shanghairen have stopped speaking the Shanghai dialect.

The lifecycle perspective for developing a sense of home and place attachment is not only based on personal experience but has roots in traditional Chinese culture. It treats home (*jia*) as analogous to "family," for example, the phrase distilling the traditional ethos, *cheng jia li jie* (form family/home first, establish career later). Thus, home is more than a place of habitation but where one's family is.[16] Such cognitive association suggests the development of place attachment could depend on an individual's stage of life, as is the case with Junlin. In her mid-twenties and single at the time of our interview in summer 2017, she mentioned:

> I don't think I will identify with this city until after starting my own family. Being alone here, away from parents, you are always alone at home. It's hard to identify, or at least not strongly. This is the place I will stay for the long term, a place I am familiar with, but it doesn't necessarily mean home. Maybe I will feel a sense of belonging when I start dating.

Junlin's anticipation is also felt by all my interviewees who attended college in Shanghai. However, even when highly educated migrants put down roots, feel that Shanghai is their home, and express strong identification with the city, it doesn't mean they regard themselves as Shanghairen, as Rong, who is a college friend of Zheng and shares a similar life trajectory, made explicit:

I don't care about the New Shanghairen or Waidiren categorization. In recent years, the concept of New Shanghairen is fading. No need to bother with it. Ultimately, [if] you spent your most important formative years here, of course, you would strongly identify with the city, otherwise you wouldn't want to stay anyway.

At the time of the interview, Rong was thirty-six years old and had spent half of his life in Shanghai since starting college. Echoing most of the interviewees in his cohort, important life events taking place in the city, and memories created and accumulated contribute greatly to a strong place attachment. When *hukou* is not an issue, time and lifecycle play a significant role in migrants' identification with the city. In the five to ten years after graduating college, most of my interviewees dated, got married, bought property, and had children. In the process, many social bonds were created and networks formed. As Agnew argues, forming and sustaining social relations and social interactions in a geographic area provides individuals a sense of place.[17] One's emotional attachment to a place grows when lived experience and relationships with others over time become fundamental to one's sense of self.

Another self-other relationship that contributes to meaningful attachment to Shanghai is employment. Its significance during formative years is beyond providing financial support and professional identity. Liu, who originates from inland Anhui province, explained:

The sense of identifying with the city started to grow after I landed the job. Before getting this job, I was not sure whether I would be able to work in Shanghai or go back to my hometown; [my life was] full of uncertainty. Now that I have secured this job, which is very stable with the college, [and] basically tenured, I have found peace of mind, knowing my life will be in Shanghai in the future. Despite my *hukou* status, or whether I can afford to purchase housing, my identification with this place is growing stronger because of my job.

The job gives her a foothold in the city, and even though her Shanghai *hukou* is still pending, she has the Shanghai Resident Permit as a safety net.

Employment serves as a strong pull factor for many young highly educated migrants. This is similar to employment-based immigration policies around the world, where young talent is welcomed into the host society. Such measures for domestic migrants fall in line with what David Harvey calls neoliberalism with Chinese characteristics,[18] which is the strategic decentralization of state interventions in the demographic, social, and economic spheres that fuel the nation's economy without the central state relinquishing control over the population.

Expanding on Gustafson pairings of self, others, and environment, certain residential neighborhoods generate specific networks and foster certain kinds of interaction, which serve as another pull factor for highly educated migrants to develop place attachment. Most native Shanghairen are nostalgic for urban-core living in Puxi, as cases in chapter 3 show. But the preference is not universal among non-natives. Rather, it is based on their varied stage in lifecycle and economic status. Jane, for example, prefers Puxi and the former French Concession area in particular for its cosmopolitan flavor, including architecture built during the semi-colonial era and stores with a global clientele. Lan, meanwhile, prefers Pudong for its car-friendly new-built environment, her daughters' schools, and the amenities in her brand-new upscale condo complex. Proshansky et al. point out the meanings of place are not universally shared, instead, place imbues symbolic and affective associations between the individual and various characteristics of the physical environment.[19] The diverse offerings in Shanghai provide different options for migrants to find "their" neighborhood, and over time, attachment is developed not only with the physical setting of a neighborhood but also through interaction with others.

Gong, in his late twenties and originally from neighboring Zhejiang province, works in a tech start-up and rents an apartment in a working-class neighborhood ten minutes' walk from his office. For him, it is the neighborliness, the sound, smell, and feel of quotidian life in the neighborhood that made him feel at home and identify with the city:

> There is a big influence from the kind of neighborhood you rent in. The neighborhood I live in is an old working-class neighborhood with typical six-floor walk-up apartment buildings. Around me are all ordinary native Shanghairen, [living a] very homey and quotidian life. You can smell the aroma of their cooking when you climb up the stairs. It makes me want to blend in, be part of their lives, so to speak.

The noises, the overheard voices, and the smells of home cooking in the walk-up building make living in Shanghai real for Gong. Attachment to a place grows out of fond memories of sounds and smells, the assurance of nurture and security, as well as simple homely pleasure.[20] Other young non-natives who haven't started their own families in the city yet echo Gong's opinion; for example, Junlin revealed that she felt lonely in her new apartment building that she had not felt when living in a walk-up. The neighborliness of old native Shanghairen six-floor walk-up buildings provides chances for young migrants to briefly interact with neighbors, such as grannies always on the lookout. It is similar to Jane Jacobs's eyes on the street, but in the case of Maoist era walk-up apartment buildings, eyes on the staircase. Elevators in newly built condo buildings not only symbolize the self-enclosure of living units but also physically prohibit such interactions.

Contrary to these warm opinions of old residential neighborhoods in historically working-class Yangpu district, highly educated migrant families with school-age children feel differently. It is the difference between feeling homey and neighborly and really being able to blend in and socialize with neighbors. The factors that explain this difference lie in both lifecycle and socioeconomic status. Despite their different preferences for either new high-rise condos in the outskirts or diverse old walk-ups near the city center, it is the social integration in residential neighborhoods catering to certain life stages that acts as the pull for highly educated migrants.

For the older cohort of highly educated urban migrants to Shanghai, who are predominantly Shanghai *hukou* holders and property owners with school-age children, a sense of community is generated organically in newly built high-rise condo complex on the outskirts of the city. It is where age, life-stage, and socioeconomic status are homogeneous among residents. Zheng, who bought an apartment in such a complex upon getting married, compared the new condo complex neighborhoods with those Gong preferred:

> A previous neighbor left our neighborhood and moved into an old working-class neighborhood of those six-floor walk-ups, so that his child can attend a better-quality public school. When he comes back to visit, he always complains to me how alienated he feels in his current neighborhood. All around him in that neighborhood are older native Shanghairen, the way they do things or the way they think are so different from his. There is no way they can hangout, because everyone "*ge guan* ge" [mind their own business].

Zheng's own experience documents the difference between the two kinds of residential neighborhoods:

> In those old six-floor walk-ups, neighbors know each other, and would say hi, but they are often of the older generation, that you don't hang out with. In my current new-built high-rise neighborhood, neighbors are of the same age group. You know, people buy a new apartment when getting married [as convention dictates], after a few years, you see all the toddlers running around in the greenery in the complex, and then they all go to the same school. Easy to feel close to [other families], for example, a neighbor would say to me, "The weather is so nice today that we are going to the nearby park. Would you and your daughter like to join us?" Or, "Let's go set up a tent or picnic in parks." Children are of similar age, so if someone shouts out from downstairs, "Anyone up for water guns?" the children will just gather to play together.

The neighborly conviviality Zheng describes is what Yan, a native Shanghairen I interviewed in 2013, reminisced about when we discussed the *shikumen* housing working-class neighborhood in Hongkou district where she grew up. Almost all of those close-knit, Shanghai dialect-speaking, and overcrowded residential neighborhoods were demolished during the massive urban redevelopment in Shanghai in the 1990s and early 2000s. In the new housing developments in the recently urbanized outer areas of the city, such neighborly dynamics reemerged. However, the *lingua franca* in those new developments is Putonghua. Shared socioeconomic status, a new-to-the-area, non-native identity, and especially their young children bring these families together. In contrast, the older walk-up neighborhoods are heterogeneous in terms of age group, socioeconomic status, and lifestyles, which family-oriented young professional migrants do not appreciate.

What also stands out in Zheng's comparison is the characteristics of native Shanghairen, the mind-your-own-business *ge guan ge*—or in the Shanghai dialect, *ge gü ge*. This quality is close to what sociologist Simmel identifies as the blasé attitude among residents in Berlin more than a century ago. That is, the sense of independence and liberty resulting from the general public's indifference. It is a trait of sharing a physical place with others, one that, according to Gustafson's categorization, contributes to meaning-making. However, this mentality and behavior pattern typical among native Shanghairen deprive non-natives the chance to develop place attachment. For Zheng and his previous neighbor, the *ge guan ge* mentality is a barrier for social integration, and to feel a sense of belonging. The undertone of Zheng's above quote corresponds to his analogy of territoriality and turf. It turns out for some highly educated migrants, property ownership as the accumulated material evidence of their belonging to and claim on Shanghai—their adopted home—is recognized but not accepted as a ticket for social inclusion by native Shanghairen.

This metropolitan mentality struck Zheng differently from other interviewees. Some upper-middle-class migrants prefer Shanghai to their hometowns for precisely the sense of personal freedom. It serves as a pull for them. Ping explained to me how much she enjoyed the kind of independence such *ge guan ge* Shanghai culture guarantees, in contrast to the traditional culture of interdependence that interfered with her personal life:

> In Shanghai, for a get-together, people would check with each other's schedule beforehand. It would be unthinkable that someone just shows up outside of your door expecting to hang out for hours. What if you are heading out for errands? Now you need to change your plans. Or what if you are very tired after a long day? Without any previous arrangement, [they] just come to visit on their whim! It just creates so much chaos for your life. I really don't like

that about my hometown, but such casualness is so important for interpersonal relations that one needs to maintain deliberately. So tiring . . . regardless of whether you like that person or not, or whether you two get along. Otherwise, you would be isolated, and people think there is something wrong with you. . . . That said, I really like Shanghai! Your life belongs to you. Your time belongs to you!

Again, what seems cold and isolating to one migrant represents liberty and freedom to others, as Ping further elaborated:

I enjoy the freedom in Shanghai; just do whatever you like without interference or constraints from others, unlike those from the massive family, friends' and acquaintances network in Wenzhou. It's comfortable, very comfortable here.

Literature on rural-to-urban migration points out how a lack of ties to natives and fellow migrants present difficulties for social integration and for developing a sense of belonging in the host society. In contrast, my interviewees of upper-middle-class background provide a nuanced look at how place attachment can be built upon weak ties or even a lack of ties with acquaintances they might otherwise feel obligations toward in their hometown.

Identifying with a place or feeling comfortable in a place doesn't necessarily lead to self-identification with it but instead could simply be a preference for that place over other places. Comparisons between residential neighborhoods, and between personality traits of dominant resident groups, echo geographer Dorian Massey's argument that what makes a place special is not necessarily its intrinsic qualities but also its comparison with and relation to the outside world.[21] A few interviewees highlighted the perceived characteristics of native Shanghairen as both the pull of Shanghai and the push of their hometowns. Besides *ge guan ge*, the other most frequently mentioned characteristic can be called professionalism.

It is the consensus among migrants in my study that the native Shanghairen they encounter in their daily lives, in business or government offices for example, are very professional and reliable. These non-natives contrast these characteristics with those of people in their hometowns. Lan and her husband, for example, came from northeastern China, and they mentioned that northeasterners often boast and fail to deliver on their promises. Ping moved from Shenzhen in Southern China to Shanghai in 2011 to help run her family's business with her husband and his brother. She contrasted the dealings with government agencies in Shanghai to those in her hometown, Wenzhou in southeastern Zhejiang province, and praised the professionalism she found in Shanghai:

The civil servants in Shanghai left a very good impression on me. Back in our hometown, you need to know people. The idea of relying on acquaintances to get things done is very strong, to get anything done. And it would happen that when you got to a government agency, there was simply no one there. But in Shanghai, everyone follows rules. It is very straightforward and well communicated, which document is needed to apply for what. But in our hometown, you need to find some acquaintance, to know someone in the office, relevant or not, for no matter what. But Shanghai is different, I quite like it here for that.

The professionalism migrants experience in Shanghai presents a sharp contrast to their impression and experience elsewhere in the country, which in their telling, relies on personal connections or favors, or a governmental official's whim. It does not necessarily mean knowing people would not help in Shanghai, but one can still get things done without knowing the right people. In her hometown or other smaller Chinese cities, it might not be the case. Hui, originating from a northeastern city, contrasted attitudes there with the orderliness that characterizes Shanghai:

I love the life in Shanghai and will never consider moving anywhere else! . . . In Shanghai, you would say, this is not good, that is not good; but as soon as you go to other places [in China], nothing there is as good as in Shanghai! Rules and convenience! For example, if you take the subway, there is always staff in the service booth during operation hours. All the rules are clear, and everyone follows them. No one would pick on you, for just because. . . . Oh, and driving! In Harbin no one drives within lanes, or signals when changing lanes, or keeps a safe distance. Every time I went back to visit, I got into traffic accidents! Not saying Shanghai is perfect, but it is surely better.

In this comparison, a feeling of safety and security in public spaces, and good management of public services contributes to Hui's psychological comfort,[22] increasing her attachment to Shanghai.

The main push factor is the environment-self relationship,[23] or what Proshansky calls place identity, which I discussed earlier in relation to displaced native Shanghairen. The flip side of the growing place attachment to Shanghai experienced by migrants is their increasing non-attachment to their hometowns. As in many parts of Shanghai, the urban built environment in their hometowns has experienced unprecedented, full-scale demolition and redevelopment, to the point that they can barely recognize the cities they grew up in. Gong, who attended high school in Nanjing, capital of Jiangsu province, explained: "So much has changed in my home city, new roads, new shopping malls, etc., all over!"

It is a push factor that makes Shanghai feel more like home, as knowledge and experiences breed familiarity for migrants. This does not mean that the urban built environment in Shanghai has not changed drastically in the last three decades, but my interviewees have lived through these changes. Unlike native Shanghairen of the same age, these migrants do not have a decades-old childhood image of Shanghai they are bound to, but instead have a childhood image of their hometown that is no longer there. In this sense, it is not only the active creation or cultivation of the attachment through day-to-day life in Shanghai that makes them identify with the city, but the swift and thorough destruction of the urban environment of their childhood neighborhoods and large swaths of the urban landscape in their native cities that leaves them no choice but to attach to their adopted home. As Jane describes her visits back to her southwestern hometown:

> The biggest problem is my home city no longer looks like the place I grew up in, the place in my childhood memory. Every time I went back there, it felt strange. Strangeness comes before familiarity. First impression is strangeness, every time. Later when you get to the quotidian level, there is still some familiarity. But such familiarity is limited to where I stay [at my parents' house] and its vicinity. As soon as I walk away from that area, I am lost [in my native city].

The dissolution of place attachment to one's hometown facilitates the construction of attachment to Shanghai. In Jane's case, she has integrated culturally, aesthetically, and linguistically to Shanghai, on top of a Shanghai *hukou* and a successful career.

However, the gradually developed place attachment to Shanghai mediated by *hukou* status and facilitated by the dynamic push and pull factors does not lead to these migrants developing a Shanghairen identity, which remains strongly associated with Shanghai dialect proficiency. Their lived experience indicates that language is the ultimate barrier for them to self-identify and be recognized as genuine Shanghairen. This persistent obstacle can be summarized by Hui's proclamation, "Since I don't speak the Shanghai dialect, who would believe I am a Shanghairen? I would never believe it myself!" Instead, they have developed what I call a flexible resident identity. In the next section, I will delineate how persistent language-based discrimination and opportunities elsewhere explain this in-between identity.

FLEXIBLE RESIDENT IDENTITY

Unlike rural-origin, unskilled migrants, my highly educated and skilled research participants would not encounter much difficulty securing stable employment and living a comfortable middle-class life in their home cities. They are often provincial capitals or big cities with more than one million population. Rather, these non-natives choose to come to Shanghai and settle down, exploring new opportunities in career and life, despite precarities related to *hukou* status. As Sassen points out, new forms of citizenship are enacted in globalizing cities.[24] In current Shanghai, as I showed earlier, qualifying for *hukou* transfers among the highly educated is akin to trying to hit a moving target. The geographical mobility and autonomy of the lucky, the highly skilled, and the wealthy are confined by national policies after all. Against the backdrop that China does not recognize dual citizenship, I use the term flexible resident identity to characterize the result of my privileged migrant interviewees' negotiations with and strategizing of their place identity. This term is inspired by Aihwa Ong's "flexible citizenship" that describes transient ethnic Chinese entrepreneurs, originally from Hong Kong and Taiwan, who choose their citizenship mostly based on economic reasons, weighing options in both their homeland and their adopted country in the West.[25] Like flexible citizenship, flexible resident identity captures the fluidity of migrants' mobility, both actual and aspirational, when living in Shanghai with a Chinese passport. Because of the flexibility, they may never identify with, or aspire to be recognized as, genuine Shanghairen.

While most migrants I interviewed regard Shanghai as a destination for future career and life, a home to settle down and to return to, Fan, in his mid-twenties, dreams of seeing the world, living and working in the United States or other countries. Since he does not make long-term plans, unsurprisingly, he has not transferred his *hukou* to Shanghai. With a bachelor's degree in information technology and science from a top university in Shanghai, Fan aspired to a travel-work lifestyle abroad in the next few years:

> [N]ot for graduate school, but work. To enhance my skills. In my field, my credentials and experience are recognized internationally. And there is a definite demand. If I land a job offer, I will just apply for a work visa. The destination would be the United States or Russia because my expertise is in data security, anti-hacking.

Responding to my follow-up question, whether such an aspiration is the reason he didn't feel that Shanghai was his home, he compared his choice with opportunities and career paths his classmates with similar education and skillset opted for:

> I am career-oriented and very open-minded. A friend of mine participated in some Australian program where he would spend the first two years in a

funded master's program, and then work there for three years after graduation. Singapore has similar programs, [of the] mandatory service after graduate school sort.[26] My friends who participated in such programs do not intend to migrate to those countries, but to accumulate experience, to be more competitive later on China's domestic job market. The job market here is extremely competitive, while in those countries, a two- or three-years' work contract is guaranteed. For them, peace of mind. But I don't feel like doing it, because I don't like to plan that much into the future. That's just who I am.

Contrary to his friends, who will return to China after obtaining further education and professional experience abroad, Fan doesn't necessarily feel attached to any place in particular. If he is able to secure a work visa to the United States or Russia, he might be able to enjoy the flexibility and on-the-job learning he wants without committing five years of his life by signing a service indenture. At the time of our interview in summer 2017, he held a Shanghai Resident Permit. But by the summer of 2020, Fan has changed his plans, moving to Shenzhen for a cybersecurity job. What he and his friends share are credentials recognized on the globalized job market, ease of relocation within China, and relaxation of emigration policies allowing Chinese citizens to living abroad temporarily, which was hard to fathom prior to economic reforms. However, without sizable wealth, his mobility merely afforded by skillset can hardly reach countries with more rigid labor migration policies such as the United States.

Similar to young migrants who possess highly desirable knowledge and skills on the globalized job market, some of the wealthy migrants who moved to Shanghai in recent years prefer to remain flexible in terms of both identity and legal status. Contrary to Lan, her fellow native Northeasterner husband keeps his *hukou* in Shenzhen, where he worked before moving to Shanghai. According to Lan, he is too lazy to deal with the point system in Shanghai even though he technically qualifies. However, in his strategic thinking, for the family of four, flexibility potentially promises more opportunities when one parent's *hukou* is in Shanghai and the other's in another globally recognized economically vibrant city like Shenzhen.

The flexible resident identity is also context-specific, since when traveling abroad, my interviewees would matter-of-factly respond to the question, "where are you from?" by saying they live in Shanghai. According to them, it is to avoid having to talk about their home provinces, which the questioner probably would not know anyway. In addition, Mei's story points out how paternal-lineage-based traditional identification *zuji* (ancestral hometown)[27] clashes with birth-place-based identification when new-generation migrants have children in Shanghai. This conflict of identifications is compounded by the possibilities for investment-based permanent residency in the West, such as the EB5 program for immigration to the United States.[28]

In Mei's family, though all four family members live in Shanghai, they each identify with a different city or province.

> When we are actually in Shanghai, I am not going to say I am a Shanghairen. At most, a New Shanghairen, or I originally come from Hunan province. My husband would say he originally comes from Jiangsu province. Those are our roots. My younger daughter [6 years of age] would certainly say she is a Shanghairen since she was born and raised in Shanghai. But it's a different story for my older daughter [20 years of age]. She was born in Guangzhou, and we moved to Shanghai when she was one year old. She would say she is a Guangzhou-ren because she was born there even though she doesn't speak a single word of Cantonese. So, your question about identification is very tricky, [is it] based on birthplace or ancestral hometown? In Shanghai, no one is a genuine native, since it is a migrant city. Everyone is a migrant or descendant of migrants.

In her mind, birthplace plays a significant role in determining the place a *ren* (person) belongs to, but interestingly, this is also mediated by local language proficiency. Mei uses her older daughter's lack of Cantonese proficiency to dispute the latter's self-claim of being a Guangzhou-*ren*, even though Mei does not equally judge her younger daughter, who does not speak the Shanghai dialect. In fact, none of the family members speaks the Shanghai dialect. This indicates the deep-rooted association between language and place identity for Chinese people. It also sheds light on not only migrants' hesitance to claim a Shanghairen identity but also native Shanghairen's rejection of migrants' potential claim to be Shanghairen. Hui's clear acknowledgement of this barrier, shown earlier, is another example. Cross-country mobility is a significant break from the idea of place-bound identities associated with ancestral hometowns that prevailed for thousands of years in feudal China. This new mobility renders the *zuji* category no longer relevant and opens opportunities for individuals to create and articulate their own place identity.

As indicated earlier, recent new-generation migrants with a bachelor's degree are only guaranteed second-tier status, a Shanghai Resident Permit. This differs from *hukou* status mostly by restricting the permit holder's children's education and their registration for nationwide college entrance exams.[29] This difference plays a big role for middle-aged and wealthy migrants, who strategize to send their children to schools overseas to avoid such discriminatory treatment. The innovative duel structure of parallel *hukou* and resident permit is both a population control and a talent-seeking measure. It aims to limit the population size of megacities such as Shanghai, while sift out needed talents for the local economy. The highly educated migrants in their late thirties and forties with sizable accumulated wealth look abroad to mitigate the legal and social precarity for themselves and their children, as Mei explained:

> You can simply go abroad to get a Green Card [through an investment-based immigration program]. Many people I know went to the United States and Hong Kong to give birth, so that after a few years, the parents can become foreign citizens.

This demonstrates firstly a misunderstanding and over-simplification of the process of obtaining permanent residency in the United States through the child-sponsored, family-based immigration program, and then an unwarranted belief and characterization of "One Country, Two Systems" in Hong Kong. Regardless, Mei's observation does align with data shown in other studies of the significant increase in Chinese students with green cards or foreign passports in international schools in Shanghai. James Farrer shows in his longitudinal study of the foreign community in Shanghai that Western parents are less and less satisfied with Chinese-dominated international schools in Shanghai.[30] Another strategy upper-middle-class parents in Chinese big cities, such as Shanghai, Beijing, or Guangzhou, employs is to send their children to private high schools in the United States to provide the young with cultural capital and flexibility for later becoming global citizens.[31]

Contrary to Mei and Lan, who had their *hukou* transferred to Shanghai relatively easily in the early 2000s, only one of the five members of the group of college-educated, affluent migrant mothers I interviewed in the summer of 2017 has had their *hukou* transferred to Shanghai. With their vague understanding of the immigration policies in the United States, and their lived experience dealing with the *hukou* system in Shanghai, they proclaimed a Shanghai *hukou* was more difficult to obtain than a permanent residency in a foreign country:

> R1: The United States' immigration policy is very different from that of China's. You get a U.S. *hukou* if you were born in the U.S., but it doesn't work this way in China.
>
> R2: That's why they say it's harder to acquire a Shanghai *hukou* than a U.S. or Canadian one.
>
> R3: Shanghai *hukou* is worth so much!
>
> R4: Especially Shanghai *hukou*! Shanghai *hukou* is the most difficult to acquire in the world—money can't buy you one.
>
> R5: I agree! Shanghai *hukou* is truly the most difficult. You can get an American Green Card for US $500,000 [through the EB5 investment program prior to November 21, 2019], but you can't get a Shanghai *hukou* with money!

With such awareness of the difficulty of acquiring a Shanghai *hukou*, none of them was actively seeking one. Rather, with the mobility and opportunities afforded by their wealth, they are tempted by various investment-based programs to acquire foreign permanent residency, circumventing the foreseen difficulty of their children's later acceptance into a top college domestically.[32]

Mei described her friends, who live a flexible resident identity lifestyle, as essentially Chinese, but since they strategically navigate two countries' systems, in a way, they are double-dipping:

> It's much easy to make money here than abroad, of course they don't want to migrate to another country; rather, they prefer to live here. They regard the Green Card as a security measure, just in case—if anything bad happens in China that they need to leave for safety, financial or other reasons, at least they have the option. The property they bought in the U.S. is just for an annual vacation, also to accumulate days living in that country—to maintain their permanent resident status. One needs to do that on a regular basis. If you ask them to settle down abroad, they would never want to.

For these affluent migrants, a foreign permanent residency is a Plan B to mitigate precarity in China, where they still hold citizenship, own businesses and properties, and live long term. Aside from the initial "investment" to obtain foreign permanent residency status, they also live in a perpetual readiness to uproot. On the one hand, their flexible resident identity alleviates the anxiety about personal or financial security in the Communist regime and the uncertainties of geopolitics and the global market. On the other hand, such freedom and fluidity indicate they hardly feel at home in either place.

Upon my follow-up question about whether those friends of hers regard themselves as New Shanghairen after obtaining a foreign permanent residency status while living in Shanghai long-term, Mei rolled her eyes to indicate how little the New Shanghairen label mattered to her friends. "[T]hey still regard themselves as Chinese. Among them, it's like, 'oh, Green card? Yeah, why not? Let's do it together!'" Such casualness makes obtaining a legal status in a foreign country, which involves millions of Chinese yuan, sounds more like organizing an oversea leisure trip or purchasing a trendy item. Limited effort or thought is spent in cultivating a sense of attachment to where they happen to or aspire to live.

In Jane's case, though Shanghai is her place of residence, the place she feels attached to, and the place she regards as home, none of that leads to her self-identification as a Shanghairen, because of her aversion to such labeling––a person of XYZ place, and her life trajectory and cultural capital:

> I never really identify as a person of my hometown [in southwestern China], or of Shanghai. . . . There is nothing wrong with Shanghai, it's just identification with a place is never my thing; . . . I don't think I have intentionally made the effort to assimilate into the local Shanghai culture, per se. . . . The environment I have lived and worked in in Shanghai has always been more foreign, like the branch of the British company I helped to establish in Shanghai. One-third of the team is Singaporeans, one-third is Westerners, such as Australians and Americans, and the last third is "locals." It's a "mixed" environment. Most people do not think I am a Shanghairen anyway. When I was in London, people thought I was Japanese. When I was in Singapore, everyone thought I was a Hongkonger. While I was in Hong Kong, people thought I was a Singaporean. And all my clients think I am a Taiwanese. So, I always see myself as a person of the world.

Aside from all the pull and push factors, Jane provides a more nuanced reflection on her place identity. It is the cosmopolitan or Western elements, for example, a mixed-origin social network and preference for Western-looking consumer spaces in the former French Concession in the city that she identifies with, instead of the vernacular characteristics of Shanghai. Her cosmopolitan identity is also communicated by her constant codeswitching between Putonghua and English during the interview: for example, the two words in quotation marks above are in English originally.

Multilingual, highly educated, and wealthy migrants, who hold upper-level managerial jobs or are entrepreneurs, see their entitlement to the city guaranteed by material wealth, regardless of *hukou* status. Their flexible resident identity is a global urban identity, though shy of global citizenship. All of them have experienced or at least are aware of the tortuous journey of acquiring a Shanghai *hukou* or the possibility of acquiring a foreign permanent residency status. The political and bureaucratic barriers present a clear contrast to the mobility and flexibility their wealth guarantees on a global scale. Even though not all of them have a Shanghai *hukou*, they appear to care less about it than their younger and less affluent counterparts in Shanghai. Such wealth-based confidence is communicated by their ease and nonchalance regarding urban residence, which could be anywhere in the world, as Hui said to me:

> I don't think there is a sense of identification with a place anywhere in the world; . . . Nowadays, most people are content with their lives. In any corner of the world, you won't think about the issue of identification. That said, I love the life in Shanghai, and will never consider moving anywhere else. All sorts of convenience, modern, it suits our generation.

Criticism of her ignorance of various kinds of sufferings in China and around the world aside, we need to acknowledge the life she enjoys is what Deng

Xiaoping envisioned as a *Xiaokang* society[33] of content, prosperous citizens when he initiated the Open Door Policy forty years ago. Contrary to what many researchers argue, Hui's contentment leads to the rejection of place identification.

The lack of identification with a place by this generation of urban migrants in China, and to be more precise, by this group who live comfortably in the global city of Shanghai, poses a sharp contrast to the ancestral home identification that prevailed for thousands of years, or the paramount importance of *hukou* status instilled in Mainland Chinese's minds over decades. Instead of a persistent melancholy for a lost home, amid societal upheavals, massive urbanization, and drastic urban redevelopment, the highly educated and upwardly mobile migrants in urban China make informed and strategic choices for their adopted homes. Nonetheless, they would never call themselves a person of that city, in this case, Shanghairen. Nor do they have the interest in learning the vernacular; perhaps because deep down, they all acknowledge that to be a true local, one needs to speak the local tongue.

LANGUAGE ATTITUDES

The inextricable linkage between language, identity, and territory manifests among native Shanghairen not only in their ambiguity regarding their children's Shanghai dialect acquisition but also their criticism of recent migrants' negative attitudes toward the dialect. Against the backdrop of the state promotion of Putonghua, and the dominant language ideology positioning Putonghua higher than regional dialects, migrants' motivations to learn the Shanghai dialect, or lack thereof, can be understood along two axes, instrumental and integrative. The instrumental motivation suggests migrants' positive attitude toward acquiring their destination's language is for practical reasons, such as qualifying for legal status, education, employment or expanding advantageous social networks. The integrative motivation stems from favorable attitudes toward the people and culture of the destination. Among the highly educated migrants I interviewed, the willingness to acquire and the actual possession of Shanghai dialect proficiency overlap place attachment to Shanghai. Their language attitudes remain independent of years of residency and are mediated by *hukou* status. Despite the overall decline of Shanghai dialect proficiency among native Shanghairen, the linkage between native identity and the vernacular is so deep-rooted that non-speakers will remain forever Waidiren, rendering the official label New Shanghairen obsolete.

Variations of Linguistic Discrimination

In the early 2000s, the Shanghai dialect still dominated the public sphere. Linguistic discrimination in its either overt or covert form was widely practiced by native Shanghairen. The responses from non-natives went either way: for some with a more pragmatic mind, the overt linguistic discrimination led to a positive attitude, regarding dialect proficiency as a plain skill to survive and live in the city. For example, the seamstress we encountered in chapter 2, or the story of the head of security guards at a performance arts venue. For those highly educated, it often led to aversion and rejection. Their negative experiences engendered the association between Shanghai dialect-speaking and bigotry and hostility. This unfavorable attitude destroys any potential motivation to acquire the dialect. For practical reasons, many migrants acquire passive knowledge of a few simple phrases such as hello and thank you, as Hui, who came from Harbin in northeastern China said in our interview:

> For those of us moved to Shanghai earlier, in 2004 or 2005, we remembered the wide usage of the Shanghai dialect, when you ran errands or dealt with government agencies. There was definitely a language barrier. We have all experienced rejection and discrimination by native Shanghairen against Waidiren, but it didn't force me to learn the dialect. I only wanted to understand it [to carry out daily activities], but I never want to learn it.

Her rejection and aversion to the dialect can be understood as her defense mechanism against the language even though speaking it could mitigate future unpleasant encounters. The changed linguistic environment, with state language policies mandating the use of Putonghua at government agencies, serendipitously justified her holding out against Shanghai dialect acquisition:

> Before, when you went to a government agency, they initiated the conversation in the Shanghai dialect, and would give you dirty looks when you asked them to repeat it in Putonghua since you didn't understand the dialect. As long as you could understand what they said, they would not be as nasty when you answered back in Putonghua. Otherwise, they were easily annoyed if you asked them to repeat their questions. Over time, since I could mostly understand the dialect, there have been fewer communication issues, and such occasions upsetting me gradually disappeared. Now it is very different. They always initiate the conversation in Putonghua. If the customer responds in the Shanghai dialect, they would switch to the dialect, otherwise the whole communication is carried out in Putonghua.

The banners, placards, and poster signs creating a Putonghua panopticon for native Shanghairen actively foster a friendlier linguistic environment for non-natives. In theory, it should prohibit Shanghai dialect-speaking in public, but as the above interview shows, in reality, it allows a degree of flexibility, as long as the staff is Putonghua-Shanghai dialect bilingual. From non-natives' perspective, the state's homogeneous language agenda facilitates their everyday lives in Shanghai.

However, outside of formal settings, all my non-native interviewees reported unpleasant encounters with native Shanghairen, especially those in their sixties or older, of working-class background or middle-aged workers in the service industry, such as independent storeowners and taxi drivers. As a college senior from northern Anhui province, who does not understand the dialect at all, put it succinctly at our interview in 2017: "As soon as they realize that you don't understand what they just said, they turn impatient and fidgety, making you feel it's your fault." Or from Liu: "When I first came to Shanghai [in 2011], it felt like Shanghairen were using the dialect to block us Waidiren, for example, in announcements on buses." Lindemann and Subtirelu stress how the burden of communication, which requires the participation of both parties, disproportionately lands on migrants who do not speak the local language.[34] Often overlooked, such phenomena blame the victim; for example, it is the non-speaker's fault if they miss their bus stop even when the announcement is incomprehensible to them. Despite the decline of Shanghai dialect usage in public, such linguistic discrimination still persists today, just in more covert forms.

Blatant linguistic discrimination against non-speaker migrants in public has gradually decreased amid the demographic changes to the city. While in the early decades of economic reforms, non-natives in Shanghai were predominantly unskilled migrant laborers. The proportion of highly educated non-natives has increased drastically in the last two decades, in part thanks to *hukou* reforms. The state's active promotion of Putonghua since 1998 and the dominant language ideology associating Putonghua-speaking with higher levels of educational attainment have changed perception of Putonghua among native Shanghairen. It results in a more tolerant and accommodating linguistic environment in Shanghai. Most highly educated migrants in my study who moved to Shanghai between the mid-2000s and early-2010s only picked up some simple phrases of the dialect. The more recently arrived found little incentive to learn the dialect, since there are almost no obstacles to face when speaking Putonghua in current Shanghai. Often, a friendly college campus community or a workplace with mixed natives and non-natives protects the highly educated migrants from overt linguistic discrimination. However, language-based social exclusion persists, as I briefly mentioned in the previous chapter about social integration between natives and non-natives at workplace. Here Junlin gave me an example from her first job after college at a local morning newspaper:

> At my previous job, more than half of my colleagues were Shanghairen. When they chatted or joked around after work in the Shanghai dialect, and you didn't understand what was so funny and asked them to repeat it in Putonghua, the mood was suddenly lost. They would comply but change the topic; the flow was broken, done. So, for non-natives like us, former classmates [staying in contact] and friends end up being all New Shanghairen, among whom you wouldn't feel the pressure.

Her experience of not being able to comprehend jokes her native Shanghairen coworkers made exemplifies covert linguistic discrimination that highly educated migrants still encounter. Instead of outrage, they internalize it as their own deficiency and a price to pay to work alongside native Shanghairen. Such language-based exclusion apparently led to social isolation and segregation as Junlin opted to socialize only with fellow non-natives, among whom she would not feel "the pressure"—in other words, discrimination. As Pillar points out, non-speakers of the dominant language, such as Lin in the Shanghai dialect-dominant environment, "are typically seen as the agents of their own exclusion."[35] Therefore, they are the ones to blame for the failure to integrate socially into the host society, even though their educational credentials and employment supposedly opened the door.

As the only interviewee in the small sample who finished college elsewhere and successfully obtained a Shanghai *hukou* through her employer, Hui explicitly expressed her dislike of the Shanghai dialect. In her words, it usually takes a few days for her to get used to the unpleasant-sounding dialect whenever she comes back to the city from a business trip or a visit to her parents in northeastern China, "it was like entering a bubble with harsh noises inside, whenever I landed at the airport in Shanghai." There are, of course, no innately unpleasant-sounding or inferior languages, and any aesthetic values associated with languages are culturally specific and ideologically.[36] Enjoyment of modern urban amenities, orderliness, and convenience in Shanghai makes Hui vow to never return to her hometown to live. However, it is safe to speculate that her distaste for the Shanghai dialect has its roots in her earlier negative experiences with native Shanghairen, not to mention her in-laws' initial opposition to her marriage due to her non-nativeness, as I showed in the previous chapter.

The aggressors in the linguistic discrimination scenarios mostly have lived in a Shanghai dialect-dominant environment their whole lives. Many of them are of the older generation who have limited Putonghua proficiency. Though they appear primarily annoyed by migrants' lack of Shanghai dialect proficiency, they are well aware of the language hierarchy and the incentives of speaking Putonghua well, as evidenced by their painstaking efforts to speak Putonghua to their school-age grandchildren. Such a contradiction does not diminish the difficulties of communication between natives and non-natives. We can attribute their shared powerlessness to recent state policies regarding internal migration and language, and to a certain extent, language education. The majority of senior citizens in Shanghai lack Putonghua competence beyond what they learned in school, where Putonghua was taught as a formal language, and primarily used in its written form. Thus, the current language conflicts are due to the quick collapse of a diglossia system in a Chinese metropolis. Both natives and non-natives are navigating and negotiating how to carry out daily and professional activities in a somewhat flexible, slightly inconvenient, but nevertheless exclusionary way based on socioeconomic status and origin.

OPPORTUNITIES AND OBSTACLES

Earlier in the book, I explored native Shanghairen's criticism of migrants' reluctance to learn the Shanghai dialect, as well as the structural reasons for the latter's lack of motivations to do so. Some migrants try to acquire the Shanghai dialect or express interest in doing so but are simply unable to master what is, essentially, a different language from Putonghua. The non-natives whom I spoke to attributed their immediate linguistic environment and their own innate language ability as the main factors for their varied success in acquiring Shanghai dialect proficiency.

Lan attributed her own Shanghai dialect proficiency to the linguistic environment during her undergraduate and graduate school years, when two close friends and dorm mates, both native Shanghairen, communicated mostly in the Shanghai dialect:

> The two of them tended to speak the Shanghai dialect in everyday conversations in our dorm. I just eavesdropped, and gradually was able to understand and to join their conversations with some simple phrases. If I felt comfortable, I would speak it; if too complicated, I would switch to Putonghua. There were incidents where strangers would be surprised with my switch, saying, "Wow, I thought you were a Shanghairen!" But I can barely speak it now, and even have difficulty understanding it . . . I no longer have the [same] linguistic environment.

She attributed both her acquisition and near loss of Shanghai dialect proficiency to environmental factors. It is not only her own domestic linguistic environment, which_since she married a fellow migrant from northeastern

China includes both Putonghua and its northeastern variation, but also the overall linguistic environment in her workplace and in public in general, where it is rare for her to hear the Shanghai dialect. Furthermore, she compared her older daughter's Shanghai dialect acquisition with her own experience, emphasizing the lack of a Shanghai dialect linguistic environment:

> Her Shanghai dialect proficiency . . . ha-ha . . . so bad! *yang jin bang*! Worse than my earlier days. She finds the dialect so interesting, but the [Shanghai dialect] linguistic environment in Shanghai [is non-existent]. . . . Another issue is domestically that even when such resources are available for my child to learn the Shanghai dialect, my husband might oppose. I very much want my child to learn the dialect, but my husband is like, meh . . . neither actively objecting, nor being supportive. He often says the kid is already overburdened by schoolwork. It's important to learn English, but why the need for the Shanghai dialect? Look at me, I am totally fine living and working in Shanghai despite not speaking the Shanghai dialect.

On the issue of their older daughter's acquisition of the Shanghai dialect, Lan and her husband each focused on one of the two functions of language: communication for social cooperation versus individual expression of identity. Her husband only sees the communication function of language, while Lan makes clear connection between her daughter's identification as a Shanghairen born and raised in Shanghai with a Shanghai *hukou*, with her regret about her daughter's lack of Shanghai dialect proficiency. Interestingly, over the interview, she stressed multiple times that her and her daughter's current Shanghai dialect proficiency level is *yang-jin-bang*, using a Shanghai dialect term that means non-standard. Her codeswitch from an otherwise Putonghua response to my interview question indicates her level of ease and comfort with the Shanghai dialect, even though she claimed her fluency had declined since college due to the lack of a Shanghai dialect linguistic environment.

Attitudes about Shanghai dialect acquisition go hand-in-hand with place attachment to the city. As shown earlier in this chapter, Lan undoubtedly regards Shanghai as home, and her attitude toward the Shanghai dialect corresponds to such sense of belonging and attachment. Her husband's unwillingness to learn the Shanghai dialect himself and his lack of interest in their older daughter's Shanghai dialect acquisition come as no surprise given his reluctance to apply to transfer his *hukou* to Shanghai and his earlier ambiguity about and hesitance to settle down in Shanghai.

The other factor to which migrants attribute their Shanghai dialect proficiency or lack thereof is their innate language ability. As Jane, who has lived in Shanghai longer than in her hometown, and who speaks nearly accent-free

Shanghai dialect, made the connection in her response, where she switched between the Shanghai dialect, Putonghua, and English:

> It's no big deal. For everyday communication, the necessary vocabulary is very limited. It's a "social language," for "dialogue." If you ask me to say "very particular" things in *Sanghai ai wo* (Shanghai dialect; originally spoken in the Shanghai dialect), I probably won't be able to. To that extent, I have no problem "understanding" it. That's enough.[37]

Compatible with her high linguistic ability, Jane smoothly included a Shanghai dialect phrase or two here and there like many native Shanghairen do, besides the constant codeswitch between English and Putonghua over our hour-long interview. Contrary to Jane's confidence in her overall linguistic ability, Junlin attributed her slowness in learning the Shanghai dialect to her overall low level of linguistic ability:

> My Shanghai dialect is really bad, very seldom I would speak it; . . . Overall, I am not good at learning languages, so I never . . . I don't feel comfortable practicing it. Even though I encounter many Shanghai dialect speakers at my previous newspaper job, and in everyday life, as long as I can figure out what the conversation is roughly about, I am good. I don't feel the pressure to learn the dialect. Even when I speak it, it sounds so weird, neither fish nor fowl, both for yourself and for others. Over the last seven years that I have lived in Shanghai, my Shanghai dialect is limited to asking for directions or saying hi to people.

Junlin had an incentive to learn the Shanghai dialect, since her first job was a reporter for a local morning newspaper, which involved interviewing various locals, including seniors who primarily speak the Shanghai dialect due to their lack of Putonghua proficiency. In addition, her brother is married to a native Shanghairen, and thus she is often invited for family dinners, where his in-laws predominantly speak the Shanghai dialect. But she still shows a reluctance to learn the dialect and attributes this to her innate lack of linguistic ability. Such explanation is rooted in the common belief that the capacity to learn a language is biological, and thus individuals are endowed with different levels of ability. Therefore, success or failure to acquire Shanghai dialect proficiency has little to do with one's will. This serves as a counterargument to how native Shanghairen view the lack of Shanghai dialect proficiency among non-natives. They accuse migrants of being lazy, and even become suspicious or question the migrants' character when the latter do not actively learn the dialect. This attribution to innate language ability is a mechanism for self-preservation against linguistic discrimination.

In workplaces in Shanghai in late 2010s, especially privately owned domestic companies, speaking the Shanghai dialect is a rarity, as Junlin, who at the time of the interview had left the local newspaper and joined a tech start-up, explained to me. Workplace demography shielded her from covert linguistic discrimination:

> When all your coworkers are New Shanghairen, or everyone speaks Putonghua, there is absolutely no pressure to understand the Shanghai dialect. In the start-up I am working at right now, everyone is Waidiren, including those with overseas experience, no one understands the Shanghai dialect. There is no Shanghai dialect-speaking environment.

The demography in the city has been rapidly changing with more and more non-natives working and living among natives. It is compounded with the fact that the younger generation of native Shanghairen rarely speak the Shanghai dialect themselves, even when they have a certain level of Shanghai dialect proficiency. All of these contribute to a more accommodating linguistic environment in Shanghai, as Junlin added: "People are used to it now that young people do not speak the Shanghai dialect, native or otherwise." The lack of pressure for non-natives to learn the Shanghai dialect to live in Shanghai comfortably can be understood as a progress, in terms of the diminished linguistic discrimination toward non-speakers. As two college seniors, who shrugged off my inquiry about their interests in learning the dialect, said, "Meh . . . I don't see why I need to."

In relationship to an individual's innate language ability, the case of Gong explains another obstacle to learning the Shanghai dialect for highly educated migrants. The non-Mandarin dialect of his hometown, Taizhou in northern Jiangsu province, is vastly different from Putonghua already, while its linguistic distance to the Shanghai dialect is also considerable. Contrary to Lan's interests and success in learning the Shanghai dialect from her college dorm mates and friends in the earlier 2000s, and Jane's pride in her overall linguistic ability evidenced by acquiring Shanghai dialect proficiency through daily interactions with native speakers in the late 1990s, Gong has never showed either interest or intention to acquire the dialect, even though two of his three college dorm mates are native Shanghairen and speak the Shanghai dialect often. Gong speaks Putonghua with an accent because of his mother tongue, and he acknowledges his non-standard pronunciation of Putonghua during our interview in a slightly timid manner. Gong's manner results from what Bourdieu calls symbolic violence,[38] which describes the force a dominant language ideology imposes on non-speakers or speakers of a non-standard variety and which makes them feel inferior. This type of violence does not need an active enforcer on site but becomes embodied linguistic capital.

Meanwhile, Gong pays no heed to the fact that he has no interest or intention to acquire the Shanghai dialect. The dominant language ideology shames those who do not speak Putonghua well, and regards regional dialects, such as his hometown dialect and the Shanghai dialect, as equally backward and inferior. To him, Putonghua is already a second language verbally, since most regional dialects in China do not have written forms. For non-natives from a predominantly Mandarin-dialect-speaking region, such as Lan, the Shanghai dialect would be her second Chinese language, while a third for Gong. Not to mention all the time and efforts supposedly invested in learning English, which is formally taught and tested from middle school up through university.

There is overall little interest among better-off, highly educated migrants to acquire the Shanghai dialect, as both my interviews and observations in Shanghai indicate. Moreover, Shanghai's recent internal migration policies, which aim to meet labor market demand and build a global financial and economic center, indirectly doom the vernacular. Upward mobility, upscale lifestyle, and community based on social class are promised and even guaranteed to the cluster of young, highly educated migrants—corresponding to the "high in educational level, high in skill level, and low in age" principle used in designing and tweaking *hukou* reform policies in the last three decades. This has resulted in the Shanghai dialect being gradually phased out in both public and private life. The right to the city is no longer associated with a linguistic insider membership but with material wealth and legal status.

In the eyes of a recent non-native college graduate, Shanghai is on track to become a true cosmopolitan city, with both a national tongue and a national palate:

> The so-called Shanghai culture is a mixture of various cultures from elsewhere. Especially the available cuisines are so diverse that Shanghai cuisine no longer dominates, for example, restaurants in Wujiaochang (shopping area). It is very rare to see a Shanghai cuisine restaurant. The same thing about language, Putonghua is getting more and more dominant that the Shanghai dialect is no longer central.

The literary analogy of what is on one's tongue, whether it be language spoken or cuisine tasted, indicates Shanghai's return to its "an ocean absorbs hundreds of streams" Hai-style character, instead of a twisted diversity placing the Shanghai dialect as default language, with other languages on the margins. Now, the Shanghai dialect and other languages, as well as Shanghai cuisine and dishes from elsewhere are equally diverse in Shanghai, with no particular one more prominent. Such equality is an agenda advocated by linguistic justice activists around the world. Ironically, the seeming achievement of it results from top-down policies in an authoritarian state. This book tells the other side of that success story that there is a price the locals pay to forgo such vernacular and their associated unique place identity. When the vernacular character of Shanghai, in both the linguistic and architectural sense, is disappearing from the city's sensory landscape, the city becomes more approachable, but bland; more diverse, but artificial; and more cosmopolitan, though rigidly confined by the central state.

NOTES

1. Liu, Ye, Zhigang Li, and Werner Breitung. 2012. "The Social Networks of New-Generation Migrants in China's Urbanized Villages: A Case Study of Guangzhou." *Habitat International* 36 (1): 192–200.

Huang, Xu, Bo Zhao, Ye Liu, and Desheng Xue. 2020. "Belonging to a Place: An Analysis of the Perceptions of Rural-to-Urban Migrants in China." *Geographical Review* 110(3): 406–24.

2. Cook-Martín, David. 2019. "Temp Nations? A Research Agenda on Migration, Temporariness, and Membership." *American Behavioral Scientist* 63 (9): 1389–403.

Du, Huimin. 2018. "Mobilities and Identities of Educated Young Adults: A Life-History and Biographical Study." *China Review* 18 (1): 35–58.

3. Di Saint Pierre, Francesca, Borja Martinovic, and Thomas De Vroome. 2015. "Return Wishes of Refugees in the Netherlands: The Role of Integration, Host National Identification and Perceived Discrimination." *Journal of Ethnic and Migration Studies* 41 (11): 1836–57.

Wang, Wenfei Winnie, and C. Cindy Fan. 2012. "Migrant Workers' Integration in Urban China: Experiences in Employment, Social Adaptation, and Self-Identity." *Eurasian Geography and Economics* 53 (6): 731–49.

4. Huang, Xu, Martin Dijst, Jan van Weesep, Yixue Jiao, and Ying Sun. 2017. "Residential Choice among Rural–Urban Migrants after Hukou Reform: Evidence from Suzhou, China." *Population, Space and Place* 23 (4): e2035.

5. Low, Setha M., and Irwin Altman. 1992. "Place Attachment." In *Place Attachment*, edited by Irwin Altman and Setha M. Low, 1–12. Human Behavior and Environment. Boston, MA: Springer US.

6. Lewicka, Maria. 2011. "Place Attachment: How Far Have We Come in the Last 40 Years?" *Journal of Environmental Psychology* 31 (3): 207–30.

7. More recent examples:

Swider, Sarah. 2014. "Building China: Precarious Employment among Migrant Construction Workers." *Work, Employment and Society*, August.

Wu, Weiping, and Guixin Wang. 2014. "Together but Unequal: Citizenship Rights for Migrants and Locals in Urban China." *Urban Affairs Review* 50 (6): 781–805.

8. Findlay, A., and Aileen Stockdale. 2003. "The Temporal and Social Embeddedness of Migration: A Methodological Exploration Using Biographical Analysis." *Geography Research Forum* 23: 4–29.

9. González, Marcela F. 2020. "High Skilled Immigrants' Pathways from Risky to Secure Legality in the United States." *Ethnic and Racial Studies*, January, 1–19.

10. Guidelines on Shanghai Resident Permit in Chinese. http://www.shanghai.gov .cn/nw2/nw2314/nw2319/nw2407/nw41492/u26aw54292.html.

11. Gustafson, Per. 2001. "Meanings of Place: Everyday Experience and Theoretical Conceptualizations." *Journal of Environmental Psychology* 21 (1): 5–16. P.9–11.

12. Tuan, Yi-Fu. 1977. *Space and Place: The Perspective of Experience.* Minneapolis & London: University of Minnesota Press. P.159.

13. Lalli, Marco. 1992. "Urban-Related Identity: Theory, Measurement, and Empirical Findings." *Journal of Environmental Psychology* 12 (4): 285–303. P.293.

14. Liu, Li, and Breitung. 2012. "The Social Networks of New-Generation Migrants," 192–200.

15. Goodman, Bryna. 1995. *Native Place, City, and Nation.* Berkeley, CA: University of California Press. P.14.

16. Liu, Liangni Sally. 2014. "A Search for a Place to Call Home: Negotiation of Home, Identity and Senses of Belonging among New Migrants from the People's Republic of China (PRC) to New Zealand." *Emotion, Space and Society* 10 (February): 18–26.

17. Agnew, John A. 1987. *Place and Politics: The Geographical Mediation of State and Society.* Allen & Unwin. P.28.

18. Harvey, David. 2007. "Neoliberalism 'With Chinese Characteristics.'" In *A Brief History of Neoliberalism*, 120–51. Oxford & New York: Oxford University Press.

19. Proshansky, Harold M., Abbe K. Fabian, and Robert Kaminoff. 1983. "Place-Identity: Physical World Socialization of the Self." *Journal of Environmental Psychology* 3 (1): 57–83. P.68.

20. Tuan. *Space and Place*, P.159.

21. Massey, Doreen. 1995. "Places and Their Pasts." *History Workshop Journal* 39: 182–92. P.155.

22. Carmona, Matthew, R. Carmona, Tim Heath, Taner Oc, and Steven Tiesdell. 2003. *Public Places, Urban Spaces: The Dimensions of Urban Design.* Oxford & Burlington, MA: Architectural Press.

23. Gustafson. "Meanings of Place," 5–16. P.11.

24. Sassen, Saskia. 2001. *The Global City: New York, London, Tokyo.* 2 edition. Princeton, N.J: Princeton University Press.

25. Ong, Aihwa. 1999. *Flexible Citizenship: The Cultural Logics of Transnationality.* Durham & London: Duke University Press.

26. According to a study by Shaohua Zhan and Min Zhou on highly skilled Chinese immigrants in Singapore, there is a narrower pathway to permanent residency and citizenship in Singapore than in the United States, Canada, and Australia.

See Zhan, Shaohua, and Min Zhou. 2020. "Precarious Talent: Highly Skilled Chinese and Indian Immigrants in Singapore." *Ethnic and Racial Studies* 43 (9): 1654–72.

27. Conventionally "*zuji*" is defined by the place a person's paternal grandfather was born and lived.

28. According to the U.S. Citizenship and Immigration Services, the EB-5 Immigration Investor Program was created by Congress in 1990 to stimulate the U.S. economy through job creation of at least ten full-time positions, or capital investment by foreign investors at minimum of $900,000–$500,000 before November 12, 2019. Conditional permanent residence to the EB-5 investor and derivative family members for a two-year period will be granted upon their admission into the United States with an EB-5 immigrant visa. The conditions will be removed from the lawful permanent resident status when sufficient evidences are provided to show job creation or investment sustainment three months prior to the end of the two-year period. See more details on the USCIS website. https://www.uscis.gov/working-in-the-united-states/permanent-workers/eb-5-immigrant-investor-program.

29. The new measure in effect from January 1, 2018, has amended this clause and grants permission for children of Shanghai Resident Permit holders to participate in the college entrance exam in Shanghai. However, it does not diminish how competitive the exams are.

30. Farrer, James. 2019. *International Migrants in China's Global City: The New Shanghailanders*. Abingdon: Routledge.P.168–97.

31. Tu, Siqi. 2020. "Destination Diploma: How Chinese Upper-Middle-Class Families 'Outsource' Secondary Education to the United States." Doctorate Dissertation, New York: Graduate Center, City University of New York.

32. The *hukou*-based nationwide college entrance exam registration requires high-school students to take the exam at the location of their *hukou*. Across the country, due to the uneven distribution of educational resources, there are eight different sets of exams, each based on different regional specific textbooks. Shanghai, Beijing, Jiangsu province, and Guangdong province each has its own exams for their *hukou* students, while the rest of the country uses the national set which has three versions. The level of difficulty of these five sets varies across regions and subjects.

33. Relatively affluent, middle-class society.

34. Lindemann, Stephanie, and Nicholas Subtirelu. 2013. "Reliably Biased: The Role of Listener Expectation in the Perception of Second Language Speech." *Language Learning* 63 (3): 567–94.

35. Pillar, Ingrid. 2016. *Linguistic Diversity and Social Justice: An Introduction to Applied Sociolinguistics*. Oxford & New York: Oxford University Press. P.162.

36. Edwards, John. 2011. *Challenges in the Social Life of Language*. Language and Globalization. London & New York: Palgrave Macmillan UK. P.73.

37. Words in single quotation marks were originally in English.

38. Bourdieu, Pierre. 1991. *Language and Symbolic Power*. Cambridge, MA: Harvard University Press.

Conclusion

In an article titled "Chengdu, China Gets a Modern Makeover" in the November 2015 issue of *Travel + Leisure* magazine, the author writes that "for many foreigners, there's a geographical hierarchy of authenticity. Shanghai is at the silicone-fake end of the spectrum."[1] The conventional understanding of authenticity lies in the unique character of a locale. How can Shanghai be seen as inauthentic, especially by foreign tourists, who expect traditional Chinese architecture, panda bears, and exotic cuisine? After all, any lack or loss of "authenticity" is itself ironically authentic, since all Chinese cities are being redeveloped to be modern, global, and nearly identical to each other.

Over the course of the last three decades, Shanghai has experienced an unprecedented transformation, as China's economic globalization and urban expansion intensified rapidly. What the article considers "fake" about Shanghai is its status as a global city and international financial center, a glossy sheen of luxury and power that suggests the non-existence of local character. From studying changes to the urban language landscape, I argue that the transformation of Shanghai is the top-down manifestation of the ideology of strengthening national identity and instilling national pride. Shanghai presents a unique case in all Asia, different from Beijing, Tokyo, Taipei, Seoul, or Singapore, in the sense that while participating in globalization with state-directed economic growth, it is not a capital city or home to a dominant national culture. In the re-globalizing process, the city has regained its status as a cosmopolitan metropolis, though one tightly controlled by the central government. To achieve this, Shanghai's own urban linguistic heritage has been sacrificed, the built environment has been remade, millions of Shanghairen are displaced and dispossessed, and millions of internal migrants have adopted the city as their new home.

The changes I have documented in this book go beyond statistics and visible architectural spectacles. I have shown a contested linguistic space, which vividly represents changes in the demography, political economy, and everyday life in urban Shanghai. Resulting from these changes, Shanghairen identity is also contested. Social processes such as these are crucial for our understanding of the impact of globalization on urban China. The effort to build global cities during the economic reform era opened Shanghai not only to the world but, more importantly, to the rest of the country. Though the city remains under the minute control of the central government, the flexibility granted by the framework of neoliberalism with Chinese characteristics[2] allowed migrants and investment capital to flow into the city, bringing about a full-scale transformation.

The uniqueness of Shanghai's transformation lies in the authoritarian state that has initiated and carefully monitored the process. In exchange for the city's global city status and improved standard of living, Shanghairen have been displaced from the urban center, their linguistic right to the city threatened, and they have experienced relative deprivation of privileges in terms of once exclusive access to top-quality social services through their urban Shanghai *hukou* status. At the same time, millions of internal migrants have settled down in the city. They have received a mixed reception from the municipal government and native Shanghairen. While their access to legal residence, employment, and social services is granted by the state, acceptance and integration into the native Shanghairen community has been less successful, especially with respect to the ultimate barrier, Shanghai dialect proficiency. In this book, natives and non-natives come together to tell a story of a transformed Shanghai, where the city's vernacular is silenced in the glittering and cacophonic global city fashioned by the authoritarian state to showcase its political and ideological success to a global audience.

I first traced Shanghai's cosmopolitan past, from the growth of its early population, to its divided landscape inherited from the city's semi-colonial era, to the contested origin of the Shanghai dialect itself. What makes the story of Shanghai fascinating is its migrant nature, uncommon among Chinese cities, which often boast more stable, millennia-long histories. The history of Shanghai gives it an East-meets-West flavor and provides a launching pad to claim a cosmopolitan future. But this time, the migrant city must speak Putonghua, sprinkled with some English if desired.

DIMINISHED LINGUISTIC SPACE

Seeing linguistic diversity as a threat to national unity and the lack of Putonghua proficiency a hindrance to economic developments across the country, the Chinese state established and forcefully promoted a language ideology that set in motion the dominance of Putonghua. This dominant language ideology portrays regional dialects, such as the Shanghai dialect, as vulgar, improper for formal settings, and incompatible with the social and economic progress of the country. With the passing of the *Law of the People's Republic of China on the Standard Spoken and Written Chinese Language,* in effect since 2001, the state made the use of Putonghua a sign of loyalty to the ruling Chinese Communist Party, making language choice a political choice. If one speaks Putonghua in Shanghai, it indicates that the speaker, being a law-abiding citizen, actively participates in achieving prosperity under the Chinese Communist Party's leadership. Conversely, the usage of the Shanghai dialect communicates a level of defiance, local pride, and in non-natives' understanding, a self-aggrandizing sense of social exclusion.

Under the state's continuous promotion of the official language through annual propaganda events and the school system, native Shanghairen have come to believe Putonghua proficiency is crucial for them and their children to achieve the "China Dream." Following Bourdieu, we see that the state has created a market for exchanging linguistic capital, represented by proficiency in Putonghua, for cultural, social, and economic capitals in the forms of educational achievement and upward social mobility. The historical, political, and societal background for the creation of this market was the shift from a planned to a market economy, which has opened up venues for such capital conversions.

Through the deployment of language laws and active construction and maintenance of the market for linguistic capital conversions, the state has successfully reduced the linguistic space of the Shanghai dialect and driven it to endangerment. Over the course of a single generation, the dialect has shifted from being regarded as the *lingua franca* of a city of millions to a local dialect incompatible with modern China. At home and in schools, a predominantly Putonghua environment is constructed for the young. Women and those of a lower socioeconomic status are more likely to cultivate Putonghua proficiency, in the hope of bettering their social position and circumstances. The state's promotion of Putonghua has been so successful that the Shanghai dialect is barely spoken among native Shanghairen born since the 2000s.

However, this does not mean the whole native Shanghairen population has abandoned the Shanghai dialect overnight. An alternative language ideology, valuing the cultural heritage and local history encoded in the dialect, and regarding the Shanghai dialect proficiency as the indicator of Shanghairen identity, has a sizable amount of supporters across generations of native Shanghairen. Against the backdrop of these two competing language ideologies, and the reality of dialect degradation, marginalization, and rapid endangerment, a Shanghai dialect preservation movement has gained traction. It started with vernacular theatre performers and intellectuals, who see high stakes of the dialect's survival for their professional lives. However, the efforts to save the dialect have led to very limited results among the general public.

The Shanghai dialect is a hybrid urban language born in *lilong* housing of Old Shanghai in the early twentieth century. Its vocabulary represents a way of life that has, to a large extent, been destroyed in the urban transformation of the last three decades. Those trying to preserve the dialect treat it as a surrogate for a Shanghai of crowded *lilong* housing and quiet streets lined with sycamore trees that will never return. Since that material base is gone, only the linguistic culture that the built environment once fostered can sustain their collective memory and Shanghai's distinct urban character. The resistance to the dominant language ideology and the uniform national identity it promotes is communicated not only through native Shanghairen's language attitudes and practices but also their viewpoint on the transformed urban built environment. To many of them, the city lost its unique character when nearly all the vernacular *lilong* housing was demolished, and in its place, rose a fake plastic global city, which they struggle to tie their place identity to. Unsurprisingly, to foreign tourists with little knowledge of Chinese languages, the Shanghai dialect as the last surviving authentic aspect of urban Shanghai is indiscernible.

INDISTINGUISHABLE URBAN SPACE

Beginning in the early 1990s, more than one million Shanghairen households were displaced from the historical urban center to make space for massive urban redevelopments and new infrastructure. In chapter 3, I illustrated the multiple social processes at work in Shanghai's urban transformation, in particular native Shanghairen's life after relocation. Renters of dilapidated state-owned properties in the historic urban center before economic reforms became owners of new apartments with modern amenities in the periphery of the city. Despite moving to better housing, the dislocation from traditional and overcrowded *lilong* housing has led to the loss of a sense of community and contributed to the dissolution of a speech community of the Shanghai dialect. Specifically, colorful idioms developed to describe daily life in *lilong* neighborhoods in most of the twentieth century have become irrelevant and obsolete.

The spectacular skyscrapers that now dominate the city's skyline were built to impress China and the world as evidence of Shanghai's global prominence. But this spectacular vision of a global Shanghai created by national elites and their delegates in Shanghai disregarded local urban history, generations of lived experience, and native Shanghairen's attachment to particular urban spaces. The urban space of glass-façade high-rises renders a sense of alienation and placelessness, as Edward Relph characterizes such modern urban built environment.[3] It has led native Shanghairen to attach their place identity to an imagined Puxi on the west bank of Huangpu River, the historical Old Shanghai. Imagined because Puxi is where the majority of urban redevelopment projects took place and where block after block of *lilong* housing and narrow meandering streets disappeared. Nostalgia for *lilong* housing no longer has a material base. It is a melancholy hidden behind the new normal of high-rise condominium buildings.

For these same reasons, many previous *lilong* dwellers reject Pudong. It had been farmland until the early 1990s but is now the skyscraper-crowded waterfront that symbolizes global Shanghai in movies, news reports, video games, book covers, and visitors' minds. Through their preference for Puxi residency and disdain for the architectural spectacles of Pudong, native Shanghairen insist on their vision of Shanghai against the state's and the world's. In turn, this attachment to place has largely served to distinguish native Shanghairen from recent migrants who are attracted to Pudong by job opportunities, modern amenities, and the "global city look." The Shanghai represented by Pudong is a three-dimensional printout designed by the state to communicate a nationalist vision, in contrast to a historically rooted Shanghai. The latter is a hybrid and dynamic urban space representing the vicissitudes of more than a century.

The destruction of this distinctive urban built environment has led many to believe that the local dialect is the last remaining signifier of the city's distinctive identity. But the influx of millions of non-speakers from across the country has disrupted the linguistic space of the Shanghai dialect and contributed to the dominance of Putonghua. With the gradual decline of structural barriers for non-natives to settle in Shanghai, geographical mobility in the economic reform era has revived Shanghai's migrant city identity. But unlike a century ago, this new cosmopolitanism now has a nationalist undertone and speaks of globalization in Putonghua.

SOCIAL INTEGRATION AND SHANGHAIREN IDENTITY

In addition to the impact of the dominant language ideology shunning the Shanghai dialect and geographical dispersion of native Shanghairen, in chapters 4 and 5, I explained another process that has contributed to the dialect's rapid decline. Under state language policies, native Shanghairen, as well as all citizens speaking local dialects across the country, acquire Putonghua as their second language. Given the vast difference between the Shanghai dialect and Putonghua, and the lack of incentives for migrants to acquire the dialect and for native Shanghairen to pass it down to the younger generation, the replacement of the Shanghai dialect by Putonghua in daily communications has turned out to be inevitable.

Shanghai has embraced migrants from all across the country for more than one and half century, starting in the mid-nineteenth century. The *hukou* system implemented in the late 1950s acted like a hiatus for that flow, till it has gradually loosened in the last three decades to meet the labor demand for globalization. To recruit a talent pool befitting a global city, the Shanghai Municipal Government circumvented the national household registration restrictions by screening and selectively granting migrants Shanghai *hukou*. This was an experimental measure adopted by other economically vital areas in the country under the umbrella of neoliberalism with Chinese characteristics. A Shanghai *hukou* is a legal status cementing Shanghairen identity, the lack of which once served as a marker for migrants' second-class status and exclusion from access to social services. By extending this legal status to highly educated and wealthy non-natives, the municipal government eliminated the institutional barrier for migrants' social integration. Indeed, my investigations have shown this group of migrants gaining acceptance at workplaces, and also in native Shanghairen social circles and families. However, this institutional inclusion that dissolves the boundary maintenance function of *hukou* status and legally treats non-natives the same as native Shanghairen backfired. It generated confusion about Shanghairen identity and triggered contention over the right to the city.

One important consequence of the transition from a socialist redistribution system to a market-based system is that more emphasis has been placed on personal financial capacity, in terms of access to housing, education, and health care. On the one hand, non-natives now have better overall chances for social integration and upward mobility since the structural barriers represented by the *hukou* system have receded; on the other hand, native Shanghairen have developed nuanced criteria anchored in dialect speaking, lifestyle, and mentality to effectively draw new social and cultural boundaries around insider membership.

Shanghai dialect proficiency and particular personality traits associated with long-term urban living, such as a blasé attitude or worldliness, function as new criteria of social distinction. The mobilization of such innate characteristics by native Shanghairen renders the officially sanctioned label "New Shanghairen" a euphemism for non-natives. Furthermore, the competing language ideologies alternately valuing Putonghua or the Shanghai dialect create fissures in the native Shanghairen community, which adds another layer to the city's language contention. There is ambivalence about membership in this group, especially among the younger generation of native Shanghairen.

Under the influence of state language policies, they speak the Shanghai dialect less and less. And more importantly, the reforms of the *hukou* system means they grew up, studied, and now work side-by-side with non-natives of similar socioeconomic backgrounds and do not necessarily see the latter as outsiders.

As for highly educated and well-off non-natives who have worked and lived in Shanghai for years, instead of a clearly demarcated insider/outsider self-identification, most of my research participants report a place identity in flux. Members of this group possess either Shanghai *hukou* or a Shanghai Resident Permit, and are granted not only legal status but also access to social services, nearly on par with those provided to native Shanghairen. Job opportunities helped them to overcome institutional barriers, either through their employer-sponsored *hukou* or through the city's new point system for a Resident Permit. Many of them have also become property owners. The reform of the household registration system in the 1990s also included provisions to allow college graduates to move around the country for jobs, unlike under the planned economy, when college graduates would be assigned by the college administration to positions locally or back in their hometowns. Such geographical mobility resulted in millions of highly educated migrants moving to economically vibrant cities, such as Shenzhen or Shanghai, where they are likely to marry fellow migrants from other parts of the country and start families in their adopted home.

Emotionally and materially, these migrants have put down roots in Shanghai, and some also articulate a sense of belonging and attachment. However, without Shanghai dialect proficiency, they do not regard themselves as Shanghairen and are not recognized as such by natives. Instead of pursuing the moving target of Shanghairen identity, more resourceful non-natives invested and cultivated a flexible resident identity beyond national borders. This in-between-ness has three components: the hometown that they no longer identify with or have desire to live in, Shanghai, where they live and work but do not fully identify with, and another country, such as the United States, where they have acquired permanent resident status through capital investments. For these selected few, their mobility and flexibility are cultivated for a sense of security and empowerment. It is a luxury and privilege that low-skilled and non-college-educated migrants, who remain the majority of non-natives in Shanghai, do not enjoy, even when they acquire some level of dialect proficiency.

With the changes to urban demography and the effectiveness of the 2001 Language Law, Putonghua dominates college campuses, offices, and other public spaces in Shanghai. The changed linguistic environment in Shanghai effectively reduced linguistic discrimination against non-natives, but also reduced incentives for highly educated and well-off non-natives to acquire the Shanghai dialect. Where dialect proficiency remains significant is in association with Shanghairen identity. The attitudes among non-natives regarding dialect acquisition indicate that changes in language attitudes are never solely a linguistic matter but are mediated by the acquisition of a Shanghai *hukou*, and the place attachment developed through years living in the city.

Promotion of the official language, transformation of the urban built environment, and selective social integration of internal migrants are the three primary state policies that converge on re-globalizing Shanghai. As it once again becomes a migrant city, Shanghai embraces cosmopolitanism with Chinese characteristics, that is, an all-encompassing, uniform Chinese identity, and an indistinguishable global city-look. Rather than presenting vernacular characters, the city turns into a mime with a painted cosmopolitan face, indistinguishable from other global cities. If it speaks, it only talks in the official language.

FUTURE OF THE SHANGHAI DIALECT

Globalized Chinese cities are the loci of international, national, and local language hierarchies and language ideologies, which manifest in language practices and attitudes of both (im)migrants and natives. The urban linguistic scene is closely monitored by national language policies, influenced by global cultural trends, and shaped by migrants past and present. In the case of Shanghai, this dynamic between languages and migrants has two dimensions. One is that the migrant experience in the city is shaped by the languages they speak when they arrive and those they learn to speak in the assimilation and acculturation process. The other is that the Shanghai dialect itself is encoded with the city's migration history and urban culture. The language conflicts and the endangerment of the Shanghai dialect I have illustrated in this book tell a story about more than just changes to the language itself, but power struggles between individuals and the state, between earlier and later waves of migrants, and between the rich and the poor.

Forces driving the rapid decline of the Shanghai dialect in the last two decades have not encountered many obstacles, though lately grassroots efforts have emerged to save Shanghai's linguistic heritage. From my investigation, the reasons for the dialect's dim prospect are threefold. First, ambiguity in associating dialect competence with Shanghairen identity; as I have shown, the younger generation of native Shanghairen rarely speak it. Second, debates within the dialect preservation community focus on the authenticity of the dialect. A similar case in Guangzhou observed by Liang shows the advocacy for correctly speaking and writing Cantonese among small activist groups.[4] Authenticity is extremely important because unlike the by-design placeless and thus universally applicable Putonghua supported by the state, the legitimacy of minority languages or ideologically defined "dialects" need ties with specific social, historical, and geographical territories to claim authority.[5] In the case of the Shanghai dialect, the spatial-temporal dimension of the claim ties to its origin story, which is a contention point within the activist's community. Dialect preservation activists compete for power, status, and fame in terms of defining the authentic version of the Shanghai dialect within the community. To a certain extent, resources and efforts are not effectively used to promote the dialect to a wider audience. And lastly, the limited resources devoted to cultural products using the dialect, such as movies and songs, if not censored by the state or market mechanisms, are often regarded as fleeting subcultural trends. Native Shanghairen who insist on the significance of dialect proficiency for genuine Shanghairen identity face the dilemma that their children and grandchildren barely speak the dialect. Nancy Dorian points out that when a language shift is already well under way, it is impossible to insist on the association between a social group's collective identity and the ancestral language.[6] Defining identity in terms of language would exclude most younger people from insider membership, since even those who do not speak the language are still legally, geographically, and ancestrally qualified to be considered native Shanghairen. Looking ahead, native Shanghairen cohorts that grew up in the 2000s and 2010s have, at most, limited Shanghai dialect proficiency or merely passive knowledge of the dialect. It would be safe to predict that without immense societal efforts to reestablish and promote dialect speaking among these younger generations, they are unlikely to actively acquire the Shanghai dialect, and later pass this linguistic heritage down to their own children.

This leads us to the issue of dialect acquisition, which relies heavily on personal motivation and access to resources. In chapter 3, we saw the popularity of a kindergarten in Pudong teaching the Shanghai dialect. Several other private kindergartens, in Puxi, have obtained permission from the municipal government's education board to use the Shanghai dialect as the medium of instruction. In addition, some native Shanghairen families have consciously exposed their children to the dialect. All these are promising signs of potential survival of the dialect. However, the new challenge lies in increasingly mixed unions in Shanghai. From my observation, in such unions, the native Shanghairen parent does not always codeswitch from Putonghua to the Shanghai dialect when speaking to the child, when they already habitually use Putonghua at work and with their spouse. It is nearly impossible to provide a constant Shanghai dialect environment for children born and raised in Shanghai, regardless of their parents' origins.

In a recent private conversation with a high-school classmate of mine, who founded one of the first private preschools in Shanghai which uses the Shanghai dialect as the medium of instruction and interaction, I learned about the other side of the blame game in terms of the Shanghai dialect acquisition among children. She founded the preschool in 2010 by using the dialect as its competitive edge to break into the market. Over the years, she encountered inquiries from parents about choosing the dialect over English and the relatively high fees she charges when there is no native English-speaking teacher, who are presumably paid more than domestic ones for creating an "authentic" English environment. How the price tag is not justified in those parents' minds suggests a language ideology locating global English higher than Putonghua and the Shanghai dialect. In response, my friend pointed out to the parents the waste and futility of a superficial English environment in those preschools when their children do not have anyone who communicates with them in English at home. On the contrary, a dialect-speaking environment at her preschool can potentially connect with the domestic environment where native Shanghairen grandparents speak the dialect and help to instill the Shanghainese way of thinking which are encoded in the Shanghai dialect.

In response to the prevailing accusation by native Shanghairen parents that their children adopt Putonghua shortly after attending preschools or kindergartens even when they were raised by predominantly dialect-speaking grandparents, the preschool principal fired back. In her defense, the culprit for either the non-acquisition or loss of Shanghai dialect proficiency is the domestic environment. This is in line with her credence of the uselessness of native-English-speaking teachers staffing preschools. Without an English-speaking environment at home or in society at large, merely a few hours a day at school, when aided by lots of body language can hardly contribute to young children's acquisition of English proficiency.It is apparent that the blame game leads nowhere when the overall linguistic environment in Shanghai has shifted from the Shanghai dialect to Putonghua. Children are not ear-muffed between schools and homes. Since the domestic, the educational, and the mass media domains are dominated by Putonghua, the diglossia system has been collapsing. It is hard to imagine a revival of the Shanghai dialect as the city's *lingua franca* for future generations.

Lastly, the role of mass media in producing theatrical, radio and television programs, and movies using the dialect, and the general public's access to these cultural goods are crucial for the fate of the dialect. For the survival of endangered indigenous languages, Grenoble and Whaley argue that economic factors, such as devoting human and financial resources to the production, promotion, and accessibility of cultural goods, are crucial.[7] Unfortunately, when mass media are under the control of state agencies like the State

Department of Propaganda or the State Administration of Radio, Film, and Television, permissions and licenses are rarely available for production in the Shanghai dialect. It furthers the dominant language ideology that has already degraded regional dialects.

Market mechanisms offer little help. To attract the largest possible audience, media production primarily uses Putonghua instead of regional dialects. A feature-length animated film released in August 2015 illustrates this market pressure. Dubbed in both Putonghua and the Shanghai dialect, "Sargent Black Cat: Emerald Star" (*heimao jingzhang: feicui zhi xin*) is a sequel to a Putonghua television cartoon series "Sargent Black Cat" produced in 1992, which was a sensation for a generation of Chinese children in the 1990s. According to an article titled "Good Idea but Hard to Promote, 'Sargent Black Cat' in the Shanghai Dialect" in the August 11, 2015, issue of the *Xinmin Evening News*, this animated film was shown on 1,530 daily screenings during initial release in Shanghai, and among these roughly 15 screenings showed the dialect version.[8] Screenings in the Shanghai dialect accounted for less than one percent of the total. In the same article, the reporter also mentioned that the audience of the dialect version was comprised mostly of Shanghairen in their thirties and forties, who explained that their children were not able to understand the dialect or were too young to read the subtitles.

It was a bold move by the studio and the local authority to produce and authorize the release of a Shanghai dialect version—especially considering the original television series was in Putonghua. Ultimately the profit-driven market determined the limited screenings and impact. This suggests a continuing downward spiral for the future use of the Shanghai dialect in mass media. With cultural censorship and the dominant language ideology ever present, there will never be a "full-fledged commitment of financial resources and manpower," which Grenoble and Whaley see as a crucial factor to offset trends toward monolingualism.[9] With fewer mass media cultural products targeting children using the dialect, the younger generation would be less exposed to the Shanghai dialect outside of family interactions, making retention of the dialect even more difficult.

Over the last few years, the Shanghai dialect or the usage of it has taken on a new life in Chinese social media. Native Shanghairen vernacular farce performer Zhou Libo—I wrote about the popularity of his show elsewhere[10]—whose phenomenal standup comedy about twentieth-century urban life in Shanghai was performed in sold-out live shows in the early 2010s. But in the last five years, live audiences have been replaced by followings and reposting of vlogs and rap songs in the dialect through Weibo, the Chinese Twitter, and WeChat, an all-encompassing social media platform, not to mention the new fad, TikTok. It appears that instead of being preserved as a cultural relic in museums, the Shanghai dialect has transformed into a counterculture or at least a medium of subculture for young native Shanghairen. Channels for media products distribution are more than ever under strict control by the Chinese state. The degree of surveillance and censorship has been more intense and fast-reacting in response to the sheer amount and speed of the spread of online contents. A Chinese term capturing such popularity on social media, *wanghong* (internet red, or rad more appropriately) is used to describe consumer products, restaurants and cafes, or influencers. In the fierce competition for attention, eyeballs or clicks, usage of the Shanghai dialect becomes a niche for brands and influencers to articulate distinction.

Two vloggers had their moments of fame in 2017 and lingered till 2019, Papi Sauce, a female native Shanghairen, and German Chubby A-fu, a male German immigrant who married a native Shanghairen and lives in Shanghai. Both won instant celebrity and attracted millions of fans online. Papi Sauce mostly focuses on the lives of young, highly educated, native Shanghairen female professionals. The rants about office life and descriptions of cosmopolitan middle-class lifestyle are delivered predominantly in the Shanghai dialect and in places mixed with English, but seldom Putonghua. German Chubby A-fu has a more domestic and quotidian flavor, unveiling the daily lives of intermarried native Shanghairen and white Europeans with a declared aim to facilitate cultural understanding between Germans and Chinese (Sohu News). He has been lauded by his native Shanghairen followers for his efforts to acquire the Shanghai dialect, especially in the eyes of those native Shanghairen who are critical about New Shanghairen's reluctance to do so. The post-colonial mentality of ranking foreigners from the West higher, thus their languages higher than Chinese languages manifests here when immigrants to the city such as A-fu, whose real name is Thomas Derkseu, overtly showcases his Shanghai dialect fluency. Similarly Bourdieu writes about a case in which a mayor "condescended" to speak the lower-status provincial dialect when giving a speech at a ceremony to honor a poet, native to the region, instead of using the official French.[11] The gesture was well received by the locals because the gesture symbolically negated the language hierarchy, however briefly.[12] Similar to A-fu's vlogs, there are other short video clips of white male immigrants in Shanghai speaking the dialect in retail settings, and acting like cultural concierges, introducing viewers to a cosmopolitan metropolis with a local flavor. Instead of the suspicions faced by Western missionaries or the so-called Shanghailanders in the early twentieth century, these immigrants enjoy online followings and applause from native Shanghairen who are alienated by the dominant language ideology belittling their native tongue.

With a very limited following that often only counts in the thousands, are rap songs with lyrics in the Shanghai dialect by native Shanghairen musicians. One of the leading figures of this trend, which started in the early

2000s, is Wang Min with the stage name Wang Changzhang (factory owner Wang). Recent native Shanghairen artists such as Mr. weezy taking advantage of this cultural market niche also performs in the Shanghai dialect, with nostalgic lyrics mixed with a hint of xenophobia. In a 2017 article about Mr. weezy by Deutsch Welle, he claims to use rap to defend the Shanghai dialect.[13] In Mr. weezy's song *The Shanghai Dialect*, a derogatory claim is made against migrants though the lyrics overtly deny the perceived accusation of xenophobia. The song first describes migrants' opinion about native Shanghairen, followed by the musician's characterization of migrants:

Shanghairen are so bad
If so, why do you still rush to be here like your life counts on it?
Try any possible means to acquire a (Shanghai) *hukou*
(We/Shanghai) give you resources
(We/Shanghai) give you space
Whatever you say/want, (We/Shanghai) provide
Ideally everything is catered to you
Sorry, Shanghai is not against outsiders but toxics
Shanghai is not where you can do whatever you want
Protect Shanghai's esteem and prestige is our (Shanghairen's) responsibility[14]

The song goes on to teach some simple terms, such as hello and thank you in the dialect, and describes characteristics of native Shanghai people as migrants themselves who adopted the dialect when settling in their new home and highlights positive characteristics of Shanghairen of different genders. The song ends with the suggestion to (non-native) listeners to learn the Shanghai dialect. The irony lies in the disjunction between the supposedly targeted audience, non-natives, and the probable audience, dialect speakers. The call for dialect acquisition in the song ends up as another instance of self-victimization, self-aggrandizement of Shanghairen identity, and language-based exclusion of non-natives.

No one should be surprised by derogatory terms or swear words used in rap lyrics. However, on a sensitive topic like Waidiren's accused behaviors and attitudes toward the Shanghai dialect, one can imagine the lack of wide endorsement or official support, even though the discriminatory tone echoes some voices in dialect preservation circles. Combined with the genre's Western origin and mostly online circulation—it is hard to imagine songs like that would be broadcast through state-owned radio stations in Shanghai—the audience reached is likely the younger generation who predominantly use Putonghua, or perhaps middle-aged listeners who are Putonghua and the Shanghai dialect bilingual. Other than a chuckle, or a repost/retweet, native Shanghairen listeners treat it as no more than one of the many fleeting online subculture fads. Such cultural products lack a critical mass to generate lasting impact on the preservation of the Shanghai dialect, or a positive message to foster meaningful changes to non-natives' mindset decoupling the Shanghai-dialect-speaking with social exclusion and discrimination, and may in fact exasperate them further. Moreover, as I have explained throughout this book, native Shanghairen themselves contribute to the decline of the dialect. Shanghai dialect rap songs or vlogs after all are transient phenomena, unable to sustain long-term interest in or promotion of the Shanghai dialect in every-day life. Echoing my findings about the ambiguity of Shanghairen identity in this book, when dialect proficiency no longer serves as the gatekeeper for material gains or access to resources or opportunities, it generates very limited traction and regresses to the state of some sort of gimmick. Not to mention Shanghairen identity as an incentive for dialect acquisition has limited appeal.

PUTONGHUA AND CHINESE
IDENTITY BEYOND BORDERS

Examining the promotion of Putonghua and the connection between local dialect and regional identity beyond the Shanghai context, I will speculate on two fronts. One is language planning in terms of fostering Putonghua profi-ciency in developing countries participating in the Belt and Road Initiative (BRI), and the other is the recent emergence of state-sponsored museums of local dialects and cultural heritage along the coast of southeast China. It is where Guangdong (Canton) and Fujian provinces, the ancestral homes of mil-lions of diaspora Chinese around the world, are located.

Against the backdrop of language shifts from regional dialects to Putonghua all over the country, a recent phenomenon caught my attention. From per-sonal communication with a scholar who originates from Fujian province and speaks Hokkien as her mother tongue, I learned about government efforts to preserve the Hokkien dialect and to build local history and cultural heritage museums in Fujian. It immediately struck me as an indication of President Xi's likely vision of an imagined global Chinese community, connecting the ancestral home with the diaspora Hokkien communities in Southeast Asia and elsewhere through shared language and cultural heritage. It manifests in the government's intention toward "integrating" the diasporic Hokkien group for China's global ambition. The measure functions simultaneously outward to link the diasporic Chinese, and also inward to connect the domestic eco-nomic migrants in other parts of China, for example the Hokkien museum in Shenzhen in Canton.[15] Shenzhen is one of the earliest Special Economic Zones initiated by the Open Door Policy four decades ago and home to mil-lions of Hokkien-speaking migrants from neighboring areas.

In relation to diasporic Chinese, Gao channels the official statement about BRI serving as the platform to spread the usage of Mandarin Chinese that

> it is also overseas Chinese immigrants' linguistic right to learn their heritage language. Moreover, the inheritance of Chinese as heritage language; . . . leads them to inherit the national characters and cultural identity behind the language. The inheritance of Chinese could be taken as the key to helping oversea Chinese immigrants and their descendants to solve the confusion between language identity, ethnic identity and even national identity[16]

The statement rejects the internal diversity of Chinese languages, and of regional and ethnic identities. The coherence of this stated goal is achieved by lumping together the assumed monolithic Chinese culture and a politically and socially constructed Chinese nation within and beyond the national border.

Recent literature on language planning accompanying the BRI citing Chinese Communist Party official speeches reveals that Putonghua is designated to play a decisive role as the medium of communication, to level off cultural barriers across societies and be adopted as the *lingua franca* along the Road.[17] In the context of bundling Putonghua usage with economic development, the explicitly stated aim is never to provoke another linguistic imperialism, as with English, but instead to promote linguistic diversity to sustain the global linguistic ecosystem.[18] Against the backdrop of the speedy measure in setting up 135 Confucius Institutes and 129 Confucius Classrooms in 51 countries along the Belt and Road,[19] in a statement by Li Mingyu, the former associate director of the State Language Commission (*guojia yuyanwenzi gongzuo weiyuanhui*), he cautioned the usage of terms such as "promotion of Chinese Language," to avoid conflict with BRI's stated goal of equality and mutual benefits.[20]

On the ground, it is a different story. An article titled "Mandarin made Compulsory in Nepali Schools" published in June 2019 by the Hong Kong-based online media platform Belt & Road News, quoted from the *Himalayan Times* that many schools across Nepal overlooked national provisions prohibiting teaching foreign languages during school hours or making foreign-language-learning mandatory by jumping on the offer by the Chinese government which covers salaries for instructors who teach Mandarin.[21] In other words, money speaks in Putonghua, and furthers China's long-term strategy aiming at fostering and exerting soft power across the region. Gao synthesizes from three volumes of *The Language Situation and Language Policy in the "Belt and Road"* edited by Hui Wang and published by Social Sciences Academic Press in Beijing that "BRI provides a platform to develop Chinese language status overtly, and makes the planning of developing Chinese as a *lingua franca* possible: the 'Greater Chinese' concept proposed in recent years is conducive to enhancing the centripetal power of Chinese and its global radiation."[22] The theoretical framework "pride and profit" developed by Duchene and Heller[23] will be useful to guide future research in examining this rising phenomenon in countries along the Road. How much economic benefits attract people in countries along BRI to acquire Putonghua proficiency? And how much the benefits will materialize?

This book documents the endangerment of the Shanghai dialect over one generation in a Chinese city that takes pride in its unique urban culture and people. Shanghai's distinctiveness is articulated by its early fame as an East-meets-West metropolis and the lasting identification with un-Chinese-ness, as much as allowed by political powers and economic interests originating elsewhere. As the city's motto, *Hai Na Bai Chuan* (the ocean absorbs hundreds of streams), indicates, the linguistic scene and the identity of the city and its people will always confront new influx and be in flux. The unique case of Shanghai and its dialect lies not only in the locale's nature as a cosmopolitan metropolis but also that the authoritarian state participates in neoliberalism and globalization. As shown in this study, in the place of vernacular culture, a national language and a state-reinvented national culture establish dominance in order to facilitate the process of globalization.

Linkage between local identity and proficiency in the vernacular is a universal phenomenon. Unfortunately, due to state language policies that vigorously promote Putonghua across the country, the significant decline and endangerment of local dialects are widely observed. Qi Shen and Xuesong Gao characterize global Shanghai as multi-dialectal and multilingual.[24] The cacophony reflects not only changing demography but also the city's new socioeconomic hierarchy. Developmental policies and the dominant language ideology impact both native and non-native Shanghairen's urban experiences in myriad ways. Various agencies are at work as urbanites navigate, negotiate, and confront institutional forces in their everyday language practices. Future research is needed to investigate the potential impact of BRI on the fates and futures of urban and regional languages along the Road, the potential of Putonghua rising to the status of a global language to compete with English, and the possibilities of new global cities in the Global South fighting to preserve and revive their vernaculars, so that they are not plastic fake after all, but authentic and unique in beautiful, audible ways.

NOTES

1. Beam, Christopher. 2015. "Chengdu, China Gets a Modern Makeover." *Travel + Leisure*, November 10, 2015. https://www.travelandleisure.com/trip-ideas/chengdu -china-modern-makeover.

2. Harvey, David. 2007. "Neoliberalism 'with Chinese Characteristics.'" In *A Brief History of Neoliberalism*, 120–51. Oxford & New York: Oxford University Press.

3. Relph, Edward. 1976. *Place and Placelessness*. London: Pion.

4. Liang, Sihua. 2015. *Language Attitudes and Identities in Multilingual China: A Linguistic Ethnography*. Heidelberg, New York: Springer. P.20.

5. Wong, Andrew D. 2019. "Authenticity, Belonging, and Charter Myths of Cantonese." *Language & Communication*, Language, Mobility and Belonging, 68 (September): 37–45. P.38.

6. Dorian, Nancy. 1998. "Western Language Ideologies and Small-Language Prospects." In *Endangered Languages: Language Loss and Community Response*, edited by Lenore A. Grenoble and Lindsay J. Whaley, 3–21. Cambridge, MA: Cambridge University Press. P.20

7. Grenoble, Lenore A., and Lindsay J. Whaley. 1998. "Toward a Typology of Language Endangerment." In *Endangered Languages: Language Loss and Community Response*, edited by Lenore A. Grenoble and Lindsay J. Whaley, 22–54. Cambridge: Cambridge University Press. P.52–53.

8. Zhang, Yi. 2015. "Good Idea but Hard to Promote, 'Sargent Black Cat' in the Shanghai Dialect [*huyuban heimao jingzhang chuangyi hao tuiguang nan*]." *Xinmin Evening News*, August 11, 2015. http://www.jfdaily.com/wenyu/new/201508/t2015 0811_1743774.html.

9. Grenoble, and Whaley. "Toward a Typology of Language Endangerment," 22–54. P.54.

10. Xu, Fang. 2020. "Chapter 11: Only Shanghainese Can Understand: Popularity of Vernacular Performance and Shanghainese Identity." In *Revealing/Reveiling Shanghai: Cultural Representations from the 20th and 21st Centuries*, edited by Lisa Bernstein and Chu-Chueh Cheng, 215–38. Albany: State University of New York Press.

11. Bourdieu, Pierre. 1991. *Language and Symbolic Power*. Cambridge, MA: Harvard University Press. P.68.

12. Bourdieu. *Language and Symbolic Power*.

13. Deutsche Welle (www.dw.com). 2017. "Use Rap to Defend the Shanghai Dialect (*yong raosheyue hanwei shanghaihua*)." DW.COM. October 23, 2017. https://p.dw.com/p/2mLjA.

14. See the full lyrics in Mandarin Chinese in the following link: https://mp.weixin .qq.com/s?__biz=MzI3MzM3MjY3MQ==&mid=2247489823&idx=1&sn=82cdd0 f21af599bbc230317b56faf9b3&.

15. "Hokkien Has Its Own Museum!" January 2, 2019. https://kknews.cc/zh-my/c ulture/l4ebye2.html.

16. Gao, Yang. 2020. "How the Belt and Road Initiative Informs Language Planning Policies in China and among the Countries along the Road." *Sustainability* 12 (14): 5506: 11.

17. Gao. "How the Belt and Road Initiative Informs," 5506: 8.

18. Gao. "How the Belt and Road Initiative Informs," 5506: 11.

19. Peters, Michael A. 2020. "China's Belt and Road Initiative: Reshaping Global Higher Education." *Educational Philosophy and Theory* 52 (6): 586–92. P.590.

20. Li, Mingyu. 2015. "BRI Requires Language Planning (Yi Lu Yi Dai Xuyao Yuyan Pulu)." People.cn - People's Daily. September 22, 2015. http://theory.people .com.cn/n/2015/0922/c40531-27616931.html.

21. Not to be mistaken with the Beijing headquartered Belt and Road News Network, which is chaired by the *People's Daily*, the official outlet of the Central Committee of the Chinese Communist Party (Albert 2019).

22. Gao. "How the Belt and Road Initiative Informs," 5506:10.

23. Heller, Monica, and Alexandre Duchene. 2012. "Pride and Profit: Changing Discourses of Language, Capital and Nation-State." In *Language in Late Capitalism: Pride and Profit*, edited by Alexandre Duchene and Monica Heller, 1–21. New York & London: Routledge.

24. Shen, Qi, and Xuesong Gao. 2019. "Multilingualism and Policy Making in Greater China: Ideological and Implementational Spaces." *Language Policy* 18 (1): 1–16.

Appendix I

Law of the People's Republic of China on the Standard Spoken and Written Chinese Language

(Adopted at the 18th Meeting of Standing Committee of the Ninth National People's Congress on October 31, 2000 and promulgated by Order No. 37 of the President of the People's Republic of China on October 31, 2000)[1]

CHAPTER I GENERAL PROVISIONS

Article 1. This Law is enacted in accordance with the Constitution for the purpose of promoting the normalization and standardization of the standard spoken and written Chinese language and its sound development, making it play a better role in public activities, and promoting economic and cultural exchange among all Chinese nationalities and regions.

Article 2. For purposes of this Law, the standard spoken and written Chinese language means Putonghua (a common speech with pronunciation based on the Beijing dialect) and standardized Chinese characters.

Article 3. The State popularizes Putonghua and the standardized Chinese characters.

Article 4. All citizens shall have the right to learn and use the standard spoken and written Chinese language.

The State provides citizens with the conditions for learning and using the standard spoken and written Chinese language.

Local people's governments at various levels and the relevant departments under them shall take measures to popularize Putonghua and standardized Chinese characters.

Article 5. The standard spoken and written Chinese language shall be used in such a way as to be conducive to the upholding of state sovereignty and national dignity, to unification of the country and unity of the nationalities, and to socialist material progress and ethical progress.

Article 6. The State promulgates standard norms of the spoken and written Chinese language, administers its use in the community, supports the teaching of and scientific research in the language in order to promote its normalization, enrichment and development.

Article 7. The State rewards the organizations and individuals that have made outstanding contribution in the field of the standard spoken and written Chinese language.

Article 8. All the nationalities shall have the freedom to use and develop their own spoken and written languages.

The spoken and written languages of the ethnic peoples shall be used in accordance with the relevant provisions of the Constitution, the Law on Regional National Autonomy and other laws.

CHAPTER II USE OF THE STANDARD SPOKEN AND WRITTEN CHINESE LANGUAGE

Article 9. Putonghua and the standardized Chinese characters shall be used by State organs as the official language, except where otherwise provided for in laws.

Article 10. Putonghua and the standardized Chinese characters shall be used as the basic language in education and teaching in schools and other institutions of education, except where otherwise provided for in laws.

Putonghua and the standardized Chinese characters shall be taught in schools and other institutions of education by means of the Chinese course. The Chinese textbooks used shall be in conformity with the norms of the standard spoken and written Chinese language.

Article 11. Publications in Chinese shall be in conformity with the norms of the standard spoken and written Chinese language.

Where foreign languages need to be used in publications in Chinese, necessary explanatory notes in standard Chinese shall be applied.

Article 12. Putonghua shall be used by the broadcasting and TV stations as the basic broadcasting language.

Where foreign languages need to be used as the broadcasting languages, the matter shall be subject to approval by the broadcasting and television administration under the State Council.

Article 13. The standardized Chinese characters shall be used as the basic characters in the service trade. Where both a foreign language and the Chinese language are used in signboards, advertisements, bulletins, signs, etc., as is needed by the trade, the standardized Chinese characters shall be used as far as the Chinese Language is concerned.

People working in the service trade are encouraged to use Putonghua when providing services.

Article 14. The standard spoken and written Chinese language shall be used as the basic spoken and written language in the following circumstances:

(1) spoken and written language for broadcasting, films and TV programs;
(2) written language for the facilities in public places;
(3) written language in signboards and advertisements;
(4) names of enterprises and other institutions; and
(5) packaging and specifications of commodities marketed in the country.

Article 15. The standard spoken and written Chinese language used in information processing and information technology products shall be in conformity with the norms of the State.

Article 16. Where the relevant provisions of this Chapter are concerned, local dialects may be used under the following circumstances:

(1) when State functionaries really need to use them in the performance of official duties;
(2) where they are used in broadcasting with the approval of the broadcasting and television administration under the State Council or of the broadcasting and television department at the provincial level;
(3) where they are needed in traditional operas, films and TV programs and other forms of art; and
(4) where their use is really required in the publishing, teaching and research.

Article 17. Whereby the relevant provisions of this Chapter are concerned, the original complex or the variant forms of Chinese characters may be retained or used under the following circumstances:

(1) in cultural relics and historic sites;
(2) the variant forms used in surnames;
(3) in works of art such as calligraphy and seal cutting;
(4) handwritten inscriptions and signboards;
(5) where their use is required in the publishing, teaching and research; and
(6) other special circumstances where their use is approved by the relevant departments under the State Council.

Article 18. The "Scheme for the Chinese Phonetic Alphabet" shall be used as the tool of transliteration and phonetic notation for the standard spoken and written Chinese language.

The "Scheme for the Chinese Phonetic Alphabet" is the unified norm of the Roman letters for transliterating the names of Chinese people and places as well as Chinese documents and is used in the realms where it is inconvenient to use the Chinese characters or where the Chinese characters cannot be used.

Chinese phonetic alphabets shall be used in primary education.

Article 19. All staff members who need to use Putonghua as their working language shall have the ability to speak Putonghua.

The Putonghua level of those who use Putonghua as their working language, such as broadcasters, program hosts and hostesses, actors and actresses of films, TV series and plays, teachers and State functionaries shall reach the respective standards set by the State; those who have not yet reached such standards shall receive different training, as the case may be.

Article 20. Putonghua and the standardized Chinese characters shall be taught in classes for foreigners who are learning Chinese.

CHAPTER III ADMINISTRATION AND SUPERVISION

Article 21. The department in charge of the work related to spoken and written language under the State Council shall be responsible for planning, guiding, administering and supervising the work related to the standard spoken and written Chinese language.

The departments concerned under the State Council shall administer the use of the standard spoken and written Chinese language in their own departments.

Article 22. Local departments in charge of the work related to spoken and written language and other departments concerned shall administer and supervise the use of the standard spoken and written Chinese language within their own administrative areas.

Article 23. The administrative departments for industry and commerce under the local people's governments at or above the county level shall administer and supervise the use of spoken and written language in the names of enterprises and commodities as well as in advertisements.

Article 24. The department in charge of the work related to spoken and written language under the State Council shall issue standards for the test of Putonghua at different grades.

Article 25. The department in charge of the work related to spoken and written language under the State Council or other departments concerned shall make arrangements for the examination of the translation of the proper nouns like the names of foreigners and foreign places and the scientific and technical terms into the standard spoken and written Chinese language.

Article 26. Any citizen may make criticism and put forward suggestions where the use of spoken and written language is at variance with the norms of the standard spoken and written Chinese language and is in violation of the relevant provisions in Chapter II of this Law.

Where persons mentioned in the second paragraph of Article 19 of this Law use the language in violation of the relevant provisions of Chapter II of this Law, the units concerned shall, by way of education, criticize the persons who are directly responsible; anyone who refuses to put it right shall be handled by the units concerned.

Where the characters used in the facilities and signboards in public places of cities and in advertisements are in violation of the relevant provisions of Chapter II of this Law, the administrative departments concerned shall give orders for them to be corrected; anyone who refuses to correct them shall be given a disciplinary warning and be urged to put them right within a time limit.

Article 27. Anyone who, in violation of this Law, interferes with other persons' learning and using of the standard spoken and written Chinese language shall be ordered by the relevant administrative departments to put it right within a time limit and be given a disciplinary warning.

CHAPTER IV SUPPLEMENTARY PROVISIONS

Article 28 This Law shall go into effect as of January 1, 2001.

NOTE

1. The National People's Congress of the People's Republic of China. Database of Law and Regulations. http://www.npc.gov.cn/englishnpc/Law/2007-12/11/content _1383540.htm.

Appendix II

List of Annual National Putonghua Promotion Week Themes 1998–2020

Table AII.1   List of Annual National Putonghua Promotion Week Themes 1998–2020. Issued by the Ministry of Education of the People's Republic of China

	Period	Theme
First	September 13–19, 1998	Speaking Putonghua, Starting from Me. [*shuo Putonghua cong wo zuo qi*]
Second	September 12–18, 1999	Promote Putonghua, Welcome New Century. [*tuiguang Putonghua, yingjie xin shiji*]
Third	September 10–16, 2000	Promote Putonghua, Walk into the New Century. [*tuiguang Putonghua, mai xiang xin shiji*]
Fourth	September 9–15, 2001	Propagate Law on the Standard Spoken and Written Chinese Language, Strongly Promote Putonghua, and Facilitate Standardization of Spoken and Written Chinese. [*xuanchuan guanche guojia tongyong yuyan wenzi fa, dali tuiguang Putonghua, cujin yuyan wenzi guifanhua*]
Fifth	September 15–21, 2002	Propagate Law on the Standard Spoken and Written Chinese Language, Strongly Promote Putonghua, Facilitate Standardization of Spoken and Written Chinese, and Welcome the 16th National Congress of the Communist Party of China. [*xuanchuan guanche guojia tongyong yuyan wenzi fa, dali tuiguang Putonghua, cujin yuyan wenzi guifanhua, yingjie dang de shiliu da zhaokai*]
Sixth	September 14–20, 2003	Strongly Promote Putonghua, Work Together to Achieve Moderate Prosperity. [*dali tuiguang Putonghua, qixin xieli beng xiaokang*]
Seventh	September 12–18, 2004	Putonghua – Link of Emotions, Bridge of Communication. [*Putonghua: qinggan de niudai, goutong de qiaoliang*]

(Continued)

Table AII.1 List of Annual National Putonghua Promotion Week Themes 1998–2020. Issued by the Ministry of Education of the People's Republic of China *(Continued)*

Period		Theme
Eighth	September 11–17, 2005	Achieve Smooth Communication, Build a Harmonious Society. [*shixian shunchang jiaoliu, goujian hexie shehui*].
Ninth	September 10–16, 2006	Putonghua: Promotion for Fifty Years, Widespread in the New Century. [*Putonghua: wushi nian tuiguang, xin shiji puji*]
Tenth	September 9–15, 2007	Construct a Harmonious Linguistic Life, Carry Forward Excellent Chinese Culture. [*goujian hexie yuyan shenghuo, hongyang zhonghua youxiu wenhua*]
Eleventh	September 14–20, 2008	Construct Harmonious Linguistic Life, Create Shared Spiritual Homeland. [*goujian hexie yuyan shenghuo, yingzao gongyou jingshen jiayuan*]
Twelfth	September 13–19, 2009	Love Spoken and Written Language of the Motherland, Construct Harmonious Linguistic Life. [*re'ai zuguo yuyan wenzi, goujian hexie yuyan shenghuo*]
Thirteenth	September 12–18, 2010	Standardize the Use of Spoken and Written Chinese Language, Carry Forward Excellent Chinese Culture and Tradition. [*guifan shiyong guojia tongyong yuyan wenzi, hongyang zhonghua youxiu wenhua chuantong*]
Fourteenth	September 11–17, 2011	Improve Competence in the Standard Spoken and Written Chinese Language, Carry Forward Excellent Chinese Culture and Tradition. [*tisheng guojia tongyong yuyan wenzi yingyong nengli, hongyang zhonghua youxiu wenhua chuantong*]
Fifteenth	September 14–20, 2012	Vigorously Promote the Use of Standard Spoken and Written Chinese Language. [*dali tuiguang he guifan shiyong guojia tongyong yuyan wenzi*]
Sixteenth	September 11–17, 2013	Promote Putonghua, Build the China Dream Together. [*tuiguang Putonghua, gong zhu zhongguo meng*]
Seventeenth	September 15–21, 2014	Speak Putonghua Well, You, I and He Realize the Dream. [*shuo hao Putonghua, yuan meng ni wo ta*]
Eighteenth	September 14–20, 2015	Promote Putonghua according to the Law, Increase the Country's Soft Power. [*yi fa tuiguang Putonghua, tisheng guojia ruan shili*]
Nineteenth	September 8–14, 2016	Vigorously Promote and Standardize the Use of Standard Spoken and Written Chinese Language, Assist the Overall Achievement of Xiaokang Society [*dali tuixing he guifan shiyong guojia tongyong yuyan wenzi, zhuli quanmian jiancheng xiaokang shehui*]

(Continued)

Table AII.1   List of Annual National Putonghua Promotion Week Themes 1998–2020. Issued by the Ministry of Education of the People's Republic of China *(Continued)*

	Period	Theme
Twentieth	September 11– 17, 2017	Vigorously Promote and Standardize the Use of Standard Spoken and Written Chinese Language, Voluntarily Pass Down and Elevate Excellent Traditional Chinese Culture. [*dali tuixing he guifan shiyong guojia tongyong yuyan wenzi, zijue chuancheng hongyang zhonghua youxiu chuantong wenhua*]
Twenty-first	September 10– 16, 2018	Speak Putonghua Well, Step into a New Era. [*shuo hao Putonghua, mai jin xin shi dai*]
Twenty-second	September 16– 22, 2019	Using Putonghua to Chant the Seventieth Anniversary; Using Standardized Characters to Write Patriotic Feelings [*Putonghua song qishi huadan, guifanzi shu aiguo qinghuai*]
Twenty-third	September 14– 20, 2020	Speak Putonghua Together, Entering Xiaokang Hand-in-Hand [*tong jiang Putonghua, xie shou jin xiaokang*]

Appendix III

2013 Interview Guide with Native Shanghairen

1) How much do you understand the Shanghai dialect?
2) How well do you speak the Shanghai dialect?
3) How well do you read the Shanghai dialect (News articles and posts written in a phonetic combination of Mandarin Chinese characters)?
4) During your school years (elementary, middle, high school, college), in which language (Mandarin Chinese or the Shanghai dialect) did your teachers teach? In which language did you communicate with teachers? With your classmates?
5) In your workplace now, in which language do you communicate? Have you seen any change in terms of the language choice over the last five years?
6) Which language do you speak with your friends?
7) At home, in which language do you communicate with parents, your spouse, and your child(ren)?
8) In public places, in which language would you initiate contact with strangers? How do you usually make the choice?
9) Have you heard about the vernacular comedian Zhou Libo? Have you gone to any of his performances? What do you think of his performances in the Shanghai dialect?
10) Have you heard about the preservation of the Shanghai dialect movement? If so, what do you think about it? What do you think about those advocates' claim that the Shanghai dialect is dying?
11) What do you think are the characteristics of being a Shanghairen; is speaking the Shanghai dialect one of them? What else counts?
12) What is your opinion on the balance between using English, Putonghua, and the Shanghai dialect, in the case of public transit announcements?

13) How do you see the future of the Shanghai dialect and the changes to Shanghai urban culture, amid Shanghai growing into a global city, especially in the face of massive internal migration?

Appendix IV

2017 Interview Guide with Non-Native Shanghairen

1) How much do you understand the Shanghai dialect?
2) How well do you speak the Shanghai dialect?
3) In your workplace now, in which language do you communicate with coworkers?
4) Which language do you speak with your friends, native, and non-native Shanghainese friends?
5) At home, in which language do you communicate with parents, your spouse, and your child?
6) In public places, in which language you would initiate contact with strangers? How do you usually make the choice?
7) Have you heard about the preservation of the Shanghai dialect movement? If so, what do you think about it? What do you think about those advocates' claim that the Shanghai dialect is dying?
8) What do you think are the characteristics of being a Shanghairen; is speaking the Shanghai dialect one of them? What else counts?
9) What is your opinion on the balance between using English, Putonghua, and the Shanghai dialect, in the case of public transit announcements?
10) How do you see the future of the Shanghai dialect and the changes to Shanghai urban culture, amid Shanghai growing into a global city, especially in the face of massive internal migration?

Appendix V

2013 Shanghai Dialect Proficiency Survey with Native Shanghairen

Questionnaire:
How much do you understand the Shanghai dialect?

- o Very well
- o Fine
- o A little
- o Not at all

How well do you speak the Shanghai dialect?

- o Very well
- o Fine
- o A little
- o Not at all

How well do you read the Shanghai dialect?
(e.g., news articles and posts written in a phonetic combination of Putonghua characters)

- o Very well
- o Fine
- o A Little
- o Not at all

How well do you write the Shanghai dialect using Putonghua characters?

- o Very well
- o Fine
- o A Little
- o Not at all

During your school years, in what language have classes been given?

	Solely Putonghua	Solely the Shanghai Dialect	Mixed with Predominantly Putonghua	Mixed with Predominantly the Shanghai dialect	Mixed with equal amount
Elementary School	○	○	○	○	○
Middle School	○	○	○	○	○
High School	○	○	○	○	○
College	○	○	○	○	○
Graduate School	○	○	○	○	○

During your school years, in what language do you communicate with your classmates outside of class time?

	Solely Putonghua	Solely the Shanghai Dialect	Mixed with Predominantly Putonghua	Mixed with Predominantly the Shanghai dialect	Mixed with equal amount
Elementary School	○	○	○	○	○
Middle School	○	○	○	○	○
High School	○	○	○	○	○
College	○	○	○	○	○
Graduate School	○	○	○	○	○

During your school years, in what language do you communicate with your teachers outside of class time?

	Solely Putonghua	Solely the Shanghai Dialect	Mixed with Predominantly Putonghua	Mixed with Predominantly the Shanghai dialect	Mixed with equal amount
Elementary School	○	○	○	○	○
Middle School	○	○	○	○	○
High School	○	○	○	○	○
College	○	○	○	○	○
Graduate School	○	○	○	○	○

During your school years, in what language do you speak at home?

	Solely Putonghua	Solely the Shanghai Dialect	Mixed with Predominantly Putonghua	Mixed with Predominantly the Shanghai dialect	Mixed with equal amount
Elementary School	○	○	○	○	○
Middle School	○	○	○	○	○
High School	○	○	○	○	○
College	○	○	○	○	○
Graduate School	○	○	○	○	○

Today, at home, in what language do you communicate?

	Solely Putonghua	Solely the Shanghai Dialect	Solely English, or other foreign language	Mixed with Predominantly Putonghua	Mixed with Predominantly English or other foreign language	Mixed with Predominantly the Shanghai dialect	Mixed with equal amount	Other
With parents or elderly relatives	○	○	○	○	○	○	○	○
With spouse	○	○	○	○	○	○	○	○
With children	○	○	○	○	○	○	○	○

Today, in which language do you speak with your friends?

- ○ Solely Putonghua
- ○ Solely the Shanghai Dialect
- ○ Solely English, or other foreign language
- ○ Mixed with predominantly Putonghua
- ○ Mixed with predominantly the Shanghai dialect
- ○ Mixed with predominantly English
- ○ Mixed with roughly equal amount
- ○ Other, please specify

In your workplace, in what language do you communicate?

	Solely Putonghua	Solely the Shanghai Dialect	Solely English, or other foreign language	Mixed with Predominantly Putonghua	Mixed with Predominantly English or other foreign language	Mixed with Predominantly the Shanghai dialect	Mixed with equal amount	Other
With boss/ supervisor	○	○	○	○	○	○	○	○
With colleagues	○	○	○	○	○	○	○	○
With clients	○	○	○	○	○	○	○	○

In public, in what language do you communicate?

	Solely Putonghua	Solely the Shanghai Dialect	Solely English, or other foreign language	Mixed with Predominantly Putonghua	Mixed with Predominantly English or other foreign language	Mixed with Predominantly the Shanghai dialect	Mixed with equal amount	Other
At government agencies	○	○	○	○	○	○	○	○
In hospital	○	○	○	○	○	○	○	○
At shopping	○	○	○	○	○	○	○	○
At leisure activities, such as gym or theatre	○	○	○	○	○	○	○	○

Your Age
| |

Your Gender

- o Male
- o Female
- o Other

Birthplace
town/city, and province
| |

How long have you lived in Shanghai
in years
| |

Your highest level of education

- o Elementary School
- o Middle School
- o High School
- o Some College
- o Bachelor Degree from domestic college
- o Bachelor Degree from domestic college
- o Graduate Degree from domestic college
- o Graduate Degree from oversea college
- o Other

Do you work?

- o Yes, full time
- o Yes, part time
- o No
- o Retired

Your type of work?
| |

Your father's birthplace?
town/city, province
| |

Your father's occupation?
| |

language your father speaks at home?
| |

Your mother's birthplace?
town/city, province

Your mother's occupation?

Language your mother speaks at home?

Bibliography

Agnew, John A. 1987. *Place and Politics: The Geographical Mediation of State and Society.* Allen & Unwin.

Albert, Eleanor. 2019. "What Is the Belt and Road News Network?" The Diplomat. October 2019. https://thediplomat.com/2019/10/what-is-the-belt-and-road-news-network/.

Alexander, Peter, and Anita Chan. 2004. "Does China Have an Apartheid Pass System?" *Journal of Ethnic and Migration Studies* 30 (4): 609–29.

Augé, Marc. 1995. *Non-Places: Introduction to an Anthropology of Supermodernity.* London & New York: Verso.

Beam, Christopher. 2015. "Chengdu, China Gets a Modern Makeover." *Travel + Leisure,* November 10, 2015. https://www.travelandleisure.com/trip-ideas/chengdu-china-modern-makeover.

Berg, Marinus van den. 2016. "Modernization and the Restructuring of the Shanghai Speech Community." *Journal of Asian Pacific Communication* 26 (1): 112–42.

Bergère, Marie-Claire. 2009. *Shanghai: China's Gateway to Modernity.* Stanford, CA: Stanford University Press.

Bian, Yanjie. 2002. "Chinese Social Stratification and Social Mobility." *Annual Review of Sociology* 28: 91–116.

Bian, Yanjie, and John R. Logan. 1996. "Market Transition and the Persistence of Power: The Changing Stratification System in Urban China." *American Sociological Review* 61 (5): 739–58.

Blommaert, Jan, and Jef Verschueren. 1992. "The Role of Language in European Nationalist Ideologies." *Pragmatics* 2 (3): 355–75.

Bourdieu, Pierre. 1986. "The Forms of Capital." In *Handbook of Theory and Research for the Sociology of Education,* edited by John Richardson, 241–58. Westport, CT: Greenwood.

———. 1987. *Distinction: A Social Critique of the Judgement of Taste.* Translated by Richard Nice. Cambridge, MA: Harvard University Press.

————. 1991. *Language and Symbolic Power*. Cambridge, MA: Harvard University Press.

Bracken, Gregory Byrne. 2013. *The Shanghai Alleyway House: A Vanishing Urban Vernacular*. Abingdon & New York: Routledge.

Bunnell, Tim. 2002. "Multimedia Utopia? A Geographical Critique of High-Tech Development in Malaysia's Multimedia Super Corridor." *Antipode* 34 (2): 265–95.

Carmona, Matthew, R. Carmona, Tim Heath, Taner Oc, and Steven Tiesdell. 2003. *Public Places, Urban Spaces: The Dimensions of Urban Design*. Oxford & Burlington, MA: Architectural Press.

Cavanaugh, Jillian R. 2009. *Living Memory: The Social Aesthetics of Language in a Northern Italian Town*. Malden & Oxford: Wiley and Blackwell.

Chan, Kam Wing. 1994. *Cities with Invisible Walls: Reinterpreting Urbanization in Post-1949 China*. Hong Kong & New York: Oxford University Press.

Chan, Kam Wing, and Will Buckingham. 2008. "Is China Abolishing the Hukou System?*." *The China Quarterly* 195 (September): 582–606.

Chan, Kam Wing, and Li Zhang. 1999. "The Hukou System and Rural-Urban Migration in China: Processes and Changes." *The China Quarterly* 160 (December): 818–55.

Chen, Ping. 1999. *Modern Chinese: History and Sociolinguistics*. Cambridge & New York: Cambridge University Press.

Chen, Xiangming. 2009. "A Globalizing City on the Rise: Shanghai's Transformation in Comparative Perspective." In *Shanghai Rising: State Power and Local Transformations in a Global Megacity*, edited by Xiangming Chen, xv–xxxv. Minneapolis: University of Minnesota Press.

Chen, Zhongmin. 1992. "Subdivisions of the Shanghai Dialect Region and Its Cultural and Historical Backgrounds (*Shanghai diqu fangyan fenqu jiqi lishi renwen Beijing*)." *Fudan Journal (Social Sciences Edition)* 4: 101–8.

Cheng, Tiejun, and Mark Selden. 1994. "The Origins and Social Consequences of China's Hukou System." *The China Quarterly* 139 (September): 644–68.

"City Centre Master-Planned Communities - Property Developments - Property Developments - Shui On Land." Accessed September 12, 2020. https://www.shuionland.com/en-us/property/Community/detail/cc.

Cook-Martín, David. 2019. "Temp Nations? A Research Agenda on Migration, Temporariness, and Membership." *American Behavioral Scientist* 63 (9): 1389–403.

Coulmas, Florian. 1988. "What Is a National Language Good For?" In *With Forked Tongues: What Are National Languages Good For?*, edited by Florian Coulmas, 1–24. Ann Arbor, MI: Karoma Publishers.

Current Affairs Correspondent East Asia. 2019. "Mandarin Made Compulsory in Nepali School´s." Belt & Road News. June 16, 2019. https://www.beltandroad.news/2019/06/16/mandarin-made-compulsory-in-nepali-schools/.

Davis, Deborah S. 1999. "Self-Employment in Shanghai: A Research Note." *The China Quarterly* 157 (March): 22–43.

Denison, Edward and Ren, Guangyu. 2013. *Building Shanghai: The Story of China's Gateway*. Chichester, England: Wiley - Academy. https://www.wiley.com/en-us/Building+Shanghai%3A+The+Story+of+China%27s+Gateway-p-9781118867549.

Derrida, Jacques. 2000. *Of Hospitality*. Translated by Rachel Bowlby. Stanford, CA: Stanford University Press.

Deutsch Welle (www.dw.com). 2017. "Use Rap to Defend the Shanghai Dialect (*yong raosheyue hanwei shanghaihua*)." DW.COM. October 23, 2017. https://p .dw.com/p/2mLjA.

Di Saint Pierre, Francesca, Borja Martinovic, and Thomas De Vroome. 2015. "Return Wishes of Refugees in the Netherlands: The Role of Integration, Host National Identification and Perceived Discrimination." *Journal of Ethnic and Migration Studies* 41 (11): 1836–57.

Dong, Stella. 2000. *Shanghai: The Rise and Fall of a Decadent City*. New York: HarperCollins.

Dorian, Nancy. 1998. "Western Language Ideologies and Small-Language Prospects." In *Endangered Languages: Language Loss and Community Response*, edited by Lenore A. Grenoble and Lindsay J. Whaley, 3–21. Cambridge: Cambridge University Press.

Du, Huimin. 2018. "Mobilities and Identities of Educated Young Adults: A Life-History and Biographical Study." *China Review* 18 (1): 35–58.

Eckert, Penelope. 1989. "The Whole Woman: Sex and Gender Differences in Variation." *Language Variation & Change* 1 (3): 245–67.

Edwards, John. 2011. *Challenges in the Social Life of Language*. Language and Globalization. London & New York: Palgrave Macmillan UK.

Farrer, James. 2019. *International Migrants in China's Global City: The New Shanghailanders*. Abingdon: Routledge.

Feng, Wang, Xuejin Zuo, and Danching Ruan. 2002. "Rural Migrants in Shanghai: Living under the Shadow of Socialism1": *International Migration Review* 36 (2): 520–45.

Ferguson, Charles A. 1959. "Diglossia." *WORD* 15 (2): 325–40.

Fincher, Leta Hong. 2014. *Leftover Women: The Resurgence of Gender Inequality in China*. London & New York: Zed Books.

Findlay, A., and Aileen Stockdale. 2003. "The Temporal and Social Embeddedness of Migration: A Methodological Exploration Using Biographical Analysis." *Geography Research Forum* 23: 4–29.

Fishman, Joshua A. 1980. "Bilingualism and Biculturism as Individual and as Societal Phenomena." *Journal of Multilingual and Multicultural Development* 1 (1): 3–15.

———. 1985. "Macrosociolinguistics and the Sociology of Language in the Early Eighties." *Annual Review of Sociology* 11: 113–27.

Fu, Zhengji. 2002. "The State, Capital, and Urban Restructuring in Post-Reform Shanghai." In *The New Chinese City: Globalization and Market Reform*, edited by John Logan, 106–20. Oxford & Malden, MA: Wiley-Blackwell.

Fuller, Michael Anthony. 1999. *An Introduction to Literary Chinese*. Cambridge, MA: Harvard University Asia Center.

Gal, Susan. 1978. "Peasant Men Can't Get Wives: Language Change and Sex Roles in a Bilingual Community." *Language in Society* 7: 1–16.

———. 1992. "Multiplicity and Contention among Ideologies: A Commentary." Edited by Bambi B. Schieffelin, Paul V. Kroskrity, and Kathryn A. Woolard. *Pragmatics* 2 (3): 445–49.

Gamble, Jos. 2003. *Shanghai in Transition: Changing Perspectives and Social Contours of a Chinese Metropolis.* London & New York: RoutledgeCurzon.

Gao, Yang. 2020. "How the Belt and Road Initiative Informs Language Planning Policies in China and among the Countries along the Road." *Sustainability* 12 (14): 5506.

Gellner, Ernest. 1983. *Nations and Nationalism.* Ithaca: Cornell University Press.

Ghertner, D. Asher. 2011. "Rule by Aesthetics: World-Class City Making in Delhi." In *Worlding Cities: Asian Experiments and the Art of Being Global*, edited by Ananya Roy and Aihwa Ong, 279–306. Malden & Oxford: Wiley and Blackwell.

González, Marcela F. 2020. "High Skilled Immigrants' Pathways from Risky to Secure Legality in the United States." *Ethnic and Racial Studies* 43(15): 2807–25.

Goodman, Bryna. 1995. *Native Place, City, and Nation.* Berkeley, CA: University of California Press.

Greenspan, Anna. 2014. *Shanghai Future: Modernity Remade.* New York: Oxford University Press.

Grenoble, Lenore A., and Lindsay J. Whaley. 1998a. "Preface." In *Endangered Languages: Language Loss and Community Response*, edited by Lenore A. Grenoble and Lindsay J. Whaley, vii–xvi. Cambridge: Cambridge University Press.

———. 1998b. "Toward a Typology of Language Endangerment." In *Endangered Languages: Language Loss and Community Response*, edited by Lenore A. Grenoble and Lindsay J. Whaley, 22–54. Cambridge: Cambridge University Press.

———. 1998c. "Toward a Typology of Language Endangerment." In *Endangered Languages: Language Loss and Community Response*, 22–54. Cambridge: Cambridge University Press.

Gumperz, John J. 1972. "The Speech Community." In *Language and Social Context: Selected Readings*, edited by Pier Paolo Giglioli, 219–31. Harmondsworth: Penguin.

Gumperz, John J., and Jenny Cook-Gumperz. 1982. "Introduction: Language and the Communication of Social Identity." In *Language and Social Identity*, edited by John J. Gumperz, 1–19. Cambridge & New York: Cambridge University Press.

Guo, Longsheng. 2004. "The Relationship between Putonghua and Chinese Dialects." In *Language Policy in the People's Republic of China: Theory and Practice Since 1949*, edited by Minglang Zhou and Hongkai Sun, 45–54. New York & Boston: Springer Science & Business Media.

Gustafson, Per. 2001. "Meanings of Place: Everyday Experience and Theoretical Conceptualizations." *Journal of Environmental Psychology* 21 (1): 5–16.

Harvey, David. 2001. "From Managerialism to Entrepreneurialism: The Transformation in Urban Governance in Late Capitalism." In *Spaces of Capital: Towards a Critical Geography*, 345–68. New York: Routledge.

———. 2005. "Neoliberalism 'with Chinese Characteristics.'" In *A Brief History of Neoliberalism*, 120–51. Oxford & New York: Oxford University Press.

Haugen, Einar. 1972. *The Ecology of Language*. Stanford, CA: Stanford University Press.

He, Shenjing. 2007. "State-Sponsored Gentrification under Market Transition: The Case of Shanghai:" *Urban Affairs Review* 43 (2): 171–98.

He, Shenjing, and Fulong Wu. 2005. "Property-Led Redevelopment in Post-Reform China: A Case Study of Xintiandi Redevelopment Project in Shanghai." *Journal of Urban Affairs* 27 (1): 1–23.

———. 2007. "Neighborhood Changes and Residential Differention in Shanghai." In *China's Emerging Cities: The Making of New Urbanism*, edited by Fulong Wu, 185–209. New York: Routledge.

Heller, Monica, and Alexandre Duchene. 2012. "Pride and Profit: Changing Discourses of Language, Capital and Nation-State." In *Language in Late Capitalism: Pride and Profit*, edited by Alexandre Duchene and Monica Heller, 1–21. New York & London: Routledge.

Hobsbawm, Eric. 1992. "Introduction: Inventing Traditions." In *The Invention of Tradition*, edited by Eric Hobsbawm and Terence O. Ranger, 1–14. Cambridge: Cambridge University Press.

Honig, Emily. 1992. *Creating Chinese Ethnicity: Subei People in Shanghai, 1850–1980*. New Haven: Yale University Press.

Hsing, You-tien. 2006. "Land and Territorial Politics in Urban China." *The China Quarterly* 187: 575–91.

Huang, Shuanfan. 2000. "Language, Identity and Conflict: A Taiwanese Study." *International Journal of the Sociology of Language* 143: 139–50.

Huang, Xing, and Yongchun Yang. 2010. "The Characteristics and Forming Mechanisms of Gentrification in Cities of Western China: The Case Study in Chengdu City (Zhongguo xibu Chengshi Shenshihua Xianxiang jiqi xingchen jizhi yi Chengdushi weili)." *Progress in Geography (Dili Kexue Jinzhan)* 29 (12): 1532–40.

Huang, Xu, Martin Dijst, Jan van Weesep, Yixue Jiao, and Ying Sun. 2017. "Residential Choice among Rural–Urban Migrants after Hukou Reform: Evidence from Suzhou, China." *Population, Space and Place* 23 (4): e2035.

Huang, Xu, Bo Zhao, Ye Liu, and Desheng Xue. 2020. "Belonging to a Place: An Analysis of the Perceptions of Rural-to-Urban Migrants in China." *Geographical Review* 110 (3): 406–24.

Hudson, Alan. 2002. "Outline of a Theory of Diglossia." *International Journal of the Sociology of Language* 2002 (157): 1–48.

Irvine, Judith T. 1989. "When Talk Isn't Cheap: Language and Political Economy." *American Ethnologist* 16 (2): 248–67.

Irvine, Judith T., and Susan Gal. 2010. "Language Ideology and Linguistic Differentiation." In *Regimes of Language: Ideologies, Polities, and Identities*, edited by Paul V. Kroskrity, 35–84. Santa Fe: School of American Research Press.

Jaffe, Alexandra. 1999. *Ideologies in Action: Language Politics on Corsica*. *Ideologies in Action*. Berlin & Boston: De Gruyter Mouton.

Jiang, Bingbing. 2006. "Bilingualism and Linguistic Harmony: Research on Shanghainese Students' Language Usage (*shuangyu yu yuyan hexie: laizi shanghaishi xuesheng yuyan shiyong qingkuang de diaocha*)." *Rhetoric Learning (xiuci xuexi)* 6: 64–6.

Jiao, Chengming. 2009. "Report on Shanghai Native Students Linguistic Behavior (Shanghai tuzhu xuesheng yuyan yingwei baogao)." *Applied Linguistics (yuyan wenzi yingyong)* 1: 27–37.

King, Anthony D., and Abidin Kusno. 2000. "On Be(Ij)Ing in the World: 'Postmodernism,' 'Globalization,' and the Making of Transnational Space in China." In *Postmodernism and China*, edited by Xudong Zhang and Arif Dirlik, 41–67. Durham & London: Duke University Press.

Labov, William. 1972. *Language in the Inner City: Studies in the Black English Vernacular*. Philadelphia: University of Pennsylvania Press.

Lakoff, Robin. 1973. "Language and Woman's Place." *Language in Society* 2 (1): 45–80.

———. 1990. *Talking Power*. New York: Basic Books.

Lalli, Marco. 1992. "Urban-Related Identity: Theory, Measurement, and Empirical Findings." *Journal of Environmental Psychology* 12 (4): 285–303.

Lee, Ching Kwan. 2007. *Against the Law: Labor Protests in China's Rustbelt and Sunbelt*. Berkeley, CA: University of California Press.

Lee, Leo Ou-fan. 1999. *Shanghai Modern: The Flowering of a New Urban Culture in China, 1930–1945*. Cambridge, MA: Harvard University Press.

Lefebvre, Henri. 1991. *The Production of Space*. Oxford: Wiley and Blackwell.

Lewicka, Maria. 2011. "Place Attachment: How Far Have We Come in the Last 40 Years?" *Journal of Environmental Psychology* 31 (3): 207–30.

Li, Mingyu. 2015. "BRI Requires Language Planning (*yi lu yi dai xuyao yuyan pulu*)." People.Cn - People's Daily. September 22, 2015. http://theory.people.com.cn/n/2015/0922/c40531-27616931.html.

Li, Xin. 2014. "Shanghai Has the Highest Percentage of Native and Non-Native Unions across the Country with Men's Average First Marriage Age at 34 (*Shanghai liangdi hunyin bili quanguo zuigao nanxing pingjun hunling 34 Sui*)." Xinmin News. February 28, 2014. http://shanghai.xinmin.cn/msrx/2014/02/28/23645449.html.

Li, Yinhe. 1997. *Rising power of the women [Zhongguo nvxing de jueqi]*. Beijing: Chinese Social Science Press.

———. 1998. *Sexuality and Love of Chinese Women [Zhongguo nvxing de ganqing yu xing]*. Beijing: China Today Press.

Liang, Sihua. 2015. *Language Attitudes and Identities in Multilingual China: A Linguistic Ethnography*. Heidelberg, New York: Springer.

Lindemann, Stephanie, and Nicholas Subtirelu. 2013. "Reliably Biased: The Role of Listener Expectation in the Perception of Second Language Speech." *Language Learning* 63 (3): 567–94.

Lippi-Green, Rosina. 1997. *English with an Accent: Language, Ideology and Discrimination in the United States*. London & New York: Routledge.

Liu, Liangni Sally. 2014. "A Search for a Place to Call Home: Negotiation of Home, Identity and Senses of Belonging among New Migrants from the People's Republic of China (PRC) to New Zealand." *Emotion, Space and Society* 10 (February): 18–26.

Liu, Ye, Zhigang Li, and Werner Breitung. 2012. "The Social Networks of New-Generation Migrants in China's Urbanized Villages: A Case Study of Guangzhou." *Habitat International* 36 (1): 192–200.

Logan, John R., Yiping Fang, and Zhanxin Zhang. 2009. "Access to Housing in Urban China." *International Journal of Urban and Regional Research* 33 (4): 914–35.

Low, Setha M., and Irwin Altman. 1992. "Place Attachment." In *Place Attachment*, edited by Irwin Altman and Setha M. Low, 1–12. Human Behavior and Environment. Boston, MA: Springer US.

Lu, Hanchao. 1999. *Beyond the Neon Lights: Everyday Shanghai in the Early Twentieth Century*. Berkeley, CA: University of California Press.

———. 2002. "Nostalgia for the Future: The Resurgence of an Alienated Culture in China." *Pacific Affairs* 75 (2): 169–86.

Lu, Yilong. 2002. "Structure and Change: The Household Registration System in China after 1949 [*1949 nian hou de zhongguo huji zhidu: jiegou yu bianqian*]." *Journal of Peking University (Humanities and Social Sciences)* 39 (2): 123–30.

Mair, Victor H., and Victor H. Mair. 1991. "What Is a Chinese 'Dialect/Topolect'? Reflections on Some Key Sino-English Linguistic Terms." *Sino-Platonic Papers* 29: 1–38.

"Map of Shanghai Municipality." 2017. Hu S(2017) No. 61. Shanghai: Shanghai Institute of Surveying and Mapping.

Marcuse, Peter. 2012. "Whose Right(s) to What City?" In *Cities for People, Not for Profit: Critical Urban Theory and the Right to the City*, edited by Neil Brenner, Peter Marcuse, and Margit Mayer, 24–41. London and New York: Routledge.

Marlow, Mikaela L., and Howard Giles. 2010. "'We Won't Get Ahead Speaking like That!' Expressing and Managing Language Criticism in Hawai'i." *Journal of Multilingual and Multicultural Development* 31 (3): 237–51.

Massey, Doreen. 1995a. "Places and Their Pasts." *History Workshop Journal* 39: 182–92.

———. 1995b. "Places and Their Pasts." *History Workshop Journal* 39: 182–92.

May, Stephen. 2011. *Language and Minority Rights*. 2 edition. New York: Routledge.

Miller, Jennifer M. 2000. "Language Use, Identity, and Social Interaction: Migrant Students in Australia." *Research on Language & Social Interaction* 33 (1): 69–100.

Milroy, James, and Lesley Milroy. 1985. *Authority in Language: Investigating Standard English*. London, Boston and Henley: Routledge & Kegan Paul.

Mithun, Marianne. 1998. "The Significance of Diversity in Language Endangerment and Preservation." In *Endangered Languages: Loss and Community Response*, edited by Lenore A. Grenoble and Lindsay Whaley, 163–91. Cambridge: Cambridge University Press.

Molotch, Harvey, William Freudenburg, and Krista E. Paulsen. 2000. "History Repeats Itself, but How? City Character, Urban Tradition, and the Accomplishment of Place." *American Sociological Review*, 791–823.

"Mr.Weezy – Shanghai Speech (Shanghai yanhua)." Accessed December 20, 2020. https://www.ximalaya.com/yinyue/6349855/174698845.

Nien, Cheng. 2010. *Life and Death in Shanghai*. Reissue Edition. New York: Grove Press.

Norman, Jerry. 1988. *Chinese*. Cambridge: Cambridge University Press.

Office of Shanghai Chronicles (*shanghai difangzhi bangongshi*). 2003. "Special Feature II: The Up to the Mountains and Down to the Countryside Movement during the Cultural Revolution (zhuanji er: 'wenhua da geming' zhong de shangshan xiaxiang yundong)." November 10, 2003. http://www.shtong.gov.cn/dfz_web/DF Z/Info?idnode=66390&tableName=userobject1a&id=62337.

Ong, Aihwa. 1999. *Flexible Citizenship: The Cultural Logics of Transnationality*. Duke University Press.

———. 2006. "Reengineering the 'Chinese Soul' in Shanghai?" In *Neoliberalism as Exception: Mutations in Citizenship and Sovereignty*, 219–40. Durham & London: Duke University Press.

Orum, Anthony M., Sidney Bata, Li Shumei, Tang Jiewei, Sang Yang, and Nguyen Thanh Trung. 2009. "Public Man and Public Space in Shanghai Today." *City & Community* 8 (4): 369–89.

Pan, Lynn. 1982. *In Search of Old Shanghai*. Hong Kong: Joint Pub.

Pearson, Margaret M. 1997. *China's New Business Elite: The Political Consequences of Economic Reform*. Berkeley, CA: University of California Press.

Peters, Michael A. 2020. "China's Belt and Road Initiative: Reshaping Global Higher Education." *Educational Philosophy and Theory* 52 (6): 586–92.

Pillar, Ingrid. 2016. *Linguistic Diversity and Social Justice: An Introduction to Applied Sociolinguistics*. Oxford & New York: Oxford University Press.

Ping, Lei. 2019. "Survival of Shanghai Urbanite Culture in the Mao Era: Bourgeois Aspirations and Practice of Longtang Everyday Life." *Journal of Chinese Architecture and Urbanism* 1 (1): 1–18.

"Plan of Shanghai 1919." 1919. Kelly & Walsh, LTD., Lithographers.

Proshansky, Harold M. 1978. "The City and Self-Identity." *Environment and Behavior* 10 (2): 147–69.

Proshansky, Harold M., Abbe K. Fabian, and Robert Kaminoff. 1983. "Place-Identity: Physical World Socialization of the Self." *Journal of Environmental Psychology* 3 (1): 57–83.

Qian, Cheng. 2012. *Qian Chen's Shanghai Accent [Qianchen de Shanghai qiangdiao]*. Shanghai: Shanghai Education Publishing House.

Qian, Junxi, Liyun Qian, and Hong Zhu. 2012. "Representing the Imagined City: Place and the Politics of Difference during Guangzhou's 2010 Language Conflict." *Geoforum* 43 (5): 905–15.

Qian, Junxi, Hong Zhu, and Yi Liu. 2011. "Investigating Urban Migrants' Sense of Place through a Multi-Scalar Perspective." *Journal of Environmental Psychology* 31 (2): 170–83.

Qian, Nairong. 1998. "On Formation of Urban Central Dialect in Shanghai [*Shanghai chengshi fangyan zhongxin de xingcheng*]." *Journal of Shanghai University (Social Science)* 5 (3): 28–35.

———. 2000. "On Changes to the Shanghai Language [*Shanghai yuyan de bianqian*]." *Social Sciences [shehui kexue]* 2: 65–66.

———. 2003. *History of the Shanghai Language [Shanghai yuyan fazhan shi]*. Shanghai: Shanghai People's Publishing House.

————. 2007. *Shanghai Dialect [Shanghai fangyan]*. Shanghai: Wenhui Publishing.

Ramsey, S. Robert. 1989. *The Languages of China*. Princeton, NJ: Princeton University Press.

Relph, Edward. 1976. *Place and Placelessness*. London: Pion.

Ren, Xuefei. 2011. *Building Globalization: Transnational Architecture Production in Urban China*. Chicago & London: University of Chicago Press.

Ritzer, George. 1999. *Enchanting a Disenchanted World: Revolutionizing the Means of Consumption*. Thousand Oaks, CA: SAGE Publications.

Robinson, Richard, and David S.G. Goodman. 1996. "The New Rich in Asia: Economic Development, Social Status and Political Consciousness." In *The New Rich in Asia: Mobile Phones, McDonald's and Middle-Class Revolution*, edited by Richard Robinson and David S.G. Goodman, 1–18. London & New York: Routledge.

Rudolph, Jennifer, and Hanchao Lu. 2008. "Mirrored Reflections: Place Identity Formation in Taipei and Shanghai." In *Urban China in Transition*, edited by John Logan, 161–81. Malden, MA: John Wiley & Sons.

Sassen, Saskia. 2001. *The Global City: New York, London, Tokyo*. 2 edition. Princeton, NJ: Princeton University Press.

————. 2011. *Cities in a World Economy*. 4 edition. Thousand Oaks, CA: SAGE Publications, Inc.

Schiffrin, Deborah. 1996. "Narrative as Self-Portrait: Sociolinguistic Constructions of Identity." *Language in Society* 25 (2): 167–203.

"Shanghai District Map." 2017. Hu S(2017) No.61. Shanghai: Shanghai Institute of Surveying and Mapping.

Shanghai Statistical Bureau. 2012. *Shanghai Statistical Yearbook 2011*. Beijing: China Statistics Press. http://tjj.sh.gov.cn/tjnj/nje11.htm?d1=2011tjnje/E0205.htm.

————. 2014. "2013 Report of Shanghai Residents' Language Proficiency Survey. (*2013 nian Shanghai shimin yuyan yingyong nengli diaocha baogao*)." February 7, 2014. http://tjj.sh.gov.cn/tjfx/20140207/0014-266714.html.

————. 2018. *Shanghai Statistical Yearbook 2017*. Beijing: China Statistics Press. http://tjj.sh.gov.cn/tjnj/20190117/0014-1001529.html.

————. 2020. *Shanghai Statistical Yearbook 2019*. Beijing: China Statistics Press. http://tjj.sh.gov.cn/tjnj/nj19.htm?d1=2019tjnje/E0201.htm.

Shao, Qin. 2013. *Shanghai Gone: Domicide and Defiance in a Chinese Megacity*. Lanham: Rowman & Littlefield Publishers.

Shen, Jie, and Fulong Wu. 2012. "Restless Urban Landscapes in China: A Case Study of Three Projects in Shanghai." *Journal of Urban Affairs* 34 (3): 255–77.

Shen, Qi, and Xuesong Gao. 2019. "Multilingualism and Policy Making in Greater China: Ideological and Implementational Spaces." *Language Policy* 18 (1): 1–16.

Sklair, Leslie. 2010. "Iconic Architecture and the Culture-Ideology of Consumerism:" *Theory, Culture & Society* 27 (5): 135–59.

Snow, Don. 2010. "Hong Kong and Modern Diglossia." *International Journal of the Sociology of Language* 206: 155–79.

Sohu News. 2017. "German Chubby A-Fu:" Being a Wanghong in Shanghai." February 13, 2017. www.sohu.com/a/126148775_115848.

Solinger, Dorothy J. 1995. "The Floating Population in the Cities: Chances for Assimilation?" In *Urban Spaces in Contemporary China: The Potential for Autonomy and Community in Post-Mao China*, edited by Deborah S. Davis, Richard Kraus, Barry Naughton, and Elizabeth Perry, 113–39. Cambridge: Cambridge University Press.

———. 1999. *Contesting Citizenship in Urban China: Peasant Migrants, the State, and the Logic of the Market*. Berkeley, CA: University of California Press.

Song, Weixuan, and Qiyan Wu. 2010. "Gentrification and Residential Differentiation in Nanjing, China." *Chinese Geographical Science* 20 (6): 568–76.

Sun, Xiaoxian, Bingbing Jiang, Yijia Wang, and Lihua Qiao. 2007. "A Survey of Shanghai Students' Use of Putonghua and Shanghai Dialect (*Shanghaishi xuesheng Putonghua he Shanghaihua shiyong qingkuang diaocha*)." *Yangtze River Academic (Changjiang Xueshu)* 3: 1–10.

Swaan, Abram De. 2001. *Words of the World: The Global Language System*. Cambridge: Polity Press.

Swider, Sarah. 2014. "Building China: Precarious Employment among Migrant Construction Workers:" *Work, Employment and Society*, August.

Szelenyi, Ivan. 1996. "Cities under Socialism: And After." In *Cities After Socialism: Urban and Regional Change and Conflict in Post-Socialist Societies*, edited by Gregory Andrusz, Michael Harloe, and Ivan Szelenyi, 286–317. Oxford & Cambridge, MA: Wiley-Blackwell.

"Table 1.6 Regional Population by Sex and Ethnicity. 2010 Census of the People's Republic of China." 2011. Beijing: National Bureau of Statistics of China.

Tam, Gina Anne. 2020. *Dialect and Nationalism in China, 1860–1960*. Cambridge: Cambridge University Press.

Trudgill, Peter. 1972. "Sex, Covert Prestige and Linguistic Change in the Urban British English of Norwich." *Language in Society* 1 (2): 179–95.

Tu, Siqi. 2020. "Destination Diploma: How Chinese Upper-Middle-Class Families 'Outsource' Secondary Education to the United States." Doctorate Dissertation, New York: Graduate Center, City University of New York.

Tuan, Yi-Fu. 1977. *Space and Place: The Perspective of Experience*. Minneapolis & London: University of Minnesota Press.

Turner, Bryan S. 1993. "Contemporary Problems in the Theory of Citizenship." In *Citizenship and Social Theory*, edited by Bryan S. Turner, 1–18. London & Thousand Oaks: SAGE Publications Ltd.

Twigger-Ross, Clare L., and David L. Uzzell. 1996. "Place and Identity Processes." *Journal of Environmental Psychology* 16 (3): 205–20.

U.S. Citizenship and Immigration Services. 2020. "EB-5 Immigrant Investor Program | USCIS." June 10, 2020. https://www.uscis.gov/working-in-the-united-states/perm anent-workers/eb-5-immigrant-investor-program.

Vendryes, Thomas. 2011. "Migration Constraints and Development: Hukou and Capital Accumulation in China." *China Economic Review* 22 (4): 669–92.

Wai, Albert Wing Tai. 2006. "Place Promotion and Iconography in Shanghai's Xintiandi." *Habitat International* 30 (2): 245–60.

Wallerstein, Immanuel. 2000. *The Essential Wallerstein*. New York: The New Press.

Wang, Fei-Ling. 2004a. "Reformed Migration Control and New Targeted People: China's Hukou System in the 2000s." *The China Quarterly* 177: 115–32.

———. 2004b. "Reformed Migration Control and New Targeted People: China's Hukou System in the 2000s." *The China Quarterly* 177 (March): 115–32.

Wang, Haiyan. 2018. "Shanghai Counselor Zhang Hongmin: '40 Years Ago, How to Solve the Most Difficult Problem in Shanghai- Housing (*Shanghai canshi Zhang Hongmin: sishi nian qian, Shanghai de tianzi diyihao nanti – zhufang nan shi ruhe jiejue de*).'" News. October 2018. https://www.shobserver.com/wx/detail.do?id =113215.

Wang, Limei, and Hans J. Ladegaard. 2008. "Language Attitudes and Gender in China: Perceptions and Reported Use of Putonghua and Cantonese in the Southern Province of Guangdong." *Language Awareness* 17 (1): 57–77.

Wang, Wenfei Winnie, and C. Cindy Fan. 2012. "Migrant Workers' Integration in Urban China: Experiences in Employment, Social Adaptation, and Self-Identity." *Eurasian Geography and Economics* 53 (6): 731–49.

Wasserstrom, Jeffrey N. 2009. *Global Shanghai, 1850–2010*. London & New York: Routledge.

Whyte, Martin King, and William L. Parish. 1984. *Urban Life in Contemporary China*. Chicago & London: The University of Chicago Press.

Wong, Andrew D. 2019. "Authenticity, Belonging, and Charter Myths of Cantonese." *Language & Communication*, Language, Mobility and Belonging, 68 (September): 37–45.

Woolard, Kathryn A. 1985. "Language Variation and Cultural Hegemony: Toward an Integration of Sociolinguistic and Social Theory." *American Ethnologist* 12 (4): 738–48.

———. 1987. "Codeswitching and Comedy in Catalonia." *IPrA Papers in Pragmatics* 1 (1): 106–22.

———. 1989. *Double Talk: Bilingualism and the Politics of Ethnicity in Catalonia*. 1 edition. Stanford, CA: Stanford University Press.

———. 1998. "Introduction: Language Ideology as a Field of Inquiry." In *Language Ideologies: Practice and Theory*, edited by Bambi B. Schieffelin, Kathryn A. Woolard, and Paul V. Kroskrity, 3–47. Oxford Studies in Anthropological Linguistics. Oxford & New York: Oxford University Press.

Wu, Weiping, and Guixin Wang. 2014. "Together but Unequal: Citizenship Rights for Migrants and Locals in Urban China." *Urban Affairs Review* 50 (6): 781–805.

Wu, Xiaogang, and Donald J. Treiman. 2004. "The Household Registration System and Social Stratification in China: 1955–1996." *Demography* 41 (2): 363–84.

Wu, Xiaogang, and Yu Xie. 2003. "Does the Market Pay Off? Earnings Returns to Education in Urban China." *American Sociological Review* 68 (3): 425–42.

Xie, Shouhong, and Yuemin Ning. 2003. "Urbanization and Suburbanization: The Dual Engines to Spatial Change of Chinese Metropolis under Transitional Era: A Case Study of Guangzhou." *City Planning Review (Chengshi Guihua)* 27 (11): 24–38.

Xu, Baojie and You, Rujie. 1988. "Initial Research on the Shanghai Dialect from Regional Gazettes [*fangzhi suo jian Shanghai fangyan chu tan*]." In *Collection of*

Thesis on Wu Language [Wuyu lun cong], 187–92. Shanghai: Shanghai Education Publishing House.

Xu, Fang. 2013. "Governance on the Production of Identity: Consuming Western High-Culture in Contemporary Shanghai." In *China and the Humanities: At the Crossroads of the Human and the Humane*, edited by Kang Tchou, 161–88. Champaign, IL: Common Ground Publishing.

———. 2020. "Chapter 11: Only Shanghainese Can Understand: Popularity of Vernacular Performance and Shanghainese Identity." In *Revealing/Reveiling Shanghai: Cultural Representations from the 20th and 21st Centuries*, edited by Lisa Bernstein and Chu-Chueh Cheng, 215–38. Albany: State University of New York Press.

Xu Mingqian. 2004. *City's context: Developing Shanghai urban central old residential neighborhoods [chengshi de wenmai: Shanghai zhongxin cheng jiu zhuqu fazhan fangshi xin lun]*. Shanghai: Xuelin Publishing.

Yao, Gonghe. 1989. *Shanghai Language [Shanghai xianhua]*. 2 edition. Shanghai: Shanghai Classics Publishing House.

Yeh, Wen-hsin. 2007. *Shanghai Splendor: Economic Sentiments and the Making of Modern China, 1843–1949*. Berkeley, CA: University of California Press.

Yeoh, Brenda S. A. 2004. "Cosmopolitanism and Its Exclusions in Singapore." *Urban Studies* 41 (12): 2431–45.

You, Rujie. 2006. "On Classification and Mixed Nature of the Shanghai Dialect [Shanghai Hua Zai Wuyu Fengqu Shang de Diwei]." *Dialects [fangyan]* 1: 72–78.

You, rujie. 2010. "Evolution of Dialects in Shanghai Suburban Districts since 1980s [Shanghai jiaoxian yuyin jin snashi nian lai de bianhua]." *Dialects [fangyan]* 3: 194–200.

Zhan, Shaohua. 2011. "What Determines Migrant Workers' Life Chances in Contemporary China? Hukou, Social Exclusion, and the Market." *Modern China* 37 (3): 243–85.

Zhan, Shaohua, and Min Zhou. 2020. "Precarious Talent: Highly Skilled Chinese and Indian Immigrants in Singapore." *Ethnic and Racial Studies* 43 (9): 1654–72.

Zhang, Li. 2006. "Contesting Spatial Modernity in Late-Socialist China." *Current Anthropology* 47 (3): 461–84.

Zhang, Qing. 2007. "Cosmopolitanism and Linguistic Capital in China: Language, Gender and the Transition to a Globalized Market Economy in Beijing." In *Words, Worlds, and Material Girls: Language, Gender, Globalization*, edited by Bonnie McElhinny, 403–22. Berlin: Mouton de Gruyter.

Zhang, Wenxin, and Liang Zhu. 2003. "The Situation and Countermeasures of Population Suburbanization in Big Cities of China." *Journal of Beijing Normal University (Natural Science)* 39 (3): 417–21.

Zhang, Yi. 2015. "Good Idea but Hard to Promote, 'Sargent Black Cat' in Shanghai Dialect [huyuban heimao jingzhang chuangyi hao tuiguang nan]." *Xinmin Evening News*, August 11, 2015.

Zhang, Yunpeng. 2017. "Domicide, Social Suffering and Symbolic Violence in Contemporary Shanghai, China." *Urban Geography* 39 (2): 190–213.

Zhao, Chunlan. 2004. "From Shikumen to New-Style: A Rereading of Lilong Housing in Modern Shanghai." *The Journal of Architecture* 9 (1): 49–76.

Zhou, Minglang. 2001. "The Spread of Putonghua and Language Attitude Changes in Shanghai and Guangzhou, China." *Journal of Asian Pacific Communication* 11 (2): 231–53.

Zhou, Minglang, and Heidi Ross. 2004. "Introduction: The Context of the Theory and Practice of China's Language Policy." In *Language Policy in the People's Republic of China: Theory and Practice Since 1949*, edited by Minglang Zhou and Hongkai Sun, 1–18. New York & Boston: Springer Science & Business Media.

Zhou, Minglang, and Hongkai Sun, eds. 2004. *Language Policy in the People's Republic of China: Theory and Practice Since 1949*. New York and Boston: Springer Science & Business Media.

Zhou, Yixing, and Yanchun Meng. 1997. "Shenyang's Suburbanization: Suburbanization Comparison between China and The Western Countries (Shenyang de Jiaoquhua Jianlun Zhongxifang Jiaoquhua de Bijiao)." *Acta Geographica Sinica (Dili Xuebao)* 4: 3–13.

Zhu, Guodong; Liu, Hong; Chen, Zhiqiang. 2008. "Go to Shanghai [*Dao Shanghai Qu*]." In *Shanghai Migration [Shanghai Yimin]*, 3–23. Shanghai: Shanghai University of Finance & Economics Press.

Zou Yiren. 1980. *Research on population change in old Shanghai. [Jiu Shanghai renkou bianqian de yanjiu]*. Shanghai: Shanghai People's Press.

Zukin, Sharon. 1995. *The Cultures of Cities*. Cambridge, MA: Blackwell.

———. 2010. *Naked City: The Death and Life of Authentic Urban Places*. Oxford & New York: Oxford University Press.

Zukin, Sharon, Philip Kasinitz, and Xiangming Chen. 2015. "Spaces of Everyday Diversity: The Patchwork Ecosystem of Local Shopping Streets." In *Global Cities, Local Streets: Everyday Diversity from New York to Shanghai*, 1–28. New York: Routledge.

Index

Page references for figures are italicized.

About the Author

Fang Xu is lecturer in the Interdisciplinary Studies Field program at University of California, Berkeley. She received an MA degree in sociology from University of British Columbia in Vancouver, Canada, and an MPhil and PhD in sociology from the Graduate Center, City University of New York. Her dissertation encompasses research on globalization, displacement, and language endangerment in Shanghai. She teaches courses in social theory, consumer society and culture, and language and identity. Her recent research publications include "Pudong is not My Shanghai: Displacement, place-identity, and right to the city in urban China" in the journal *City & Community* and "Only Shanghainese Can Understand: Popularity of Vernacular Performance and Shanghainese Identity" in the edited volume *Revealing/Reveiling Shanghai: Cultural Representations from the 20th and 21st Centuries.*